Sheridan's Troopers on the Borders

LIEUTENANT GENERAL SHERIDAN

Sheridan's Troopers on the Borders
The Winter Campaign of the U.S. Army Against the Indian Tribes of the Southern Plains, 1868-9

De Benneville Randolph Keim

LEONAUR

Sheridan's Troopers on the Borders
The Winter Campaign of the U.S. Army
Against the Indian Tribes of the Southern Plains,
1868-9

by De Benneville Randolph Keim

First published under the title
Sheridan's Troopers on the Borders

Leonaur is an imprint
of Oakpast Ltd

Copyright in this form © 2010 Oakpast Ltd

ISBN: 978-0-85706-256-7 (hardcover)
ISBN: 978-0-85706-255-0 (softcover)

http://www.leonaur.com

Publisher's Notes

The opinions of the authors represent a view of events in which he was a participant related from his own perspective, as such the text is relevant as an historical document.

The views expressed in this book are not necessarily those of the publisher.

Contents

Preface	7
A Letter From Lieutenant General Sheridan	9
Arrival at Leavenworth Fort	11
Beyond the Pale of Civilization	17
The Indians	22
Events Which Preceded the Outbreak of 1868	26
War Inaugurated	31
An Adventure	35
A Night in a Frontier Town	39
Off for Fort Wallace	43
Forsyth's Battle of the Arrickaree Fork	48
Return to Fort Hays	55
An Old Fashioned Buffalo Hunt	61
A Brute Army	65
Arrival of Osage Warriors	71
Ready to Take the Field	75
Arrival at Fort Dodge	80
Hunting-Parties	85
Custer Takes the "War-Path"	91
The Battle of the Washita	98
Safe Arrival of the Volunteers	107

California Joe	113
Fiendish Mutilation	125
The Flight of the Savages	134
Arrogance of the Savages	141
Christmas Day	147
The Occupants of the Country	154
The Apache (Lipans)	160
Justice	167
On the Move	176
War	183
Intellectual Development of the Savage	189
Traditions	194
An Exploring Expedition to the Witchita Mountains	201
Legends of Medicine Bluff	207
A Race For Life	213
An Unpleasant Predicament	219
A Hunt by Moonlight	229
Closing Events	237
The Administration of Indian Affairs	246
The Administration of Indian Affairs Continued	253
Off for Camp Supply	259
Homeward Bound	266

Preface

Civilization extending in opposite directions, westward across the great valley of the Mississippi, and eastward traversing the auriferous regions of the Rocky Mountains, presents two extensive fields of American industry, approximating each other, and demanding a more convenient and rapid intercourse. Railways and telegraphs have boldly penetrated the solitude of the plains, and the wild passes of the mountains reverberate to the rumble of moving trains. The two oceans are already linked together by an iron highway. The savage, alarmed at this new encroachment, is ready at any moment for a desperate, probably a final effort to drive out the invaders of his hunting-grounds. Fearful of his future he opposes such encroachments, for in them he sees no benefit to the remnant of his race, who have taken refuge on the plains and in the mountains.

The struggle has come, to solve, for all time, the question whether the white or the red man shall prevail in the vast intermediate region between eastern and western civilization. The exigencies of modern civilization point to the inevitable doom of the aboriginal people of the United States. Their savage natures, incapable of restraint, render them by instinct foes to progress and the cause of humanity. As with the buffalo the approach of civilization is to them the knell of destruction. As the murderous bullet of the white hunter ruthlessly slaughters the buffalo, so the vices of civilization carry off those of the red men who have outlived their kindred.

The following chapters contain a narrative of more than six months spent on the Southern Plains, observing the operations of the army personally directed by Major, now Lieutenant General Sheridan against the refractory savage on the Republican, the Arkansas and the Washita.

The curiosity of friends, as well as a seeming general desire to know something more of the country constituting the unexplored hunting-grounds of the Comanche, the Kiowa, the merciless Cheyenne, and Arrapahoe, and these predatory people themselves, are the considerations that have induced me to give my somewhat rough and novel experience in this form.

The campaign was an exceptional one. There was much in it that had never characterized any previous undertaking against the savages. The season of the year was against all precedent for active hostilities. Most of the country was entirely unknown. These people, in a majority of cases, had come in contact with but a few semi-savage traders, or with the white settler, during their murderous depredations upon his cabins. The object was to show to the savages the ability of the "white man's soldiers" to brave the storms of winter, and to surmount this barrier, which had in former years protected them. In my narrative I have endeavoured to combine useful information with entertaining reading. In this view I have given much of the soldier's life on the plains.

Hoping, therefore, that this volume will possess some feature that will recommend it, and in a measure supply the wants of a large number of persons who appear to have suddenly turned their attention to the Indian and the country he inhabits, the writer submits these pages.

I add my acknowledgments of the courtesy of F. C. Newhall, Esq., for the use of the admirable portrait of General Sheridan, found in the beginning of this volume.

Keim

Washington, D. C., 1870

A Letter From Lieutenant General Sheridan

The following letter was received from Lieutenant General Sheridan as this volume was about going to press. The author is induced to publish it, in this connection, in view of its accord with his own views expressed on the Indian policy.

Headquarters Military Division of the Missouri, Chicago, Ills.,
April 28, 1870.

Mr. De B. Randolph Keim.

Dear Sir: I have carefully read the proof-sheets sent me of your forthcoming book, (Sheridan's Troopers on the Borders,) and think well of it.

I may say in reference to the management of Indians, the reservation system is the only one offering any prospects of success, but all experience has shown that the wild Indian will not adopt it until he is forced to do so. All the tribes on the Northern Pacific coast had to be subdued and forced on the reservations, which was accomplished between the years 1855 1860, Then peace ensued. Latterly the same policy has been pursued in regard to the Comanches, Kiowas, Cheyennes, and Arrapahoes.

After the wild Indians are put upon the reservations a strong military force will have to be kept there to protect the. agents and others required in the work of civilization, and also for the subordination of the Indians, and their protection against the encroachments of the white settlers, who otherwise would take possession of their lands.

Very truly, yours,   P. H. Sheridan,
              Lieutenant General.

Chapter 1

Arrival at Leavenworth Fort

Less than a year and half ago, one midnight, the writer of these pages entered the distant western town of Leavenworth in the state of Kansas. Three sooty lanterns east a dubious light upon a dozen passengers groping their way amongst threshing machines, barrels and boxes, towards a rickety and battered coach. Said coach had the appearance of having migrated, by slow stages, all the way from the Atlantic sea-board, keeping pace with the advance tide of civilization, and shunning railroads as relentless intruders. The coach had, evidently, last seen paint east of the Alleghany mountains, and in its western march of progress had become quite bare of those embellishments which, doubtless, formerly attracted so much attention and observation among the children. In the dim flicker of lanterns it was a spectre of a coach.

About an inch of candle, stuck to the floor, in the front end, was suggestive of the necessity of haste, or the inevitable and speedy succession of darkness. The interior cushions and fittings had the appearance of the coach being converted, nightly, into a sleeping apartment. In this machine, the writer and his fellow-travellers set out for the hotel about a quarter of a mile distant, on the top of the bluff. A crack of the whip, and a few words of encouragement from the driver, fired the quadrupeds in front with astounding vivacity. They bounded off, over several railroad tracks, into several ruts, altogether with such unexpected velocity, that the hulk of the coach groaned and laboured, pitched and rolled, like a ship at sea, while the occupants, baggage and all, were jostled about in the most unsatisfactory manner.

Arriving at the hotel the nightly nuisances, at all hotels, were still about gazing at each individual as he blinked out of the darkness, into the office. Knowingly they watched each stranger put his name upon the register, and immediately after rushed up to farther gratify their sense of importance and provincial curiosity. The writer having been provided with apartments, impressed into his service a yawning, half-a-sleep negro, who just at this timely moment made his appearance through a window looking into the coat-room. Led off by this same sable youth, he soon found himself comfortably, (that is for nearly fifteen hundred miles west of Atlantic tide water,) provided for the recuperation of his physical forces.

Wonderful indeed it was to reflect upon the sudden transition and great lesson of the age. In the brief space of four days, traversing six States of the Union, and a distance of twelve hundred and thirty-five miles, I now stood upon the west bank of the Missouri. Less than twenty-five years ago to accomplish this same distance would have been the toil of months. A century ago civilization had not yet ventured away from the Atlantic seaboard. Such has been the marvellous progress of American Industry and Enterprise. Opulent cities and thriving towns and villages, linked together by a network of iron highways and electric wires, now cover all the vast region sweeping away from the Alleghanies to the confines of the great plains in the very heart of the continent.

Thus remote from the older seats of civilization and settlement is the town or city, I believe is the term, intended to dignify the place, of Leavenworth. It is a fine, thrifty community with a population of about fifteen thousand souls. It is beautifully located on a series of bluffs, overlooking the muddy waters of the Missouri. It possesses some very fine buildings. The Public School would compete with any structure of the kind in a city ten times the size. The new Catholic church bears the same relation to Leavenworth notions of the wonderful, as the great organ does to the extreme ideas of Boston. The building is really an ornament and an enterprise of just pride. Leavenworth society, properly speaking, is good, and is principally composed of the old settlers, persons of moderate means generally, but hospitable. The transient circles are composed of interlopers, government contractors, Indian agents, and Indian feeders. The place is a famous winter resort for Indian men and is a sort of general base of operations for anything that turns up in which the government is a principal party.

Several miles out of town, on a bluff overlooking the Missouri, is situated Fort Leavenworth. This is one of the early posts built when civilization with feeble steps, began its march across the continent. Fort Leavenworth is now properly a station for troops and depot for the supply of the posts on the upper Missouri and on the Plains. It is therefore easy to account for the class of people, generally "sharpers" who make their "stopping place" at Leavenworth or as it is some time symbolically represented "11worth." The fort is made up of a collection of barracks, officers quarters, an Arsenal, stables, haystacks and board piles. The buildings are well constructed and substantial. To prevent encroachment the government retained a. large plot of ground probably over a thousand acres, known as the "Reservation." As the country around has become well settled, for several years past a number of patriots and public economists have been at work with Congress trying to effect the passage of a bill authorizing the sale of the premises.

It will prove a large profit to someone or set of worthies, who always display so intense an interest to relieve the government of a share of its responsibilities.

The day after my arrival at Leavenworth I rode to the fort to make inquiries about the proper objective point, in view of the particular part I proposed to play in the campaign, as well as to learn the whereabouts of the commanding general. All information I readily obtained from the assistant adjutant general of the department, General McKeever, who had been left to take charge of the office work at headquarters, while the general himself was in the field. Owing to the hostilities on the plains, the troops had been almost entirely withdrawn from Fort Leavenworth, leaving but a detachment of the Fourth Artillery as a garrison. In other respects the place was quite lively. Generals Card and Morgan, the former chief quartermaster, and the latter chief commissary of the department, were up to their ears in business, making contracts for forage and other supplies and organizing the necessary transportation.

From what I learned, Leavenworth was no point to serve my ends, so the next day I took the train on the Kansas Pacific Railway on my route further west. The same night I was delayed at the town of Lawrence, a neat flourishing place, forty miles from Leavenworth, and on the trunk road connecting with the Missouri Pacific Railroad at Kansas City.

This town and Leavenworth are rivals for fame and importance. Leavenworth has the advantage of the proximity of a military post, Lawrence can claim the workshops of the Kansas Pacific railway. If the public economists, already spoken of, succeed in selling the government reservation, Leavenworth "stock" is bound to decline. Lawrence has a little chapter of history, also, to which the people revert with a sort of mixture of sadness and pride. The town and its people were well nigh destroyed by the notorious guerrilla Quantrell, and was again reduced to a dilapidated condition by another raiding party from Missouri. Lawrence is a smaller town than Leavenworth and with fewer fine buildings.

The next morning at ten o'clock I resumed the journey westward by rail. The train was composed of a number of stock cars, laden with horses destined to the various posts to furnish a remount for the dismounted men of the cavalry regiments, a few freight cars carrying quarter-masters and commissary stores and two passenger cars.

As time wore on and the train sped over its iron path, the evidence of civilization became more rare. The country began to present that monotonous configuration incident to the plains generally. During the day we passed Fort Riley, at the mouth of the Republican River. This fort is one of the old time military establishments of the plains. Built on a high ridge it commands a vast stretch of vision. In early days, though not many years ago, this fort was the centre of military operations on the plains. It was then far beyond the very utmost limits of civilization, and was only reached by the slow means of wagon transportation. It was here for a long time the extensive trains loading for New Mexico fitted out. The glory of the old post has departed. Frontier settlements have sprung up around it in the fertile valleys of the Kaw and the Republican. The wolfs mournful howl no longer is heard. The whistle of the locomotive breaks upon the air suggestive of the miraculous transformation. There was a time when the trooper arrayed for battle might have been seen leaving the protecting walls of Riley to scour the surrounding country in pursuit of a savage foe, or returning to rest from the fatigues of his task, profitless in honours or promotion. Today the decrepit and exhausted cavalry horse here finds rest and abundance. A squad of infantry soldiers to watch the premises constitutes the garrison.

Further west we passed a hotel, a few shanties and a number of cars upon a side track. The country for some distance was covered with herds of cattle, each with its herders, like so many mounted maniacs darting about, yelling furiously, and cutting right and left with their enormous whips. This point was recorded upon the "schedule" under the sentimental name of Abeline, and I learned was the great rendezvous and shipping post for Texas cattle. Annually immense droves are brought here across the plains, from a distance of not less than five hundred miles and shipped to the eastern markets—St. Louis, Chicago, and the great cities of the Atlantic.

Towards evening an odd buffalo or a small herd of antelopes appeared in the distance, but not in sufficient proximity to get even a good sight.

At eight o'clock the train reached Fort Harker. Here we were delayed some minutes awaiting the special train of the commanding general from the west. We then pushed on to Ellsworth, three miles further.

Owing to hostilities and the presence of Indian war parties along the line of road beyond, the running of trains except by daylight had been abandoned. We were therefore booked for the night. Leaving the train and walking a few hundred feet across an open space covered with boxes, broken barrels, tin cans, and every other variety of rubbish, we reached the "first class" hotel, known as the Anderson House. We were received at the door by a wizen-faced, spare individual, who was afterwards found to be the proprietor The hotel was a frame structure about forty feet front and two stories in height. The accommodations were not of the most commodious character, though this inconvenience was obviated by the hospitality, for a pecuniary consideration, of the citizens of the place. Those who could not be accommodated at the hotel, were taken in tow by a seedy African and escorted to some neighbouring house or tent to be provided for.

Being the first to reach the hotel I had the first chance of accommodation, and was accordingly assigned to room No. 1. The other passengers were provided for to the extent of five persons in three rooms. The rest of the passengers, now reduced to twenty, either were billeted on the citizens or slept in the cars.

After a supper on buffalo steak, antelope ham, soggy bread, and a cup of warm water, flavoured with a grain of coffee or a leaf of tea, the passengers gathered in the hotel office, a small room eight by ten and furnished with a counter and several dilapidated chairs. The proprietor presided. Seating himself on a three-legged chair and cocking his feet on the stove he entertained himself spinning yarns laudatory of his own prominent career, throwing in occasionally a bit of history connected with the laying out and subsequent growth of the town of Ellsworth. He had not only purchased the site of the town and sold much of it out in small lots, thereby greatly expanding his financial condition, but was also justice of the peace, and in his own idea, the most important personage on the plains.

According to his accounts, when the railroad was being constructed up to that point, some preliminary buildings having been thrown together in anticipation of that event, the population consisted of rather a miscellaneous assortment of human beings. Nor was the order of the place any better. Shooting at each other upon trivial grounds was a common pastime, and to kill on an average a man a night was an expected and ordinary occurrence. Drinking shops and gambling dens were the only profitable places of public amusement. Since the railroad had been pushed further west, the town had become quite orderly and the population had at the same time suffered a material diminution. During the night our attention was several times attracted outside by violent yells, accompanied with salvos of uproarious oaths and the usual demonstrations of the scientific use of the fist, but as no one was killed the reputation of the place was not effected, and the parties were allowed plenty of room to finish it out in true frontier style.

A notification that the train would depart at four o'clock in the morning, put a period to the edifying talk of the proprietor, as he found his last listeners were about to try the experiment of slumbering upon all his terrible stories. One rough old customer delivered his valedictory by informing the proprietor, "that it would be just as much as his life was worth to let him miss the train."

CHAPTER 2

Beyond the Pale of Civilization

By three o'clock the next morning the passengers were rallied at the hotel, by two coloured boys who patrolled the town for that purpose. All bills had been settled in "advance." The landlord a few moments before the starting of the train, informed us that "the cooks had overslept themselves, we would have to excuse them but it would be impossible to get breakfast before the train left;" with a parting benediction upon the landlord's head most of the passengers retired to an adjacent "rum mill" and "stowed away" a "slug" or two of "mountain dew" to keep up their spirits. Being thus provided they got on the train, a few minutes ahead of time. The locomotive whistled "up breaks" and away we started westward.

We were now fairly upon the vast expanse of country known as the Plains. The last traces of civilization had disappeared, unless we except the Iron road over which we were running, at the rate of twenty miles an hour, instead of by the earlier emigrant train, at the same rate per day. This made the wildness and solitude of the surroundings even more effective. Far in advance the road could be traced winding along over the rolling waste, rarely a straight line for any considerable distance, but taking advantage of natural depressions, avoiding the higher swells, thus saving time, labour, and capital. Nowhere were to be seen grateful visions of farmhouses, gardens, fields of waving grain, green pastures, and cattle or sheep.

The country was one vast sweep, extending as far as the eye could reach. Even that luxuriant natural growth, known popularly as the "Prairie Grass" which was found further east, had given place to a new variety. An occasional woodpile or water-tank, watched by two or three men and a squad of soldiers constituted the railway stations. A dilapidated freight car answered the double purpose of sleeping quarters and defence for the railway employees, while the soldiers occupied a few tents outside.

The reader has frequently heard of the great American Plains yet very few have ever seen them and consequently the idea the term conveys is anything but a correct conception of their natural character or their vast extent. Four hundred and twenty two miles west of the Mississippi, at St. Louis, or the ninety seventh meridian, these Plains properly begin. For a distance of nearly five hundred miles westward, or to the one hundred and fifth meridian, this vast and monotonous region stretches away to the base of the Rocky Mountains. It extends from the Red River in the south, to the Nebraska or Platte in the north, a distance of fully five hundred miles, or from latitude thirty-four to forty one degrees. This immense region embraces the western portion of the Indian Territory, western Kansas, southern Nebraska, eastern Colorado, eastern New Mexico and north-western Texas.

With the exception of the beautiful and fertile strip of country between the Red and the Washita Rivers and a few isolated and limited valleys, the country presents no features of configuration to interest the eye and no qualities of soil to invite the settler. Wave after wave rolls in endless sameness, an ocean of earth, terminating where its billows strike the immense mountain walls on the west. The soil generally is composed of an extremely sandy loam, with extensive patches of gravel, red clay and shale. Here and there are met surface indications of large beds of *gypsum*, and *strata* of sandstone and limestone.

Five large streams having their fountains within or near the spurs of the Rocky Mountains, flow the entire width of the Plains, from west to east. These are the Republican, the Arkansas, the Cimmaron, the Canadian and the Red. There are four lesser streams, the Solomon, the Smokey Hill, the north fork of the Canadian and the Washita. Besides these, innumerable tributaries answering more the purposes of an extensive system of drainage during the rainy season, than permanently flowing currents, are to be found everywhere.

A peculiar feature of all the plains streams, is the effect of the seasons upon their size. During the summer the largest rivers dwindle into utter insignificance and the fact that they were ever anything more, is only observable by their dry sandy bed covered when the streams are swelled by the melting snows and spring rains. When the larger streams are effected by the excessive lack of rain, it is easy to imagine that the tributaries and smaller water courses are lost entirely. It frequently happens that the water loses itself in the sand and at intervals of a few miles will rise again to the surface, forming a chain of ponds with no apparent communication with each other. In some of the streams the water is exceedingly impregnated with alkaline substances and is very unpalatable, as well as injurious to either man or beast. This is particularly the case with the Cimmaron region.

Timber is the rare exception, rather than the common representative of the vegetable kingdom of the plains. The traveller pursues his way for mile after mile, without seeing a single tree, nor even a shrub. Where trees are found at all, is upon the banks of some of the larger streams and then a very sparse growth. The Indian when it is possible establishes the seat of his families where wood and brush are to be had, while his hunting-parties build their fires of buffalo chips. The emigrant trails have generally been laid out with a view to the streams presenting the advantages of timber and water.

The only vegetation which thrives, is a tenacious, diminutive, but very nutritious growth called the "buffalo grass" and by some set down as a variety of mesquite. With this grass the entire country is covered, until within a short distance of the mountains where the sage brush predominates.

The traveller in passing over this country naturally asks himself the question, will this immense domain forever remain a barren waste? Extreme heats and sand storms in summer and terrific visitations of winds, snow and rain in winter are certainly not climatic considerations the most inviting. The hot winds of summer, have repeatedly demonstrated the precarious tenure of any vegetable growth, except the buffalo grass This grass driving its roots far down into the earth, seems in this manner to derive ample moisture to keep up the requisite supply. To look at the buffalo grass not over an inch in height and really resembling moss rather than what its name indicates, persons unfamiliar with its nutritious qualities would at once remark the country as worthless as a desert, though experienced frontiers-men declare that the time is not far off when stock grazing on these very plains will be a profitable and extensive employment and lands now considered not worth taking as a gift, will have their value. If this prove correct, these plains alone will graze enough cattle to feed half a dozen states. It is certain they afford sustenance to vast herds of buffaloes, which keep in wonderfully fine condition.

As daylight dawned on our way towards Fort Hays, several dark indefinable spots on the horizon were pointed out as small herds of buffalo. They were entirely too far distant to enable us to make a minute examination of the monstrous beast. We who had never yet had the pleasure of feasting our eyes upon a live buffalo, excepting some unfortunate representative of the species in a menagerie, were left at least to the gratifying reflection that we had some evidence that there were buffaloes in the country arid that such an animal had an existence, and we a very good prospect of verifying the fact.

It was not long before several shots fired from the window of the forward car created some excitement. As the savages had appeared in sight of the railroad several days before, each man seized his rifle which he loaded and kept near at hand ready for a brush. In the car in which I was seated I observed twenty-five stand of arms, breech-loading rifles, and a large chest of metallic centre primed needle-cartridges, provided by the railroad company, for the use of the employees to defend their trains against Indian attacks.

As soon as the firing commenced several of the train men rushed into the car in which I was seated, snatched a rifle from the rack, rammed a couple of handfuls of cartridges in their pockets and darted back again into the forward car.

At this juncture as I thought things were getting serious I re-examined my own rifle, buckled on a pair of pistols, slung my cartridge box over my shoulder and started forward to look into the cause of all the commotion. At this moment a shout "Buffalo crossing the track" was heard and bang! bang! bang! simultaneously went several pieces. Poking my head out of the car window I observed a small herd of six buffalo bulls running at full speed parallel with the train, about a hundred yards ahead and not more than sixty feet from the track. The stupid animals seemed bent upon crossing, but finding the locomotive pursuing too closely, at the last moment turned and attempted to get out of reach. While the pursuit was going on, a number of shots were fired but without effect.

As the herd left the track, the engineer slackened the speed of the train. A fusillade now began in earnest. Each person vied with the other in firing the most shots. Two of the animals were wounded, one mortally. The locomotive whistled "down breaks." Without waiting for the train to stop every one, engineer, conductor, brakesman and passengers, leaving only the fireman, jumped off the cars and gave chase. The wounded buffalo still on his feet, with great effort was trying to make his escape. He had been shot in the thigh and though retarded, made good progress, when another ball taking effect in the other leg, let his hind-quarters down upon the ground. Nothing daunted the wounded animal made every exertion to drag himself off, on his two fore feet, when a ball under the shoulder put an end to his sufferings and his efforts to rejoin his companions.

A cheer wound up the railroad chase, when the busy knives of "professionals" in hip-joint operations, soon had the "rumps" severed and after cutting out the tongues and a few strips of "hump" the rest of the two immense carcasses were left as a dainty and abundant re past for the wolf. The meat was put on the train, and again we continued our journey. Both the animals killed were bulls, and, judging from the rings on their horns and their long shaggy manes, had already outlived the ordinary life-time of their species.

Without further delay at about noon the train reached Hays city. Here for the present was the termination of my journey.

Hays city was, and probably is still if not migrated farther west as is a peculiar habit of plains towns, located on the rail-road, three hundred miles from the eastern state line of Kansas and five hundred and eighty three miles west of St. Louis. Its population, composed of Americans, Germans, Swiss, French, Jews, Mexicans, and a few women, numbered not more than two hundred souls. The place when the terminus of the road, could have mustered a much stronger force, but with the railroad, all the restless spirits pushed farther west. Even the houses were taken down and carried to Phil Sheridan station, a hundred miles away. The houses still standing at the time of my visit were the depot, the hotel, a dozen "rum holes" and a few shops, mainly kept by Jews, a drug store, a lawyer's office and the post-office. These were all built of wood in the most economical manner, frequently with canvas roofs. The citizens occupied *"doabee"* huts and tents.

Wonderful stories of an excessively sanguinary character were told me concerning the early ages of Hays city, that was about twelve months before. Drunken brawls, murders and robberies, were the everyday enjoyment of the citizens.

CHAPTER 3

The Indians

Leaving the train, and stepping upon the platform extending along the track, I had the good fortune to meet Lieutenant Kelley, of the "Thirty-eighth." In his company I rode over to the fort, about a mile distant. Fort Hays, the headquarters of the department in the field, was built on a high ridge rising from Big Creek, a stream twenty feet in width, and tributary to the Smokey Hill. In point of location and design, for those consigned to the isolation of life on the plains, I conceive this to be a most desirable place. The quarters consisted of a row of eight double frame houses, one and three fourths stories high, neatly furnished and painted both within and without, and had a decided appearance of comfort. These quarters fronted on one face of the parade, while the other three sides were enclosed by the frame barracks for the troops. The hospital, quartermaster's and commissary's buildings, and the corral, occupied positions apart from the fort proper. On the left were sheds with accommodations for the horses of a cavalry squadron. The country, however, in the vicinity of the fort was perfectly uninviting, and an excellent sample of the worst features of the plains; high swelling divides, covered with buffalo grass in bunches, and not a tree in sight, excepting a few scattered specimens on the banks of Big Creek.

I was kindly tendered comfortable quarters, and at the same time having made some arrangements in regard to rations, I soon felt perfectly at home. I have frequently since thanked my good fortune in meeting Lieutenant Kelley. It was to his unexpected and preliminary courtesy that I owed much of the pleasure I experienced, in more than a month's residence at the fort.

At the time of my arrival, General Sheridan, the Commanding General of the Department, was absent, but was momentarily expected from Fort Harker, where I passed his special car the night before.

The remainder of my first day I quite agreeably occupied in making the acquaintance of the little community of officers and their families. The post was commanded by Major Yard, 10th cavalry. The other post-officers were Brevet Major Kimball, Quartermaster; Dr. Buchanan, Surgeon, and Lieutenant Reed, 5th Infantry, Adjutant. The garrison consisted of Ovenshine's company, 3rd Infantry, Clous' company, 38th Infantry, and Brotherton's company, 5th Infantry. Lieutenant Borden, commanding.

The commanding general, as his military family in the field, was at this time accompanied by Brevet Brigadier General Forsyth, (Tony), Major 10th Cavalry, Inspector General; Brevet Lieutenant Colonel McGonnigle, Captain and Quartermaster; Brevet Lieutenant Colonel Crosby, 1st Artillery. Acting Assistant Adjutant General, Brevet Lieutenant Colonels Moore, Captain 40th Infantry, and Sheridan, Captain, 7th Cavalry, Aids-de-Camp, and Dr. Asch, Staff Surgeon.

After the outbreak of hostilities the only amusements away from the post, that of a gallop over the plains, or an occasional buffalo hunt, were cut off, owing to the possibility of encountering a band of warriors, or more likely being cut off by them. The society of the post was enlivened by the presence of three estimable ladies, wives of officers, Mrs. Major Kimball, Mrs. Dr. Buchanan, and Mrs. Captain Ovenshine.

During the same evening I enjoyed the honour of an introduction to the commanding general, who had now returned. Although, during the fall of 1864, I visited the Shenandoah Valley, while he was in command of that region, I was prevented, by illness, from overtaking him, in time to witness his brilliant victories, and becoming personally acquainted with him.

The conversation, of course, was on the subject of the war. Indian fighting was evidently not a new thing to the general, and his plans were so arranged as to accomplish the greatest results with the least means. His military department embraced the states of Missouri and Kansas, Colorado, New Mexico, and the Indian Territory, an extent of country equal, in area, to nearly a half dozen ordinary states. The Pacific Railway, it is true, was convenient, as communicating with the base of operations, and enabled him to establish large depots of supplies at the forts on the line. This was the least portion of the labour. Stores had to be shipped to the posts away from the railroad, and that too, within a limited time, before the setting in of the wintry storms.

Government wagon trains, as well as "citizen" trains, were constantly passing between the railroad and Forts Dodge, Wallace, and Lyon. Large contracts were also given out for the supply of Fort Bascom, from New Mexico, and Fort Arbuckle, from Kansas, and the Cherokee county. This was literally going back to warfare according to first principles. The general, certainly, had now a fair opportunity of making up his mind as to the utility, convenience, and economy of railways, as compared with wagon trains, in conducting warlike operations.

The theatre of war was so extensive, that there were about the same chances of scouting parties finding the Indians, as for a fleet of vessels at sea to encounter an enemy's squadrons. The general had thoroughly made up his mind that it was a profitless task to undertake to punish hostile bands when the grass was in a condition to afford nourishment for their ponies. At such a time he felt that they would be able to protract the war indefinitely. He resolved to make the experiment of a winter campaign. It was very certain, when the grass lacked its nutritious properties, the Indian pony would soon weaken and break down.

During the winter season he well knew the savages suspended all warlike expeditions, in a word were paralyzed. Their families could not move with the same facility as in summer, and in certain conditions of the weather it was impossible to move their lodges at all. A bold dash into the heart of the Indian country, though at the risk of much suffering to the men and loss of animals, was certain to effect some beneficial results. If it demonstrated to the savages no more than the fact that they were safe at no season of the year, that the "soldiers" could travel on the war-path when they themselves could not fight nor run away with their families, the effect would unquestionably make a deep impression on their minds.

It was still several months before winter could be considered as having fairly set in, and to start before that time would be a waste of energy and material with little chance of return. It was necessary, however, to keep advised, as far as possible, of the movements of the savage war parties, as indicated by their trails, which could be easily tracked on the plain by experienced Indian fighters. The general was particularly anxious to watch the savages north of the railroad along the Republican and its tributaries, and, by constant demonstrations, hoped so to alarm them as to cause their movement towards the south, lie would then have all the refractory bands well in hand for an excellent chase and sure punishment. At the same time the line of railroad defended, even by a small force, would be entirely safe for the passage of trains. For these reasons the majority of the preliminary movements of the campaign were directed towards the north.

It will be interesting here to furnish some statistics respecting the Indians who were hostile or contributed to the war. While the war was going on at the south, the Sioux sent parties, not only down as far as the Platte to commit depredations along the Union Pacific railroad, but a large force of warriors extended their hostile movements to the Republican, joining the northern bands of Cheyennes and Arrapahoes. With due allowance, the number of Sioux actually participating, may be set down at one thousand. This gives the following estimated results:

The bands north of the Arkansas—	
Sioux	1,000
Cheyennes	1,800
Arrapahoes	750
	3,550
The bands south of the Arkansas—	
Cheyennes	1,500
Comanches	1,500
Kiowas	1,086
Arrapahoes	860
Apaches, (Lipans)	281
Total	8,777

Out of this aggregate of all ages and sexes, the five bauds, together with the Sioux, could muster about two thousand warriors. Within the limits of the department was an aggregate Indian population, embracing friendly Indians on reservations and the wild tribes above mentioned, amounting to over ninety thousand souls.

CHAPTER 4

Events Which Preceded the Outbreak of 1868

In this connection, I desire to contribute a few preliminary historic facts respecting the Plains Indians, for the information of the reader, before proceeding farther into the events which I have to narrate. The great Indian families that once occupied the entire North American continent have presented, at different times, excellent types of intellectual and moral eminence in the leaders of the powerful coalitions of Indian valour and martial skill frequently formed to repel the aggressions of the white race. Indian history furnishes repeated instances of fierce and sanguinary wars excited by the fears or superstitions of warriors who foresaw the inevitable destiny of their race, had the heroic courage to lift their arms to check the surging wave, and were ready to die in defence of the hunting grounds of their progenitors Against the obstacles thus thrown in the way of civilization and the security of the frontiers, the white settlers continued to spread over the country, the Appalachian chain was soon crossed, and today, less than three centuries since the establishment of the first white settlement on the shores of America, the remnants only of these primitive Indian families are to be found, confined within the restricted limits of reservations west of the Father of Waters, far remote from the seats of their ancestors.

Still farther west, in the depths of the great plains extending away to the base of the Rocky Mountains, we find a savage people of the same race, but governed by widely different instincts and superstitions. Their habits vary from the other representatives of their race who lived along the great rivers of the Atlantic and in the expansive valleys of the western slope of the Alleghanies. These people of the plains are literally nomadic, and in their habits show many points of resemblance to the barbarous hordes that roam over the steppes of Central Asia.

Until within the past few years, these nomads of the great American plains, protected by the vastness and inaccessibility of the country they occupied, experienced no sense of external danger, and pursued their habits of life undisturbed and without fear. The complete seclusion of these primitive people may be judged from the fact that even now little is known of those who first came in contact with the pioneers of civilization, and there are bands at this late day that have never had any direct intercourse whatever with the whites. The aggregate population of the Indian tribes is estimated, or rather computed, at very nearly three hundred thousand souls, of which number a little more than one third dwell upon the great plains.

The census of tribes is either by actual count, upon Indian authority, or by approximation, taken for the convenience of distributing annuities to the Indians having treaty relations with the government. In some cases the census of a band is taken by the Indian chiefs themselves. This they do by requiring the heads of families to furnish a small stick for each human being in the lodge. These sticks are tied in a bundle with a strip of rawhide, and by the chief handed to the proper government officer. The chiefs always allow a liberal margin, and instances are mentioned where they did not fail to include in their count all the perceptibly prospective progeny of the band, and likewise dropped in a dog or two as an allowance for contingencies.

The feeling of security entertained by the wild inhabitants of the mountains and plains, dissipated by the encroachment of the whites, has naturally conduced to inimical relations between the two races.

The Plains Tribes have, as yet, presented no prominent warriors in the character of leaders. Their mode of living, and the precarious means of obtaining a supply of food at certain seasons, rather indicates the impracticability of ever organizing in large masses, though a confederacy of co-operating tribes would be a possibility, and, under the organizing and authoritative voice of a chief equal to the emergency, would result in a protracted, merciless, and intricate war. The plains are well adapted to the part of border hostilities, and the wild tribes that inhabit them, mounted on fleet and hardy ponies, and familiar with every foot of the monotonous waste around them, would be capable of keeping up a constant annoyance of the frontiers, retiring upon the approach of danger. The success of a campaign, in a country so extensive, would depend entirely upon the co-operation of different columns, and conducted in the winter season, in spite of wind, and rain, and snow. The possibility of such a campaign has been demonstrated in that which I am about to narrate.

In reviewing some facts in Indian affairs during the past two years, it is certain that the prosecution of our inter-oceanic railways has developed a more determined and restless spirit of opposition than that which existed against the ordinary old-fashioned emigrant trains, and will henceforth demand more enlarged efforts and vigorous measures to secure the peace, quiet, and security of the country on both sides of these great highways. The discoveries of gold and other metals, constantly enlarging our acquaintance with the auriferous regions of the far west, and the presence of government surveying parties, combine to increase this uneasiness.

To avert, if possible, the calamity of an Indian outbreak, during the summer of 1867, Congress authorized the appointment of a Board of Commissioners clothed with ample powers to treat with the Indians manifesting signs of hostility, and to seek, if possible, a practical and peaceable solution of the impending difficulties. This Board was known as the Peace Commission. To avoid all clashing of authority, the operations of the army, by order of the Executive of the nation, were made to conform to the suggestions and wishes of the Commission. Thus, with every facility open for the accomplishment of the humane wishes of the government, the Commissioners commenced the work before them. The reservation system appeared the most simple and feasible method of solving the question. It was, therefore, proposed to remove the Indians from the routes of travel and settlement, and to maintain them at the expense of the national government. To accomplish this end, it was proposed to lay out two extensive reservations—one to lie north of the State of Nebraska and west of Missouri River; the other, south of the State of Kansas and west of the Arkansas River.

With this theory in mind, and confident of the success of what they considered a plan which the Indian could easily comprehend and would be willing to accept, the commissioners made their appearance in the Indian country during the month of October following. On the twenty-first day of that month they met many of the chiefs and headmen of the Kiowa and Comanche tribes at the Council Camp on Medicine Lodge creek, seventy miles south of Fort Larned. This creek, a tributary of one of the forks of the Arkansas, was a favourite resort of the Indians on occasions of ceremony, and received its name from the practice of making "medicine" there to serve for good luck in important undertakings.

The council "talk" resulted in a treaty, so called, or agreement, to which all the chiefs and headmen of the two nations present appended their marks, and in return received some tangible evidences of the friendship of the government.

A very brief synopsis of this treaty may not be ill timed, as these documents are entirely novel, except to a limited class of officials, contractors, and speculators, particularly interested in them. The treaty provided for the protection of human life and the punishment of offenders; defined the limits of reservations; encouraged the cultivation of crops; provided for the erection of agency buildings, the transfer of lands, the payment of bounties, the employment of a physician, farmer, blacksmith, carpenter, engineer, and miller, and for the education of the Indian; defined the annuity articles to be annually distributed as follows: for each male person over fourteen years of age, a suit of good substantial winter clothing, consisting of coat, pantaloons, flannel shirt, hat, and a pair of home-made socks; for each female over twelve years of age, a flannel skirt or the goods necessary to make it, a pair of woollen hose, and twelve yards of "domestics;" for boys and girls under the ages named, such flannel and cotton goods as might be needed to make each a suit, as above, together with a pair of woollen hose for each provided for a census and the necessary appropriations to carry out the provisions of the treaties, and for the issue of hunting permits.

In regard to the security of the railways and settlements, important stipulations were entered into.

At the same time and place, the Apache (Lipan), tribe was confederated with the Kiowas and Comanches, and placed on an equal footing with them in every respect. They agreed to accept the reservation of the Kiowas and Comanches as their own, and pledged themselves to make no settlements outside.

On October twenty-eighth following, at the same place, the commissioners met the chiefs and headmen of the Cheyennes and Arrapahoes and consummated a "treaty" similar in all respects to the other, presenting only a different reservation.

Having completed their negotiations with the wild tribes of the southern plains, in the following spring the commissioners proceeded to Fort Laramie, Dakota Territory, and, at that point, arranged a "treaty" with the northern Cheyennes and Arrapahoes. Those Indians agreed to the same terms as determined with the southern bands, and also promised to occupy the northern reservation or join that portion of their people living along the Arkansas.

The main source of the uneasiness felt by the Plains Indians, as displayed in their councils, was the encroachments of the whites upon their hunting grounds. It was with a keen sense of their fate that they contemplated the opening of roads. The Sioux took a decided stand, and in very plain terms alluded to the consequences if the whites persisted in opening the road through the Powder River country, declaring that that section constituted the only hunting-grounds they had left, and that they would defend them. It was by this route that it was proposed to open communication with the upper settlements in the far west. The construction of the Platte railroad now obviated the necessity of passing through the Powder River country, and it was determined by the commissioners to comply with the wishes of the Indians by abandoning that section entirely.

Early in 1868, in compliance with this action of the commission, the general of the army gave the necessary orders for the evacuation. This surrender of territory, in compliance with the wishes of the Indians, was immediately construed into a compulsory evacuation, and even while the public stores were being removed the tribes along the route of march began open depredations. These raids were carried on as low down as the railroad and into Colorado.

The commissioners had now withdrawn and returned to Washington to make their report. They had, it is true, made "treaties," and their fulfilment was confidently anticipated. Meanwhile the northern Indians gloried in what they considered a triumph. Runners were at once dispatched to communicate with the tribes in the south, to inform them of the success of their demands for the surrender of their hunting-grounds, and advising a warlike attitude, which they declared would lead to the abandonment of the Smoky Hill country.

There is no question, that, had the commission acted on the principle of yielding nothing that had once been accomplished and contented themselves with making no new demands, except to secure the railways from attack, the result would have been different. The Indian, naturally enough, interpreted the action of the Commission to fear, because it was a part of his training to recognize such influences as the only way to bring about concessions.

CHAPTER 5

War Inaugurated

Until midsummer unusual quiet prevailed in the south. Most of the Indians had withdrawn from the vicinity of the military posts to more remote and inaccessible regions. A party of two hundred Cheyennes, four Arrapahoes and twenty Sioux, for sometime in camp on the Pawnee, north of the Arkansas, suddenly took the war path, as they asserted, against the Pawnee Indians. The movements of the savages were watched with suspicion. They had retired west of the Fort Dodge road, and with great ceremony performed the first step to a great undertaking, making "medicine." About the twelfth of August, this same party appeared in the valley of the Saline north of Fort Harker. The settlers unprepared for such a visit, treated the visitors with great kindness, hoping to dissuade them from the execution of any evil intentions they might have in view. But the savages soon threw off their guise of friendship and stood forth in their real attitude. They inaugurated their depredations by assuming a dictatorial manner. The next step was to force their way into the cabins. They now commenced to pillage and murder, and committed every form of outrage upon men, women, and children.

Two days later the same force visited the settlements on the Solomon, destroyed the houses, drove off stock, killed thirteen men, and perpetrated other barbarities. The band now broke up into detachments and scattered over the country, some moving off towards the north, along the Republican, while the main party commenced depredations along the line of the Smoky.

Intelligence of the conduct of the Indians on the Saline and Solomon was conveyed, by the fugitive settlers, to Fort Harker. The garrison was at once put in condition for active service. As a hasty means of relief to the settlements, Lieutenant Colonel Benteen, was ordered out with one company of the 7th Cavalry. On August fourteenth, he arrived at Spillman's Creek, while the Indians were attacking. His unexpected appearance so alarmed the savages that they took to flight, thus sparing the lives of the settlers at that point.

The news of the outbreak was at once communicated to General Sheridan who was at his headquarters at Fort Leavenworth. With his customary celerity of action, he resolved to take the field and inaugurate a series of movements in hopes of punishing the offenders. Fort Harker on the line of the Kansas Pacific railway, was selected as the point for headquarters in the field, removing soon after to Fort Hays, farther west. Thither the Commanding General repaired by special train. Reports were constantly coming in of other depredations. An attack was made on a Mexican train, at Pawnee fork, above the Cimmaron crossing, and a war-party of savages appeared in the vicinity of the town of Sheridan, at the terminus of the railroad; the Denver stage coaches were pursued and acts were committed which could not be misconstrued. Up to this time but two tribes, the Cheyennes and Arrapahoes, were known to have taken up the hatchet.

The commanding general at his headquarters at Fort Harker saw plainly that all peaceable efforts to secure the return of the refractory bands to order were fruitless. His only course was a resort to force. On the twenty-fourth of August, he accordingly issued a general order which served as a declaration of war. By the middle of September, the Indians in hostile numbers had made their appearance in all parts of the Department west of Fort Riley, north as far as the Platte river, to the Arkansas in the south, and westward into Colorado. The lines of travel demanding protection were the Kansas Pacific railway, for a distance of over two hundred miles, the stage routes, and lines of travel from the terminus of the railroad to Denver, nearly two hundred miles, and into New Mexico, over four hundred miles. Besides these the settlements on the Saline, the Solomon, the Republican, and the Smoky Hill, needed some means of defence, while the posts of Forts Riley, Harker, Hays, and Wallace, along the railroad. Forts Lyon and Bascom in the west. Forts Dodge, Lamed, and Zarah on the Arkansas, with an outpost at the mouth of the Little Arkansas, and Forts Arbuckle and Gibson, in the Indian Territory, required suitable garrisons.

To meet these demands upon the military force of the department, the commanding general had, as his whole available strength, nine companies of the Seventh Cavalry, eight companies of the Tenth Cavalry, eleven companies of the Third and parts of the Fifth and Thirty-eighth regiments of Infantry, a total of about twelve hundred cavalry and fourteen hundred infantry. After the distribution of this force in guarding the railroad, garrisoning the different posts, and protecting the settlements, the only force for duty in the field, consisted of eleven companies of cavalry, seven of the Seventh and four of the Tenth, making eight hundred men. Early in the preceding spring, Grierson had been sent with four companies of the Tenth Cavalry to Fort Gibson. The garrison at Fort Arbuckle was also strengthened by an increase of two companies of infantry.

With this insignificant force, available for field duty, that is eight hundred cavalry, active hostilities were commenced. The country over which the savages roamed up to this time, covered an area of at least two hundred miles from north to south, or from the Republican to the Arkansas, and almost five hundred miles from east to west, or from Fort Riley to the Rocky Mountains. The country was entirely in a state of nature, and supplies were only to be conveyed, by the tedious process of wagon transportation, at immense distances. The Indians familiar with these vast stretches of plain, and moving from place to place on his hardy pony, was not easy to find and when found was even more difficult to overtake or bring to an engagement, except with great odds in his favour.

The troops were hastened into the field, and scouting parties were sent in all directions. Colonel Forsyth (Sandy), with fifty scouts moved to the Republican on the north; Sully, towards the Cimmaron, and North Fork of the Canadian on the south, Graham conducted an expedition in the direction of Denver; Penrose pursued a party from Fort Lyon. Owing to the increasing magnitude of the war, a regiment of volunteers from the State of Kansas, was recruited by Governor Crawford, upon the authority of General Sheridan. By the latter part of September, the savages had killed eighty persons. The frontiers were now entirely abandoned by the settlers. A reinforcement of seven companies of the fifth cavalry was brought from the east, a corps of scouts was organized, and preparations were made to accumulate a large store of supplies at the principal forts.

In order to make an effort to keep the other wild tribes in peaceable relations, the commanding general met some of the leading warriors of the Arrapahoes, and about ten days later, also, met a few of the chiefs of the Kiowas, Comanches and Apaches. The savages withdrew promising to return. They kept their promises of peace by inaugurating a general attack along the line of the Arkansas. This attack was led by the Cheyennes and Arrapahoes, assisted by war-parties from the bands which had then but recently expressed in the most solemn form, their pledge of friendship. It was evident now to the satisfaction of all that the Indians were bent upon a war, and there was no alternative but to fight them.

Chapter 6

An Adventure

The "end of the track" was one of those indefinite expressions in plains parlance, having reference to the terminus of the railroad, somewhere in the wilderness of waste, far to the westward. In times of active construction on the road the expression was particularly applicable, for the last traveller would find himself penetrating regions which his itinerary predecessor of but a few days before had never thought of and probably no white man before, except the surveying party, had ever visited. The "end of the track," therefore, meant precisely where the locomotive stopped running.

At eleven o'clock on the morning of the second of October, the train for the west arrived at Hays City. I was one of a party of about half a dozen persons who had been awaiting its arrival for two long and monotonous hours.

My fellow passengers altogether numbered about twenty persons. A fiercer, hirsute, and unwashed set I never saw. With the exception of two ladies, wives of officers, the rest were just the characters a person would expect to meet so far in advance of civilization. And yet with all their rough exterior, there was traceable in most of them an honest, a wild, unrestrained independence, a frankness of temperament, a fullness of soul, somewhat surprising. It was only when the fearful flames of passion, impelled by motives of revenge or enmity, were allowed to find vent, that the worst features of their natures broke forth. For my part I found them pleasant companions, under the circumstances, and felt well satisfied I might have fared worse.

The conductor of the train was a man of sense and good address. He had much experience in life on the plains and was the man for the position he held. He always had his rifle by his side and pistols, either about his waist, or where he could conveniently put his hands upon them. He was an excellent shot, and had several bullet scars as mementoes of early conflicts.

We had hardly proceeded fifteen miles on our journey when we came in sight of several large herds of buffaloes, each numbering not less than two thousand animals. We were promised a "wonderful sight" of the beast by the conductor of the train. Indeed, so marvellous were his stories that he was listened to with evident incredulity.

As we increased the distance from the last settlement, buffaloes, rapidly grew in numbers. Thirty miles on the way the country was literally overrun. The main herds lay on the northern side of the track and as far as the eye could reach, not less than a distance of ten to fifteen miles, the plain was perfectly black with them. The herds nearest the track alarmed at the strange sounds issuing from the locomotive, set off at a rapid lope, heading towards the north, in turn setting in motion the herds before them. The huge animals raised such a dust that for some minutes it was impossible to see more than a long line of hindquarters and elevated tails. A number of isolated smaller herds which had crossed to the south upon the approach of the train, invariably raised their heads, looked at us for an instant, and then with heads down and tails up galloped towards the track making extraordinary exertions to get across ahead of the locomotive. In trying this strategic feat one specimen found himself forcibly lifted into the air and thrown into the ditch, where he lay upon his back, his cloven feet flourishing madly.

Several animals had been shot from the cars out of this herd. The train now stopped to afford time to bring in a few "rumps." While this operation was going on, a party of six or eight of us started down the track to dispatch the buffalo, still kicking and bellowing with a mixture of suspense and rage, displaying certain serpentine and spasmodic motions of the dorsal column, which indicated an effort to get on his feet. When our party got within fifty yards a shot was fired at the animal which seemed to have a peculiarly vitalizing effect. At all events it called the buffalo to a sense of his ludicrous and unnatural position. With one desperate effort the old beast regained his feet. Several more shots were instantly fired, but none seemed to take effect. Instead of retreating the irate quadruped made for our party coming at a "full jump" head down, tongue out, bleeding and frothing at the mouth, eyes flashing, and to cap the climax of his terrible exhibitions of infuriation, roared fearfully.

As there was no time to lose, and to fire at him "head on" would be but a waste of ammunition, the party scattered in all directions. For my own part, I took occasion to make a few long and rapid strides across the track into the ditch on the other side. The rest of the party imitated this dexterous movement without many moments of reflection. Losing sight of us, the enraged animal, smarting under the blow he had received from the locomotive, and the tickling he had sustained from our rifles, reaped his anger upon the opposite side of the embankment of the railroad by rending great furrows in the earth, stamping on the ground, raising a great dust, and making a terrible noise.

It was very certain there was no time to waste. Should his lordship of the plains spy any of us he would doubtless renew the offensive. Raising up so as to get a partial sight of his carcass, not over thirty feet off", three of our party fired, the rest holding in reserve. Every ball seemed to take effect. Almost instantly the animal fell upon his knees. The rest then fired, when the animal rolled completely over. His tenacity of life was perfectly wonderful. By this time he must have had a dozen bullets in his body. Notwithstanding all this he struggled and swayed to and fro until he again brought himself to his feet. But all power to harm had fled. Planting himself firmly, moving his head to the right and left, his eye still full of fire, the noble beast looked even more defiant. From his nostrils ran streams of blood.

To put the animal out of misery was the first sense of recovery from our stampede. Repeated shots were fired into his body. Thug, thug, the bullets could be heard penetrating his thick hide. As each ball entered, a slight turn of the head and switch of the tail were the only external indications of the effect of the bullet. At length after having been literally "peppered" with lead, a sudden quiver passed over the animal's entire frame, he staggered and fell. One deep gasp, a convulsive motion of the jaws, one sudden flash of the eye, a quantity of dark clotted blood ejected from the nostrils, and the buffalo was dead.

Never before had I seen such an exhibition of tenacious rage and vitality. Had the animal been less injured by the locomotive, it would be difficult to say what would have been the result of his charge upon our party. It is a question, however, whether a buffalo would attack from the mere impulse of destruction. I have found the buffalo, compared with his remarkable physical strength, rather disposed to be timid. Several horsemen could ride into the midst of a herd of ten thousand with comparative safety, select their game and dispatch it; but when wounded the whole nature of the animal seems changed. He turns upon his pursuers, and death it is to him who ever falls into his power. Not satisfied with goring his victim until he is a mangled mass, he frequently plunges upon the remains until mashed into a perfect jelly. The vital spot in a buffalo is immediately under the shoulder, penetrating the heart or the lights. On the forehead the bullet of the most powerful rifle has no effect whatever, the force being entirely expended on the immense mat or "mop" of hair, eight or ten inches in length, between the eyes.

After our somewhat exciting battle, taking a last look, and I must say I felt a pang of shame as I left the inanimate carcass a useless waste, we hastened back to the train which was ready to move on and had been signalling us for some minutes.

For sixty miles the same great multitudes of buffaloes appeared in sight without signs of diminution in numbers. Beyond this, as we approached Sheridan station, the herds grew less in size and more isolated until they disappeared from view. 1 computed, during the entire day there were in sight from the train, not less than two hundred thousand animals of all ages.

At six o'clock in the afternoon we reached the end of steam travel on the Kansas Pacific railway. The end of the track presented all the appearance of work very abruptly terminated. At the very extreme point was a plain wooden mile-post painted white, with the characters "*405 to S. L,*" 405 miles to the State Line, that is of Kansas, at Kansas city The objective point of the road, contemplated in the law, is the Pacific ocean with a branch to Denver. The Pacific is to be reached by a more southerly route passing through Alburquerque, New Mexico, Southern Arizona, into Southern California. The length of the road from its initial point will be over two thousand miles.

CHAPTER 7

A Night in a Frontier Town

Owing to the dangers of travel on the lines of communication with points farther west, I found myself booked for the night at Sheridan. The Santa Fe coach was announced to leave the following morning. The prospect was anything but agreeable. I was, however, fortunate enough to make the acquaintance of Colonel Stone, the agent of the coach line, and enjoyed in his company quite an interesting evening. Colonel Stone (how he got his title I did not learn) was a man of tall, sinewy form, and, judging from a half-hand which he displayed every now and then, seemed to be a character after the true style of the country. According to his account, he had experienced all the "ups and downs" of frontier life, and, though he got through with his life, he bore off numerous scars and other souvenirs of his eventful career.

Among the wonders of Sheridan then on exhibition, were the remains of a saurian animal discovered near the town by a Swiss watchmaker named Brandt. Most of the bones of the monster, in a fine state of preservation by means of petrifaction, were in the possession of the Swiss. For the convenience of the curious, the remains were arranged on a table in the rear of his shop. The reptile measured, when alive, at least forty-five feet in length—the Swiss insisted upon one hundred and forty-five feet! The lower jaw must have been over four feet in length, and the teeth, some of which were very well preserved, were perfect cones in shape—the largest about an inch and a half in height and one inch in diameter at the base. Several about eighteen inches in length. Several sections of the vertebra measured seven inches in diameter. The reptile was found in a *cañon* about three-fourths of a mile from the town. It was lying near the surface, with a portion exposed.

According to the Swiss's description, the monster was moving across the canon at the time of its death, and lay with its head on one side and its tail on the other, while in the centre a space of several feet was washed away. The country around Sheridan I found wonderfully prolific in petrifactions of all kinds. The rocks which appeared upon the surface were frequently rather remarkable, presenting a variety of marine shells. There was no doubt in my mind, from the numerous exhibitions of submarine formations, that, at some remote period, the entire country formed the bed of a vast inland sea.

Sheridan compared very favourably with other plains towns. It contained a population of one hundred and fifty souls, and from accounts all were desperate characters. After the suspension of work on the railroad, the population, which at one time was much larger, suddenly diminished. Frequently the citizens were put to great straits to secure a maintenance. Many lived by poisoning wolves and selling the skins, for which they realized a dollar, or a dollar and a half, each, according to size. It was hardly the proper season for this work, although parties were engaged in it, and found no difficulty in disposing of their stock. I was told by one person that in the winter he could make from seventy-five to a hundred and fifty dollars per month out of the wolf skins he could secure. The wolf family is rather large on the plains, and a liberal application of strychnine evidently would not be seriously fell for some time to come.

Ten o'clock in the evening I discovered was the regular hour for the public entertainments to begin, which consisted of a skirmish with pistols, or a series of pugilistic encounters, in which it rarely happened that both parties come off with their lives, or at least without receiving a damaging and indelible remembrance of the contest. I had already heard fearful stories of the "quiet and orderly" town of Sheridan, and, as much as possible, kept clear of the streets from fear of some stray pistol ball, by mistake, finding a lodgement in my own person.

The week before, the Sheridanites, according to their own accounts, had had "a beautiful time." During that week six men had been shot in drunken brawls. On the Sabbath night the honour of two more specimens was brought into antagonism over the flowing bowl. Pistols were produced, and the "popular tragedy" opened. One was mortally wounded. The other set out with a view to escape. He was closely pursued. The pursuers fired repeatedly, which was responded to by the fugitive. After a lively chase and considerable firing the pursued was overtaken. He fought desperately, but without avail. A rope was procured; one end was fastened around the victim's neck, the other to a cross-tie in the tressel railroad bridge at the town. The victim was then forcibly ejected between the ties into space below, and was there left to shuffle off this mortal coil; which was more readily done than to shuffle off the coil which had been prepared for him by his peculiarly justice-loving fellow-citizens.

The business of Sheridan was monopolized, almost exclusively, by that enterprising, homeless race, the Jews. The universality of enterprise of these modern representatives of that ancient and numerous family circle is probably more completely illustrated upon the plains than anywhere else. It would seem, from their appearance, manner, and want of knowledge of the language, that it was only the new importations from Germany, particularly, who constituted the specimens sent out. It was the rare exception to find an Americanized member of the family exposing himself to the dangers of a scalpless *pate*, or to the discomforts and isolation of frontier society. How they managed to subsist was a mercantile problem which I could not penetrate nor unravel.

The favourite branch of business to which they devoted their attention was the sale of clothing and cheap notions, and generally had a stock equal to the emergencies of a community of ten times the gross invoice of that which really existed. If any Indians, of a friendly band, happened near at hand they drove a fair trade by bartering their cheap commodities at high rates for skins at low rates. These pioneers of business were, generally, the representatives of large establishments in the east, and were evidently set up in trade by advancing a supply of goods on easy terms, and were sent out into the remote regions of the plains to "cut their eye-teeth," and otherwise show themselves meriting the reward of increased confidence.

At the time of my visit, Sheridan was in a state of siege. Several days before, a large war-party of savages had appeared upon two buttes near the town and opened fire upon the inhabitants. Everybody rushed to arms, and for the larger part of the day a spirited fusillade was kept up. The people of the place at once organized a regular corps of defenders, and detachments were on the watch day and night. On the more prominent eminences pickets were posted to signal the approach of war-parties. At night the guard was doubled so as to completely encircle the town.

The first thing upon my arrival I negotiated for quarters at the "hotel." There being but one in the place, the choice was not difficult. At bedtime I was escorted to a small enclosure immediately over the bar-room. The establishment below was of that enterprising character that kept no count of time. During the entire night I enjoyed, quietly, not only one of those phases in human life which is to be found nowhere else but in the bar-room, but also a vivifying anxiety and trepidation in anticipation of a pistol ball or two finding its way through the thin floor into my bed. This sort of bedfellow I certainly had no desire to cultivate. In the midst of all the frontier slang, crudely-fashioned oaths, and unpolished vulgarities inspired by oft-repeated charges of "chain lightning," which electrified the boisterous crowd below, my attempts at slumber were anything but satisfactory.

CHAPTER 8

Off for Fort Wallace

At an early hour on the following morning, an unusual din below suggested that the day's duties had commenced, a routine invariably inaugurated with cocktails "all around." A voice from the foot of the stairs proclaimed "breakfast—ye better be dusting up thar—stage—Santa Fé—time up." These incongruous observations were instantly obeyed, and in very few minutes the lodgers dropped down stairs with a rush.

By the time we had "tossed" in a breakfast, composed of half-cooked meat, as tough as India rubber, and boiled potatoes as hard as bullets, the announcement was made that the "stage" was ready to get off. There were three passengers besides myself—a government land surveyor, a Pennsylvanian, travelling without any special object, a delightful recreation, indeed, in such a country, and a Jew. On account of hostilities I found that the daily line had been abandoned and two coaches were run together on alternate days, one for passengers and the other for a military guard, freight, and the mails. The time of departure having arrived, the baggage and mails were stowed away in the boot and on the driver's box of the first coach.

With pistols and rifles, my fellow-passengers and myself took possession of the interior of the same vehicle. The second coach carried the heavier packages and the guard, consisting of six "brunette" soldiers. The coaches were modelled after the American pattern, and were each drawn by four horses. The inside accommodations were for six persons on two seats. Both coaches were painted red, and in a bold and artistic display of white paint were portrayed the words "*Overland Stage Company, Santa Fé.*"

As soon as the driver mounted the box, there began a series of equine quadrilles, swingle-tree, and bar exercises, with an enlivening

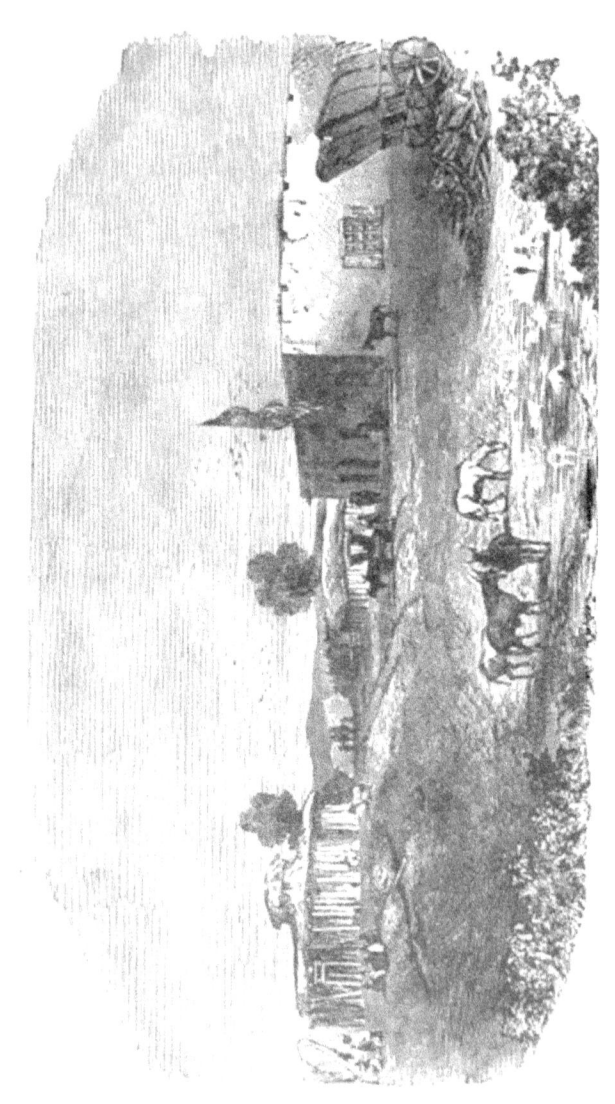

A STATION ON THE STAGE ROUTE

admixture of feathery and fantastic aerial performances of the nether hoofs. The driver with great ceremony from his seat, bade "goodbye" to all the crowd of persons who had gathered around, probably having in his mind, not only the usual interchange of courtesies, but the uncertainties of stage-driving in that exciting country. He evidently felt relieved after complying with this last act of friendship, and seemed to feel little anxiety as to whether he should ever greet the familiar and expectant faces awaiting him at the other extremity of his perilous journey. The silent and lamb-like passengers within the coach were seriously disconcerted at the cool formality. It shivered four frames with dreadful visions of reeking scalping knives, tomahawks, spears, and all sorts of implements of savage greeting on the plains.

The conversation immediately turned upon the latest barbarities, with refreshing details. The government surveyor, who "had been on the plains before," was the oracle and cyclopedia of information combined. He graphically narrated a few of the peculiar customs of the wild tribes, for instance, the Apaches, when they took a prisoner tied him up to a tree by the heels and built a slow fire under his head, in which tedious manner the fires of life were choked, smoked, and burnt out. He also stated, that generally the women, probably under the direction of one of that love-sighing, poetized maiden class, did the torturing, such as throwing spears, and shooting arrows into the carcases of their victims and otherwise entertained them, while the warriors sat around and admired the ingenuity of the partners of their *wigwams*. It was not with sentiments of the highest appreciation that these illustrations of savage customs were contemplated. The portable arsenal which each one of our party represented, was re-examined and suggestions were interchanged as to the best mode of defence. Each one made up his mind precisely what he would do in event of attack, all of which were human impossibilities.

While this serious and contemplative state of affairs existed inside the coach, the driver on the outside preserved his outward hilarity. Whether the same feelings penetrated his interior, could not be detected. These brave, reckless, rollicking men, so inured to every danger, accept the situation philosophically, and instead of consuming the peace of mind in endless anxiety, look confidently upon the future. The moment of actual danger is sufficient for them. The past is forgotten, the present is their immediate concern. The future beams full of hope. They live the philosopher, and meet their often fearful fate under the same rigid teaching which the severe lessons of their lives afford them.

Whack! whack! the huge strip of "rawhide" used as a whip, descended upon the impatient and expectant quadrupeds, literally "making the fur fly." Hi! Hi! ejaculated the driver, who was responded to with fit vocal demonstrations by the citizens, by way of a parting and enthusiastic peroration. The uproar, as well as the smarting influence of the lash, was electric. The animals set off with a bound. The sudden *impetus* of the start was met by an adverse motion, causing the occupants of the front seats inside to lose their equilibrium and the whole contents of the coach were suddenly deposited with considerable emphasis towards the rear. The horses dashed wildly out of the town, accomplishing that feat literally in about four jumps and in a few moments were ascending the gradually rising plain in the direction of the Smoky Hill.

Having exhausted our powers of imagination in portraying for our own benefit and mental preparation for emergencies, such lively pictures of the hazards of "staging it" in the savage countries, the least we expected was a distant view of the noble warrior of the plain, say upon some remote swell in the vast expanse, from which stand-point he was known to possess many features for interesting and vigilant observation. Such, however, was not our fortune. The horses galloped along at a lively gait. The coaches or "prairie clippers," as they are called by the denizens of the country, pitched and jolted. The broad plain spread around. Not a sign of life was visible. But two days before the trail was watched by a large party of larking warriors. The eye now wandered to the utmost limits of vision in vain. Alarmed at the activity of the troops, the war parties had evidently withdrawn to a safer distance, thus dissipating our anticipations of a cordial and warm reception into the "wild country."

The arrival of the coach at the fort was the occasion of a general turn-out of the officers of the garrison. The first inquiry was after the mail and while that was being assorted, in the sutler's store, a group assembled around asking after every item of news from Sheridan, as if that enterprising "city" were in the heart of business, trade, and fashion. Fortified with a letter of introduction from General Sheridan to Colonel Bankhead, commandant, at the earliest moment I singled out that gentleman and presented the document.

Fort Wallace resembled Fort Hays in design, but was greatly inferior in construction. The site occupied a swell in the plain, which gave it a commanding view of the country for miles in every direction. It was exclusively a military post. Several companies of infantry and a squadron of cavalry, commanded by Colonel Carpenter, constituted the garrison. The nearest settlement was Pond City, quite an extravagant appellation for a relay station with a community of about a half a dozen semi-barbarous inhabitants. Exclusive of this frontier emporium and Sheridan, about fifteen miles distant, there was not a settlement within a hundred miles of the fort.

As may be imagined, the arrival of a stranger, and particularly a visitor so recently from "the States," was a rare and important event in the daily routine of the garrison. It was, therefore, not many moments before the writer found himself, and most readily too, the target of a diversity of interrogatories embracing a bewildering range of topics.

CHAPTER 9

Forsyth's Battle of the Arrickaree Fork

At Fort Hays having learned that the scouts, who had fought the savages on the Arrickaree, had returned to Fort Wallace, the time of my visit to that post was hastened. As soon as the civilities incident to my arrival were over, I seized the earliest moment to mingle with the scouts in their own camp, and at his own request afterwards, met their brave commander in the hospital. From the scouts themselves I learned the following particulars of this brilliant and heroic achievement; I allude to it, somewhat in detail, because it is a sample of the ill-requited, but desperate character of warfare on the plains.

During the latter part of August, 1868, General Sheridan authorized the organization of a body of scouts, for the purpose of making a thorough reconnoissance of the country towards the north, between the Republican and the Smoky Hill Rivers, in order to discover the movements of the savages who had committed the depredations on the Solomon and the Saline. Forty seven picked frontiersmen were found willing to undertake the hazardous mission. Colonel Forsyth, and Lieutenant Beecher, of the 3rd Infantry, were assigned to command, and Dr. Moers attended the party as surgeon. A body of men had never assembled better adapted to the work. The majority were old plain's men, accustomed to every hardship and "dead shots" with the rifle. The party set out from Fort Hays moving towards the Solomon, and scouting westward, brought up at Fort Wallace. This preliminary movement was without incident worthy of note.

After refitting at Fort Wallace, on September 10, the expedition set out once more. Two days after, a small war-party of Indians was discovered but was not considered worth pursuing. Three days more were consumed in reaching the Republican, and following its winding: course until arriving at the Delaware or Arrickaree Fork. During this time but few savages were seen, though the indications of the recent presence of large numbers were unmistakable.

At daylight, on the morning of September 17, before the scouts had saddled their horses, shouts of Indians! Indians! were given. An advanced party of twelve savages dashed towards the scouts yelling fiercely, firing and weaving their blankets, in hopes of stampeding the animals. Seven horses made their escape and were taken. The rest were seized and, with great difficulty, prevented from getting away. After brisk firing the attacking party was driven off. Orders were then given to saddle and mount, but before the command could be complied with the country, in the vicinity, literally swarmed with warriors. From their trappings, they were discovered to be Cheyennes, Arrapahoes and Sioux.

The position occupied by the scouts was greatly exposed. The valley in which they stood was covered with high grass, under protection of which the Indian sharp-shooters, with comparative safety were enabled to approach within easy range The scouts, therefore, fell back and took position on a small island in the stream nearby. The new ground had the advantage of an open space for some distance on all sides. Closely pressed, in making this movement, they were compelled to abandon what few supplies they had left, and also their medicines.

Upon reaching the island, the men tied their horses to a few stunted trees, and immediately prepared for action. The savages finding themselves foiled in what they evidently relished as an easy capture of their prey, were mad with rage; or two hundred of their number were dismounted to act as sharpshooters, while five hundred of their bravest warriors remained in the saddle and prepared to charge. The mounted savages disrobed themselves of all useless trappings. With faces hedaubed with war paint, bodies bare to the waist, with shields, bows, arrows, spears, rifles and pistols, flourishing in the air, they presented a fearful scene for the contemplation of the beleaguered party.

The old war-chief addressed his warriors. The "big medicine" man galloped up and down in front beating his drum and exclaiming "the white man's bullets will melt before you." The women and children gathered on the hills around to see their people scalp the pale face. Some danced and shouted, others pressed closely upon the rear of the warriors, determined to follow and share with them their bloody work.

These were breathless moments on the island. The day was bright and cheerful. The savage warriors were seen upon the plain making their final dispositions preparatory to an attack.

It was now nine o'clock in the morning. A few desultory shots had been fired. The women could be heard chanting their songs of victory. The old men narrated the deeds of their forefather's to excite the emulation of the young. The medicine man shouted and beat his drum.

The war-chief with all the dignity of command, now waved his weapons, and gave the fierce war-whoop. With one responsive yell the warriors dashed across the plain. On the island all was quiet. Each man held his weapon firmly and calmly for a desperate defence. With yells, and violent gestures, on came the surging savage hordes. As the advanced line plunged within range, the quick rifles of the scouts greeted them. Suddenly a wall of fire rose to check the tide. Many a warrior bit the dust. The savage front quivered, for a moment it hesitated. Every instant was in favour of the scouts. Their fire grew more rapid and their aim steadier and more deadly. Astounded at the opposition the savage line halted, and the next moment was sent reeling back out of range. Within ten feet of the position of the scouts were several bodies of the "red skins," either lifeless or writhing in the agonies of death, while others were being dragged off by their fellow-warriors.

The scouts also suffered. The first one of the party hit was Forsyth, the ball lodging in the upper part of the leg. A second ball struck him in the calf of the left leg, fracturing the bone about the centre, and passing out in front. At the same time Beecher received a ball in the side, which passing through the body, fractured the spine, proving mortal. Dr. Moers was shot in the head and died three days afterwards.

All the officers were now either killed or wounded. The savages, undaunted at the warm reception they had received, were evidently resolved to try another attack. Notwithstanding his wounds Forsyth continued in command, giving his orders through his trusty chief of scouts, Grover, or "sharp Grover," as he was designated by his comrades. Grover was just the man for the desperate emergency.

The lull in the conflict was improved by digging rifle pits, which was accomplished with sheath and jack-knives. Grover enlarged the area of his pit, so as to afford protection for his commander.

The savages were ready to attack a second time. The chief, with a bearing of command, and in a voice of authority, addressed his people. "Young warriors, we are many and the whites are few. The white bullets are wasted. Once more and we bring the white man's scalp to our fires."

The warriors yelled assent. Grover, understanding the chiefs language, took an opportunity to respond to the royal savage. At the top of his voice he shouted, "Hello, old feller, got any more people to kill? This is pretty tough, ain't it?" The surprised chief involuntarily shouted back, "you speak right straight."

Just before noon the Indians made their second attack. The scouts, better protected, took cooler aim. The Indian line again reeled and fell back. Immediately a renewed effort was made but was again unsuccessful. In these attacks two of the scouts were killed.

Failing to accomplish their purpose the warriors opened fire upon the horses tied to the trees. After a considerable consumption of ammunition, the death of the last animal was announced by a young warrior, who sprung from behind a bunch of grass about a hundred yards distant, exclaiming in good American, "there, the last d——d horse is shot."

Between ten and three o'clock in the afternoon, the savages again attacked, but in their own mode of fighting, by circling around the scouts, indulging in bravado, and gesticulating violently. This was the last regular attempt of the day.

Forsyth now found his condition to be anything but cheering. Himself disabled, his lieutenant dead, his surgeon barely alive, three men killed and fifteen wounded, all this out of an aggregate of fifty. The savages were still besieging him. His horses were killed and his command was almost out of food. It was necessary, at all hazards, to notify the troops at Fort Wallace of his condition. Two daring young men, Stillwell and Truddell, volunteered for the dangerous mission. With their trusty rifles in hand and a scanty supply of food, the messengers disappeared in the darkness of night. In their success rested the only hope of escape. As they were departing, borne upon the still air, were sounds of woe from the savage camp. The songs of victory in the morning were now turned to the sorrowing tones of wailing. The dead were receiving the last offices of the living, and the wounded, in their moments of agony and death, heaped imprecations upon their pale-faced enemy.

Early the next morning a party of savages dashed upon the island, probably imagining the scouts had left. A well-directed volley, not only changed the direction of their gallopade, but two warriors were brought to the ground as a punishment for their temerity.

No regular attack was made during the day, which gave the scouts an opportunity to sink wells and make other preparations to sustain a siege. The most alarming danger which now made itself felt was the scarcity of food.

On the third day a war party was seen stealthily peeping over the hills, evidently looking for a chance to make a dash. On the same afternoon, twenty-five warriors approached, bearing a white flag. The scouts motioned to them to keep off. Forsyth remarked, "tell them this is no peace commission, shoot the first red devil who comes within range." Three dead bodies of their warriors were lying on the island. It was supposed the object of the party with the flag was to secure them, but Indian treachery was too well known. The savages retired.

It was now evident the Indians had no disposition to renew the conflict. A few of the scouts visited the old camping-ground. Several camp kettles were found and brought in, with some grains of coffee picked out of the sand. Fires were made out of the Indian arrows gathered in the vicinity and on the island. A refreshing but scant allowance of coffee was distributed among the wounded, which seemed to revive their energy and gave them a new lease of strength to endure their privations and sufferings. Fires were built in the trenches, and large quantities of horse-flesh, cut from the dead animals were jerked, after the fashion of the Indians, thus affording a supply for at least several days. Graves were dug and the bodies of the dead were gathered for interment. No martial note, no tread of sorrowing comrades, no religious form, marked this closing scene of mortality. The wolf's low howl and the sighing north wind alone sings their requiem.[1]

From these sad and rude rites of burial, the living turned to thoughts of self. The same night two more messengers, Donovan and Plyly, were sent to seek relief.

Four long and weary days had passed. A small party of warriors remained in the vicinity watching the movements of the scouts, the main body, however, had departed. The well men, relieved of the constant watching, now gave some attention to the wounded. Their injuries, which had grown very painful, were rudely dressed. Soup was made out of horse-flesh. Shelters were constructed protecting them from the heat, damp, and wind.

---

1. A party sent out from Fort Wallace the following winter to bring in the bodies returned, having been unsuccessful. The graves were found but no signs of the bodies, the savages evidently having exhumed them.

On the sixth day the wounds of the men began to show more decided and alarming signs of neglect. Maggots infested them and the first traces of gangrene had set in. To multiply the discomforts of their situation, the entire party was almost overpowered by the intolerable stench created by the decomposing bodies of the dead horses. Their supply of meat was nearly exhausted. Under these trying circumstances, Forsyth assembled his men. He told them they "knew their situation as well as he. There were those who were helpless, but aid must not be expected too soon. It might be difficult for the messengers to reach the fort, or there might be some delay by losing their way. Those who wished to go should do so and leave the rest to take their chances." With one shout the men resolved to stay, and if all hope vanished to die together.

At last the supply of jerked horse-meat was exhausted and the chances of getting more were gone. By this time the carcasses of the animals were a mass of corruption. There was no alternative. Strips of putrid flesh were cut and eaten. The effect of this offensive diet was nauseating in the extreme. An experiment was made to improve the unpalatable flesh with gun-powder, but without avail. The men allayed only their most extreme cravings of hunger, trusting still that succour might reach them before all was over.

On the morning of September 25, the sun rose with unusual splendour, and upon its bright colours seemed to play the brighter effulgence of the ray of hope. The solitary plain, receding in all directions, possessed a deeper interest than ever before, though still it showed no signs of life, and presented the same monotonous expanse upon which the heroic band had gazed for so many days. Across the dim and indefinable distances which swept around the eye often wandered, wondering what might be the revelations of the next moment. Suddenly several dark figures appeared faintly on the horizon. The objects were moving. The question was, are they savages or the messengers of relief?

As on such occasions of anxiety and suspense, time wore on heavily; yet every moment brought the sufferers nearer to the realization whether this was their doom or their escape. Over an hour had elapsed, when the objects were distinctly defined to be troops, and probably the relief party. The strong set up a shout such as men seldom utter. It was the unburdening of the heart of the weight of despair. The wounded lifted their fevered forms and fixed their glaring eyes upon the now rapidly-approaching succour, and in their delirium involuntarily reiterated the acclamations of their comrades.

As soon as the scouts made a signal of their presence. Carpenter and Fitzgerald and the scout Donovan, with thirty men, dashed ahead and were soon in the midst of the little band whose joy and relief now knew no bounds.

The day following, Bankhead arrived with supplies, while Brisbin, with a detachment of the Second Cavalry, arrived accidentally from the north.

The immediate demands of hunger were allayed, and the injuries of the wounded received a primary dressing. Preparations were made to return to the fort at once. The more severely wounded were put into ambulances. Those slightly, together with the well, were placed in wagons. After a march of several days, the rescuers and the rescued arrived at Fort Wallace. The entire loss of the scouts, including Lieutenant Beecher and Dr. Moers, was five killed and fifteen wounded. The savages lost not less than seventy-five killed and wounded. The bodies of five Cheyenne warriors killed were found by the troops on their way to the relief.

CHAPTER 10

Return to Fort Hays

The warm reception which greeted Forsyth's little band on the tributaries of the Republican, had the effect of increasing, to the highest degree, the determination of the commanding general to punish the refractory tribes, not only to convince them of their weakness when brought into collision with the strong arm of the government, but to reduce them to such a condition of feebleness and fear that they would see the folly of opposition and be content to remain upon their reservations.

Sheridan, taking a practical view of the trouble, advocated a sound thrashing as the first step to quieting the tribes on the war-path. The government had been paying large annuities in goods and granting liberal supplies of food, as bribes, to keep the savages at peace. At the same time, the Indian trader subject to no responsibility, sold arms and ammunition. In 1867, it was an offence, subject to trial by court martial, to shoot an Indian under any circumstances. The savages naturally grew arrogant and insulting, while the soldier, under the rigid rules of discipline, was compelled to submit to his humiliation.

On one occasion some Indians asked for rifles and powder; they were told they could have neither, as they would "shoot soldiers." They replied, "no, no, me no usee to puff soldiers, me usee kill buffalo heap; me chase soldier and drive way with sticks." Such was the contempt inspired by a pacific course. Sheridan's control of affairs, in connection with the new outbreak, promised activity, summary punishment, and a conquered peace, three things novel in the history of our Indian wars.

The few days which I passed at Fort Wallace was not one of the most unpleasant experiences, but it certainly was one which I would not court as a steady duty. The quarters were small and well ventilated by a series of cracks, and other openings, which suggested no allowance in the construction for shrinkage. About a dozen officers, and three ladies, constituted the society of the post. In order to wile away the dreary hours off duty, all sorts of recreations were invented. Prolonged conversations upon a diversity of subjects, together with a sociable pull at the garrison pipe, absorbed more regularly and more largely that daily burden called time.

Books, newspapers, and occasional letters, were a pleasing reserve. Owing to the hostility of the Indians, the manly sport, the chase, was almost excluded from the list of pastimes, and when participated in by a few of the more daring, was confined within a very limited radius, the fort constituting the centre. The buffalo, alarmed by the martial demonstrations constantly invading his haunts, had left for more remote and secluded localities, leaving only a few herds of timid antelope, and an abundance of sneaking wolves, for those who were fond of hazarding a chase.

A military fort on the plains suggests very forcibly the peculiar inspiration of a ship at sea; isolation within and desolation without. The same rigid enforcement of discipline unremittingly exacted, as if in the face of the enemy. The commandant, a sort of supreme authority, executive, legislative, and judicial. All the forms of military etiquette observed. The flag hoisted every morning at sunrise and dropped at sunset, attended by the same roll of the drum, and the same reverberations of the evening gun. A furlough or brief "leave" was one of those pleasures in anticipation, which seemed to compensate for the lack of other mental relief. If there be any who deserve the sympathies of those who enjoy comfortable and secure homes in the settlements, they are the officers and soldiers condemned to the isolation of duty on the plains.

During my stay at the fort I had an opportunity to witness one of those atmospheric demonstrations peculiar to the plains. It was one of those windy and turbulent conditions of the ethereal sea called "northers," for convenience, probably, as they are known to blow at various times from all directions. Early in the evening the sky blackened up as if about to deluge the earth with a storm of ink. At about seven o'clock a fearful roar was heard, sounding like the surf beating upon a rock-bound shore. There was about as much stir and excitement in the garrison as might be expected on ship-board on a sudden indication of a squall. Windows were fastened down and doors barricaded. In a few moments a terrific volume of wind came thundering up, causing the frail pine dwellings, occupied by the officers, to creak and sway as if the very next moment would see them shivered into fragments. The wind brought with it a variety of waifs, in the way of sticks and pebbles, which pelted against the sides and roofs of the quarters like the rattle of musketry. Clouds of fine sand filled the air, almost to suffocation, and beat into the buildings through the most diminutive apertures.

The next morning, the force of the storm, which had now spent itself, was discernable in a variety of visible exhibitions. Unroofed sheds, boards scattered in every direction, tents blown away, a battery of howitzers forced several feet from their position, ambulances and wagons blown some distance across the parade or out on the plain, some overturned and others with their covers rent into shreds. Indeed it took the garrison several days to gather up the debris and repair damages.

The commanding general having arrived, a few days late to make a personal inspection of the buildings and garrison, I took the opportunity of his departure to return to Fort Hays. After a hasty cup of coffee, in the gray of the morning, in an ambulance, drawn by four sprightly mules, and followed by an escort of cavalry, we dashed out of the fort. A drive of two hours brought us to Sheridan, where a special train was in readiness.

On the return, the general took occasion to stop at several stations to examine the defences, which the detachments of coloured troops distributed along the railroad, had built for themselves, and in which they had displayed wonderful skill and ingenuity. These defences they very aptly termed "underground monitors." The process of building one of these ingenious little defensive works was first to dig a hole ten feet square or more, according to the number of men to be accommodated, and about breast deep. The soil, being very compact, made excellent walls. Upon the surface a sod breast, about eighteen inches thick and a foot high, was built on each face of the square, and over head a plank roof was thrown, covered with a thick mass of earth, rendering the top bullet-proof In the sod walls and angles a number of loop-holes were cut, allowing free scope for firing in every direction. These works were reached by a subterranean passage, with the entrance as much as thirty feet distant. Where several were built they were connected also by subterranean passages.

A test of the defensible qualities of the "under-ground monitors" was made by a large party of warriors attacking one occupied by five soldiers. The savage party had stumbled upon the "monitor," and approached it out of curiosity. Their curiosity was considerably disturbed upon being received with a volley of bullets. After attempting all sorts of ruses and expedients to dislodge the soldiers, the savages left, having suffered a loss of several of their number. This single experience had a marvellous effect, eliciting a profound and distant recognition for all similar contrivances.

An amusing incident is mentioned, in which the invulnerability of the "monitors" was placed in a very dubious light. One day all except the lookout had retired to the "monitor," which had also the recommendation of affording fine protection from the intolerable heat of the sun. The men were lounging upon bunks which they had constructed within. Quite unexpectedly a huge "diamond" rattle-snake made his appearance. The entire garrison hastily decamped. The hideous old serpent coiled himself on the ground and began a vigorous presentation of fangs. The late occupants were now on the outside looking in through the port-holes. The triumph of the venomous intruder was short lived. The men opened a volley from without and soon dispatched him.

The "monitor" had achieved such a popularity that it was introduced, very generally, at the stations west of Fort Hays, by the railroad employees, as a place of refuge in an extremity of danger.

At a woodpile I observed one evidently built for the accommodation of a single person. While stopping to "wood up," I entered into conversation with an old man who seemed to be sole monarch of the establishment, wood-pile included. I inquired of him whether he had any fears of the Indians. He replied: "No; I am an old man, and have not many years longer to live anyhow; if they come around these parts and get me out there, it will only be cutting off a life already more than most people live." This was, indeed, philosophy reduced to a fine point. The old fellow appeared to be perfectly resigned and cheerful, whatever might be the fate awaiting him.

During the entire journey, we were passing through immense herds of buffalo. As the chances for shooting were admirable, I left the general's car, taking my rifle and posted myself on the cow-catcher, or rather buffalo-catcher of the locomotive. After proceeding about ten miles, we struck a large herd crossing the track. The locomotive pursued its course without diminution of speed. Approaching the herd rather rapidly, I did not favour the idea of receiving a buffalo in my lap, a fact growing momentarily more probable. The herd had passed.

One animal lagging in the rear out of bewilderment, or reckless daring, planted himself in the middle of the track, with his head down as much as to say, "Come on whoever you are and we'll try."

As I felt no relish to be a party to any such cranial collision, and finding no other convenient place, took a conspicuous but uncomfortable position on the steam-chest, holding on by the rail, I found the temperature as far as my feet were concerned anything but desirable, but in momentary anticipation of a rare display of buffalo-meat, kept a sharp lookout for the pieces. At this moment, the whistle blew. The buffalo, startled at the shrill sound, made an effort to get out of the way. He succeeded, so far as to have his posteriors pretty well damaged, that is minus his tail, and to wind up with a series of acrobatic exercises over the embankment.

Upon his return to Fort Hays, the commanding general received dispatches from different parts of the department, indicating greater boldness of the savages than had as yet characterized their operations. A body of one thousand Kiowas, attacked Fort Zarah, on the Arkansas, but were driven off, after a brisk fight. From Fort Lyon in Colorado, it was reported that demonstrations of small parties were daily events. At Fort Harker, on the railroad, seventy-five savages made their appearance, to the consternation of the settlers in the vicinity.

While the Indians were thus occupying themselves, the commanding general was busily engrossed in perfecting the plans of the campaign, and making every necessary provision for the success of his movements when the proper time should arrive.

The insufficiency of the military force within the department occasioned the calling out of twelve companies of volunteer cavalry from the State of Kansas, to serve for six months unless sooner discharged. As an additional measure to secure success, by the employment of proper guides and trailers, the General opened negotiations with the Osage and Kaw tribes of Indians in Kansas, and the Utes in New Mexico, asking them to furnish a number of warriors, stipulating to pay them for their services, and giving them liberty to take and keep all Indian ponies they might capture in the campaign. Each of these tribes promised to send some of their best men.

The Utes and Osages were particularly the mortal enemies of the Kiowas and Cheyennes. During the previous summer a war party of Utes left their haunts in New Mexico and, after marching on foot a distance of over five hundred miles, fell upon a band of Kiowas, completely routed them, captured a number of ponies, took many scalps, and, more calamitous than all, got possession of the "medicine" of the band. As might be inferred, the Kiowas had a superstitious dread of the very name Ute. The employment of these people, therefore, would be a valuable accession to the army in the special duty for which their assistance was solicited.

Chapter 11

An Old Fashioned Buffalo Hunt

To relieve the monotony of inactivity the commanding general, much to the pleasure of a number of the officers of the staff and garrison at Fort Hays, proposed a "genuine" buffalo hunt. The diversion was also in part out of compliment to Captain Merryman, of the U. S. revenue cutter *M'Culloch*, then on a visit to headquarters. A bright day in October was fixed for the sport. Accordingly at an early hour the horses were sent to the railroad and put on the cars. Leaving Hays City we ran up the track, a distance of thirty miles. Here, by means of a gangplank, the horses were led out of the cars and saddled by the orderlies. Leaving the guard, the general had brought with him to protect the train, we mounted and "lit out," as rapid locomotion is called in that locality. Each person wore a brace of pistols for close work, and carried a breech-loading rifle to use at greater distance.

After a lively gallop of several miles, passing within the cordon of watchful sentinels, always found on the outskirts, we struck a herd numbering several thousand animals. Our approach had already been signalled and the herd was moving off at a rapid pace. There was no time to lose. Each one of the party singled out his animal, and putting spurs to his horse dashed after, striving to get abreast his game at a distance of a few paces, in order to deliver his fire. The general led off in the charge followed by Merryman, who, accustomed to salt water navigation, swayed from side to side. He, however, maintained a vigorous hold upon the pummel of the saddle, bounded into the air and returned emphatically, but not always gracefully, into his saddle with every leap of his horse.

The general, after considerable manoeuvring, managed to separate a fine cow from her companions The chase was quite spirited for several hundred yards, but a well directed shot under the shoulder, which very summarily suspended the powers of locomotion on the part of the buffalo, put a termination to the race. Several of the party soon became busily engaged on their own account in the exciting sport. One young bull, of irate temper, finding himself selected as a target, undertook to show fight and turned upon his pursuer. For some minutes the characters were reversed, and, judging from appearances, it might have been supposed that the buffalo was the hunter. In the course of an hour five animals were killed. Most of the horses, however, were perfectly "green," and consequently no use whatever, except to follow, giving the rider an opportunity to witness the sport without participating in it.

There is something majestic and formidable in the appearance of a buffalo. It is therefore not surprising that but few horses will readily approach sufficiently near to enable the hunter to make a close shot. Some horses rebel, notwithstanding every effort to allay their alarm. Others, by a proper course of training, carry their riders, without any direction, into just the position desirable. Such an animal is a treasure in the esteem of a plainsman. He talks about his "buffalo horse" with more pride than he would of himself, had he accomplished a feat ever so wonderful. It was interesting to watch the movements of the trained horse. He approached the buffalo rapidly but cautiously. His eyes were steadily fixed upon the animal and watched every motion. Should the buffalo expedite his pace, the horse did likewise, regulating his increased rate of speed so as to get alongside without unnecessarily alarming the animal.

As the horse came abreast, the buffalo naturally swayed his course away to the right or left. This was the dangerous part of the chase. Should the buffalo after moving away, the horse following, turn suddenly, a collision would be almost certain. This the horse seemed to know be perfectly that he changed direction on a long turn. After firing, should the animal fall, the horse kept up his speed, described a circle bringing him back to the carcass of the dead or wounded buffalo.

Timid horses and awkward riders run great risk of their lives by not knowing how to avoid any hostile demonstrations on the part of the buffalo. The latter has the advantage, and by not keeping a close watch, fatal results are sure to occur. An old hunter, mounted on a "buffalo horse," in every sense of the term, dashing fearlessly across the plain in pursuit of this truly magnificent game, presents a picture the very culmination of manly sport.

During our own attempts to make a fair show of knowledge of the subject, there were several very narrow escapes as regarded personal safety. Two of our party being in pursuit of the same animal, there was quite a competition as to who would get the first shot. The rider in the rear, in the excitement had his pistol go off out of time. The ball passed within a very few inches of the front rider's head. Both were alarmed, and the race terminated by the one apologizing, and the other feeling around to see whether he had been hurt.

While our own sport was going on, two Mexicans with us, were to be seen in the very midst of the herd following up the younger animals. Each rider had his *lariat*, holding the coil in one hand and with the other swinging the loop above his head in order to get the proper momentum. It was short work. At the first attempt, each man had his noose over the head of a fine yearling. The horses gradually slackened their gait, while the terrified buffaloes made every effort to escape. One of the *lariats*, unfortunately, parted and off went the animal with it dangling at his heels. The other calf was secured and sent to the train.

After several hours occupied in the exciting amusement of the chase, we returned to the cars. The horses, much blown, were unsaddled and put aboard, A party of soldiers were sent out to bring in the meat.

On our homeward journey a fine herd of antelopes was discovered ahead, close to the track. By a little skilful calculation of time, distance, and velocity, the engineer brought us within three hundred yards. A perfect fusillade was opened out of the car windows, during which, one of the beautiful little animals was seen to fall. The train stopped and the "meat" was brought in. This terminated the day's sport. At nine o'clock in the evening we reached Fort Hays.

I may, in this connection, make a few passing notes upon the resorts and habits of the American bison or buffalo, as he is popularly designated. With the savage nomad, he constitutes the actual and aboriginal occupant of the plains. The movements of the immense herds of buffaloes regulate the locations of the savage tribes. They constitute the commissariat of the Indian, and govern frequently his ability for war or control his desire for peace.

Prior to the opening of the country to the settler, the buffalo roamed over the entire territory from the Missouri river to the Rocky mountains, and from the plains of western Texas to the headwaters of the Missouri in the north. Today the buffalo is rarely seen south of the Red river, or within two hundred miles of the Missouri, at Kansas City, In numbers he is evidently rapidly diminishing, though the countless herds, found during the summer along the railroads, would seem to indicate that the race is far from running out.

The buffalo is migratory in his habits and subject to two influences in his movements, the seasons, and the abundance or scarcity of pasturage. The migrations of the herds appear to be simultaneous. I have seen herd after herd stretching over a distance of eighty miles, all tending in the same direction. During the early spring months they are generally to be found in the regions south of the Canadian, as far as the Red. Here the winters are short and the grass shoots early. As the pasturage makes its appearance towards the north, the herds follow, moving across the Cimmaron, the Arkansas, the Smoky Hill, the Republican, and beyond the Platte.

Cases frequently occur where small herds becoming detached from the main bodies, and particularly the old bulls and cows unable to travel, remain north of the Platte, and manage to eke out an existence through the coldest winters. Other small herds are found in different localities far south during the summer. These exceptions, to the general rule of their habits, are always the result of causes, such as inability to follow the main herd, or being detached and driven back.

CHAPTER 12

A Brute Army

In all his habits the buffalo displays an instinctive sense of organization and discipline which alone could accomplish the wise provisions of nature in subsisting such enormous masses of animal life. Not only does the great herd, as a mass, preserve a remarkable concert of action "on the move," but it is subdivided into smaller herds, which seem to be composed of animals having peculiar affinities. These small herds have each their leader, always a fine young or middle-aged bull, whose fighting qualities had won for him the ascendancy over all other male competitors. In the black mass presented by the great herd a space, sometimes as limited as a hundred yards, can always be detected between the sub-divisions. Each herd always preserves its relative position to the others, and, in case of alarm, takes flight in a single mass. It also preserves the same relation in galloping to water.

As a precaution against surprise, each herd has its *videttes*, through which the alarm is given upon the appearance of danger. Approaching a herd, groups of buffaloes in fours and fives are first seen. These, taking the alarm, gallop towards the common centre. The ever-watchful and suspicious young males immediately on the outer edge of the herd receive the movements of the *videttes* as warnings. They sniff the air, and with piercing vision scan the plain. If the cause of alarm be discovered, the herd-leader, heading the way, sets out, followed by the cows and calves, while the males form a sort of rear guard and flankers. For the sake of protection, the females and the young occupy the centre of the herd. By a wise instinct, the young are thus secured from the ravenous wolf, and the natural timidity of the cow is guarded against sudden or unnecessary alarm.

The evening is the usual time for the herds to set out for water. When moving for this purpose, they may be seen in single-file, following their leaders, travelling at an ambling gait. Frequently they travel eight or ten miles to the nearest stream or pond. The passage of large numbers of buffalo in this way 'over the same ground soon marks out a well-beaten track, resembling a footpath, and known to hunters as the "buffalo trail." On the banks of the streams running through the buffalo country these trails may be seen converging from all directions, some faintly marked, while some are worn eight and ten inches in depth. These trails not only follow the most direct course to a given point, but always lead to water or a watercourse.

The traveller on the plains is frequently obliged to take to the trail of the buffalo in order to reach water. In many places the "buffalo wallow" furnishes a supply of stagnant water which, though extremely unpalatable, has often saved life. The buffalo wallow is a circular, dish-shaped, hole in the earth, about twelve feet in diameter and a foot deep at its greatest concavity. During the warm season, immense clouds of dust are to be seen rising over a herd quietly grazing. Like other animals of his species, the buffalo frequently amuses himself by wallowing in the fine sand or ploughing up the earth with his horns. The surface once broken, the place becomes a common resort, until the wallow assumes the shape above described. In the wet season, the rain fills up the wallow, and, unless consumed, standing water is to be found there far into summer.

Among the young buffalo bulls there seems to be a remarkable aspiration to secure the leadership of the herd. This question of rank is annually settled by a test of strength. Certain ambitious males set themselves up as competitors. The first opportunity that offers is accepted. The contests are stubborn and severe—frequently fatal. If the old leader gets the upper hand, he is doubly a hero, and his claims to pre-eminence are greater than ever. Next in rank to the herd-leader are a number of young buffalo, courtiers and gallants, who have free range of the herd so long as they do not come in contact with the leader, or trespass upon his privileges. Between the young and the old males there is an inveterate hostility. As the young grow in ability to cope with the fathers of the herd, a regular conflict takes place. If it terminates in favour of the former, the old buffaloes are unceremoniously driven out.

Thus banished from their associations when strong and active, the old animals form a sort of hermit order on the outskirts of the herds, where they constitute the outer guard. These competitive encounters are constantly taking place. As one generation of males succeeds another those, driven out can never return, but live an exiled existence until age, the hunter's bullet, disease, or the ravenous wolf, finishes their days.

The females display, most remarkably, the attachments of maternity. In one instance, I remember, our party shot and badly wounded a fine calf about six months old. As the calf fell, the mother turned and looked upon it with an expression of absolute grief. Her offspring made repeated efforts to rise, but without avail. The mother, in perfect despair, ran around her young, uttering low moans. As we approached, the mother's nature was entirely changed. She stamped upon the ground as if to warn us to "keep off." Although she made no direct attack, she manifested a disposition to defend her young, which was only exceeded by the shouts and firing, which seemed to terrify her. To put the calf out of its suffering and relieve the distress of the mother, and insure our own safety, both animals were dispatched.

Always in the vicinity of the buffalo herd the hunter encounters that beautiful little animal, the antelope. Shy and timid, with an acute scent and far-reaching vision, it is difficult of approach. An old animal is killed now and then by a long-range rifle. Like other timid animals, the antelope had a remarkable development of that too-often fatal instinct, curiosity. By taking advantage of this failing, the experienced hunter succeeds in taking the game. The usual means resorted to is "still hunting." A red flannel flag, fastened to a short stick, is, posted in a conspicuous place. The hunter then secretes himself and waits for an opportunity. This is always a slow process; but, with a proper degree of patience, if anywhere in the vicinity of antelopes so that the flag can be seen, he is sure "to bring a haul."

The wolves and the coyotes are the inveterate enemies of the antelope, and continually waylay its path. The fleetness of the animal, however, is its complete protection until weakened by age, or, probably, it has been crippled. In times of danger, if possible, the antelope takes refuge within the lines of the nearest herd of buffaloes. Its excessive fright at these times often causes whole herds of the mighty beasts to take to their heels as if a battalion of hunters were on their tracks.

Probably one of the most perfect pictures of desertion and despair, is the aged and enfeebled buffalo. Driven first from the herd as if it were a mortal offence to live beyond a certain period of summers, or his inability to follow its movements, he is left alone to wander feebly about, without companions, and an object of patient, sometimes decidedly impatient, watchfulness on the part of the wolf. When the buffalo has arrived at such an advanced age, he will be found near a constant stream where grass grows in abundance. Isolated, shy in his movements, and alarmed at the slightest indications of danger, he seems to lose his customary boldness, and becomes an easily terrified and suspicious, animal. He loses his vigorous appearance, and, literally becomes worn down and decrepit. The timidity of age grows upon him, and the solemn stillness and solitude which surrounds him is calculated to increase rather than diminish this instinctive terror.

Few of these superannuated specimens come to a natural end. The starving wolf and his diminutive companion the coyote, are ever ready to take advantage of the first favourable opportunity of hastening the demise of the object of their solicitude and observation. Under the goading impulse of hunger, the wolf does not hesitate to attack any buffalo who may have strayed from the herd. As if tired of waiting for the natural course of the expiring fires of nature, his wolfship, with a few comrades begins a regular series of battles until his victim is overpowered.

On one occasion while present with a small detachment of scouts, we suddenly drew to the summit of a "divide." In the valley below an old buffalo, and a pack of seven large gray wolves, were evidently in the act of engaging in a mortal fray. The old buffalo, as if realizing his situation, stood with his head down and confronting the wolves. At times he threw his head up and down, dropped out his blackened tongue, and constantly uttered a low hoarse roar. We determined to witness the conflict, which was evidently at hand. We halted and *lariated* our animals, The buffalo so much engrossed in his own safety failed to discover our presence, though not more than several hundred yards off. The wolves saw us. This only sharpened their appetite, and seemed to hasten their desire to secure the feast which they had before them. The wolves were seated upon their haunches and formed a sort of semi-circle in front of the buffalo. They resembled so many wise men in council. The buffalo stood a few paces off, very careful to keep his moppy head towards his starving tormentors, and his hind-quarters in an opposite direction, free from any demonstration in the rear.

By way of response to the fierce gutteral effusions of the buffalo, the wolves at times set up a mournful chorus. No sooner did the wolves see us than they slyly deployed for action. Finding his rear thus in danger, the buffalo made a dive at the nearest wolf, tumbling him over and over. During this movement, however, the rest of the pack pounced upon the hind legs of the buffalo, snarling and snapping, and tearing at his hams. Their object, evidently, was to hamstring their antagonist. These attacks in the rear diverted the attention of the buffalo from the hapless victim of his first charge. The animal turned to attack in the opposite direction, but his tormentors were once more at his vulnerable point.

The contest after these opening performances grew lively and exciting. The buffalo evidently fully appreciated the situation, and the wolves were not to be robbed of their meal. The hindquarters of the buffalo streamed with blood, and the animal showed signs of exhaustion. He did not dare to lie down for that would be fatal. The wolves had three of their number *hors de combat*. The noise of the contest had attracted quite an audience of coyotes, and a few interloper wolves, sitting at a distance, licking their chops, and impatiently awaiting the issue, evidently expecting an invitation to participate in the feast. The buffalo made several efforts at flight, but soon found that that was a useless manoeuvre. The battle test had been going on more than an hour, and having no more time to devote to that sort of recreation, a well directed volley laid out several of their wolfish excellencies. The buffalo did not stop to thank us for our timely assistance, but took the first moment of relief to hobble off. The animal was evidently badly injured, and doubtless our interference was merely prolonging the burden of life, now doubly an encumbrance.

A wolf feast over the carcass of a buffalo is one of those sharp-toned entertainments, which could only be compared to an old fashioned tea-party, composed of snappish octogenarian, paralytic, and generally debilitated characters of both sexes, with a fair sprinkle of shrivelled virginity, and a few used up celibates of the masculine gender. Each one guzzling to his heart's content, and growling, and finding fault with his neighbour.

The construction of railroads has developed a new and extensive field for pleasure seekers. The facilities of communication now opened with that strange and remote section, the plains, and, at the same time, the opportunity afforded of seeing the buffalo, that animal above all others associated from our earliest years with everything wild and daring, now invites visitors from all parts of the country. From the cities of Chicago, Cincinnati, St. Louis, and other less important points during the autumn of 1868, excursions were made up at low rates of fare.

The following announcement of an excursion I found at one of the railroad stations. I give a copy of it as one of the peculiar and progressive innovations made by the railways.

RAILWAY EXCURSION
AND
BUFFALO HUNT.

AN EXCURSION TRAIN WILL LEAVE LEAVENWORTH, AT 8 A. M. AND LAWRENCE, AT 10 A. M. FOR

SHERIDAN,

ON TUESDAY, OCTOBER 27, 1868, AND RETURN ON FRIDAY. THIS TRAIN WILL STOP AT THE PRINCIPAL STATIONS BOTH GOING AND RETURNING. AMPLE TIME WILL BE HAD FOR A GRAND BUFFALO

HUNT ON THE PLAINS.

Buffaloes are so numerous along the road that they are shot from the cars nearly every day. On our last excursion our party killed twenty buffaloes in a hunt of six hours.

All passengers can have refreshments on the cars at reasonable prices.

Tickets of round trip from Leavenworth. $10.00.

The inducements, at these rates, to any one anxious to visit the plains, and see a live buffalo, and perhaps a "live injun," not so acceptable at that time, were certainly very tempting, as the full expense of the above trip, at the regular rate of fare, would not have been short of seventy dollars. A quarter of a century hence, the buffalo and the Indian will have entirely disappeared from the line of the railways. The few that still survive will have then been driven to the most remote, inaccessible, and uninhabitable sections, if not entirely exterminated

CHAPTER 13

Arrival of Osage Warriors

While the commanding general was deeply absorbed in completing his preparations for the contemplated movement towards the Washita River in the south, the savages on the Republican were kept in constant alarm and uneasiness. About the middle of October, a squadron of the 10th cavalry, one hundred and fifty men, while acting as escort to Brevet Major General Carr, Major 5th Cavalry, *en route* to his command in the field, supposed to be on the Beaver, was attacked by a large party of Indians, numbering nearly five hundred warriors. The savages exhibited great boldness, approached close to the column, and fired with deliberate aim. The engagement began early in the morning and ceased at two o'clock in the afternoon, inflicting a loss of ten warriors killed and many wounded on the part of the savages, and three enlisted men wounded in the command.

From a warrior, wounded in the fight, information was obtained that their camp was on the Solomon, at Chalk Bluff, and that they had left it the night before, that it consisted of eight hundred lodges of Cheyennes, Arrapahoes, and Sioux, and stated that a large war-party had gone to the Saline,

Hardly had the savages recovered from their discomfiture on the banks of the Beaver, than they again found themselves unexpectedly confronted by a more powerful force. No sooner had the commanding general learned this acceptable information, than he ordered a new movement from Fort Wallace, putting every available man in the field. By a fortunate coincidence, the 5th Cavalry, under Colonel Royal, had just returned to the railroad for supplies. As this was the column in search of which Carr had moved north with an escort, the general joined it and hastened preparations for a new start. Some reinforcements were sent forward. The entire force when it moved, consisted of companies A, B, F, H, I, L, and M, 5th Cavalry, and Pepoon's scouts, Carr, commanding, in all about four hundred and eighty men.

It was Friday, October 23, when the troopers started afresh. The line of march lay in a north-westerly direction, towards the Little Beaver. The weather was delightfully clear and bracing. The plain, hardened by recent rains, rendered the marching less toilsome than before.

Two days had elapsed. The column pushed forward with rapid steps, the animals instinctively hastening towards watering places and camp. Officers and men scanned the country in every direction, in expectation of spying some detached band of savages watching their line of march, and indicating their proximity to the scene of fresh encounters. But the bold horsemen did not appear. Immense herds of buffaloes, with all the appearance of a sense of security, were seen far and near, grazing upon the broad undulations which swept away on all sides. The aged bulls, banished from the herd like so many trusty sentinels, at times snuffed the air, and seeing nothing to excite alarm, returned to their accustomed habits. The cows, and their progeny in the inner circle, confiding in the watchfulness of the outposts of the herd, grazed with perfect composure. The antelope, startled at imaginary dangers, could be seen galloping in the distance. The diminutive prairie dogs rushed to and fro, vigorously wagging their stumpy tails, barking fiercely, and popping in and out of their subterranean dwellings. The wolf might be seen lying in wait for his prey, or skulking out of the way of something more formidable than his questionable prowess would tempt him to encounter.

All of the second day the column moved onward. The rapidity of the march was accelerated by the destruction of fifteen wagons. The signs of Indian war-parties were growing more frequent, but as yet no hostile warrior had been seen. It was four o'clock in the afternoon as the column reached the summit of a "divide." Two hundred warriors, mounted and painted, with bows strung, now rose as if by magic. It was evident from their actions that they had no disposition to attack, their object being to retard the movement of the column. They resorted to the practice of firing the dry grass to the windward as an impediment to the march.

Detachments of troopers, well mounted, made several dashes, but the savages, with their usual skill, avoided an encounter. From the persistence exhibited in declining an engagement, it was apparent that their main body had not as yet come up, and, until they were ready, it were a fruitless task to essay forcing an action. The troops, therefore, pushed forward, carefully protecting their flanks and rear from surprise.

The third day, the column, in battle array, with trains in the centre, moved out of camp at an early hour. An engagement was surely expected A distance of ten miles having been traversed, a strong party of savages took position in front as if determined to dispute, with firmer resolution, the further progress of the troops. A squadron of cavalry, under Kane, Schenofsky, and Forbush, was ordered forward on the charge. The savages withdrew, while the troopers, for a distance of three miles, kept up a vigorous pursuit. The squadron now halted, and fell back to the main body. The Indians, in turn, charged. At this juncture, Pepoon's scouts were also ordered to the front. The engagement now become more general, A number of men, dismounted, advanced as skirmishers. The savages fought on horseback, galloping along the front of the skirmishers, dodging behind their horses at an imaginary bullet, or firing as a favourable opportunity offered.

As the column reached the summit of a commanding eminence, immense clouds of dust, rising in the distance, indicated another large body moving away in great haste. There was now no doubt of the fact that the savages in front were a strong covering party to delay the advance of the column, while their families, lodges, and stock were being hastened out of the reach of danger.

With these inducements ahead, the men used every exertion to overtake and fall upon the moving villages. A dash made at this time brought the troops in possession of hundreds of cedar lodge-poles, four hundred dried buffalo hides, and a large amount of other abandoned property. These were destroyed. Late in the evening, utterly exhausted in the chase, the column went into camp. During the day, the savages sustained a loss of ten warriors and seventy ponies killed, while on the side of the troops but several men were wounded. During the entire night, by the light of the burning plain, the flight of the savages could be traced for miles in the distance.

The following morning, the column resumed the pursuit without opposition. During the night the savages had withdrawn, and were miles away. The country had become more broken and difficult to travel. Further pursuit was in vain. After several day's fruitless marching, the command retraced its steps to Fort Wallace.

The successes of the troops on the Republican and its tributaries, compelled the savages to resort to a new mode of tactics. By experience they had been taught their inability to cope with any considerable force. Parties, numbering twenty-five to a hundred warriors, set out on expeditions in different directions, but having a common point of rendezvous. Several of these detachments appeared along the line of the railroad, seriously threatening, for a time, the safety of communication with the western posts. The guards west of Fort Hays were strengthened, and cautioned to preserve the strictest vigilance. On the last day of October, a war-party succeeded in throwing a train from the track by hacking off the ends of the ties for the length of a rail, but beyond this accomplished nothing.

About this time, twelve friendly Indians of the Osage nation arrived at Fort Hays, in response to a letter from the commanding general inviting their people to unite with the white man against their enemies. War and disease had reduced the Osages to a mere handful. They occupied a fine reservation in the south-eastern portion of Kansas, and lived principally at the expense of the government; occasionally "raided" into the hostile Indian country, stole from the settlements, and, when these sources of obtaining a livelihood failed, literally starved to death.

Upon the agreement that their people should be fed by the army, and that they would receive a certain sum of money for services, a squad of Osages agreed to serve. The new arrivals were arrayed in all the paint and finery their rude toilet could afford.

At the head of their party was Cha-pa-jen-kan, or Little Beaver, the second chief of the nation. Little Beaver was a remarkably fine-looking Indian, sixty years of age, over six feet in height, spare built but muscular, and straight as an arrow, aquiline features and a thoughtful expression. Next in rank was Wen-tsi-kee, or Hard-rope, the chief counsellor, celebrated for his prowess in battle, as well as for his wisdom in council, He was an old man of heavy frame. The most prominent of the "soldiers" was Koom la-manche, or Trotter, celebrated as being the fleetest runner and best shot in the nation. The balance were young men of fine physique, and were selected for their fitness for the duty it was designed that they should perform.

Chapter 14

Ready to Take the Field

A few days after their arrival, the friendly Indians received their arms and proposed celebrating the occasion by giving a grand wardance. After dark a party of officers and ladies from the post, repaired to the spot selected for the purpose. At the foot of a gentle slope in the plain, upon the banks of a small stream, and in the midst of a grove, the savages had built a large fire. In a semi-circle, facing the fire, they had seated themselves, their eyes with thoughtful and solemn expression were fixed upon the flame. The chief, Little Beaver, had established himself upon a rude dais of sticks, from which he gazed about him with inward pride and satisfaction. He was puffing away at a huge pipe, and in the intervals of smoking he murmured over a few incomprehensible sounds which were responded to by his warriors with an *ugh! ugh!!*

Each savage was decorated with due "pomp and circumstance." Their mahogany-coloured bodies were gorgeously covered with paint and highly burnished Their faces were bedaubed in varied colours and streaked with black, forming devices, suggested by the taste of the person. A breech-clout, leggins and moccasins, constituted all the dress they wore. Their heads were a forest of feathers, and from their scalp-locks were suspended long trains, composed of a number of small silver plates. In their hands they held their bows, arrows, spears, and war-clubs. One of the party had a small drum, while another, seated by his side, held a large Indian rattle.

When the time had arrived for the dance to commence, the old chief stood up and said a few words, by way of an introduction. As soon as he had finished and seated himself once more, the warriors with the drum and rattle stood up. Stepping towards the fire, they began a mournful refrain, simultaneously drumming and rattling vigorously. This prelude lasted but a few seconds, when the rest of the warriors, with a fearful whoop, sprang to their feet, all joining in a chorus of the wildest description. With each utterance the dancers assumed a new and grotesque attitude, stamping their feet in the most excited manner. Frequently one imitated the neigh of a horse, which was responded to by others with a whoop. The sounds, uttered in the refrain, resembled the following:

Ah-ha-ha-haah, haah,
Haah-haah, haah-haah,
Aha, aha, aha, ahaah,
Ha-ha, ha-ha.

In the height of the excitement, the old chief, warming up, harangued the dancing warriors. His words were always received with yells of approbation.

The dance was divided into four parts, at the expiration of each of which the warriors took a respite of a few moments for a blow. The first scene was a general invocation of the great spirit to have success attend their expedition and enable them to slay large numbers of their enemies. The second was "in search of the trail." Here the gestures and positions of the body were suggestive of an actual occurrence, some of the figures were in the attitude of listening to an alarm, others were stooping with their attention fixed upon the ground, others were lying down with their ears to the earth. After enacting all these forms, observed on the war-path, the scene terminated in violent gesticulations and wild shouts. The trail had been discovered.

Taking again a few moments rest, the *tom-tom* beater and rattler rose and led off in the third scene, "on the trail." This opened by making a minute examination of all the characteristic features of the trail, the number of the war-party, and by some unknown marks, of what tribe. After this preliminary form was consummated, the dancers set up a shout, the *tom-tom* beat more rapidly, the rattle clattered more vigorously, and the whole party imitated running, jumping, and made a variety of noises. Occasionally they halted, and with their hands shading their eyes, appeared to be gazing at objects in the distance, and then again they set off as before, as if in pursuit of their foes, and rapidly closing upon them. They finally overtook the enemy and a fight took place, in which whooping and yelling, denunciations, bravadoes, and terrific gesticulations composed the chief features.

The closing scene was "the return of the war-party." This was, of course, a celebration of victory. The dancing was irregular and without any concordance of sounds. The musicians pummelled the *tom-tom* and shook up the rattle with all their might. The dancers bounded high into the air and jumped about in the most lively manner. Some indulged in loud declamations, recounting their imaginary deeds, how many scalps they had taken, and how many hair-breadth escapes they had had.

This terminated the dance. The savages now gathered about the fire and appeared to be in the best kind of humour. Laughing and conversation, took the place of their late severity of countenance and formality of demeanour. The scene, upon the whole, was peculiar, novel, and interesting. Not a breath of wind stirring, the dull notes of the *tom-tom*, accompanied by the studied sounds of savage voices, fell upon the still night air with startling effect, the blazing fire lighting up the surrounding space, and in full glare radiating upon the savage warriors arrayed in all the hideousness of battle attire, added a weird effect.

The old chief, desirous of letting himself be heard, or rather wishing not to be forgotten in the midst of the excitement, commenced an harangue for the benefit of warriors and visitors. His words, however, were little heeded, notwithstanding the vigour of voice and gesture he infused into them.

Late in the evening our party strolled back to the fort, having enjoyed an entertainment, certainly in keeping with the surrounding circumstances of time and place.

The warlike preparations, which had been vigorously pushed forward, under the immediate supervision of the commanding general, were now nearly completed. For two months five hundred government wagons had been in constant employment transporting supplies from the line of the railroad to Fort Dodge, on the Arkansas, accumulating supplies with a view to provide the depots, which were to be established in the heart of the Indian country. Already everything had been accomplished, necessary to a campaign of six months. The troops, assigned to duty in the field, were remounted, as far as necessary, to replace horses condemned as unfit for the service before them. The men were examined with a view to their own capacity for sustaining the trial of a hazardous and trying campaign in the midst of winter. Their arms and ammunition were thoroughly inspected so as to secure the most effective results.

The reports from the different scouting parties were eminently satisfactory. Large bands of savages from the north had crossed the railroad and the Denver stage route going south. A body, supposed to be Sioux, were also reported crossing the Platte, going north. The harassment to which they had been subjected in the vicinity of their old haunts, along the Republican and its tributaries, had so completely dissipated their feelings of security, that the northern bands had almost entirely abandoned that section and were in search of new seats for their villages and their families. The season was far advanced and aside from their repeated disasters, their desire to be let alone was now gaining strong hold on the savage mind. Sheridan, however, as the cold weather approached, became more active in his preparations, and the time to strike came nearer.

By November 5th, ten companies of the 19th Kansas Cavalry, the volunteer organization, one thousand strong, ordered out for the campaign, moved from their rendezvous at Topeka *en route* for Camp Beecher, at the mouth of the Little Arkansas. The next day two companies of the same regiment, two hundred strong, arrived at Fort Hays, and several days after were ordered, by way of Fort Dodge, to overtake Sully's column, about to move south, into the Canadian river country. The same day ten Kansas, or Kaw Indian scouts arrived.

On November 13, the 5th Cavalry, under Carr, left Fort Wallace for Fort Lyon, Colorado Territory, which was used as the point of departure, of an independent column, to advance into the Cimmaron country. From Fort Bascom the news was favourable to a start, at the proper moment, into the Washita country. Instructions were also issued to the commanding officers of posts along the railroad. This completed the preparations for the campaign.

The commanding general now announced to his military family that the time had arrived to leave for the front, and all should be ready to set out at a moment's warning. Although preparations, with a view to personal comfort, had been going on for several weeks, the prospect of an immediate departure occasioned considerable excitement and hurry to accomplish in the shortest space, many things that had been delayed.

The novelty and severity of a campaign in a wild and unsettled country, and in the midst of winter, required no little judgment in getting up a suitable "outfit." A couple of good horses and equipments, warm clothing, buffalo robes, and blankets for sleeping, a good rifle, a brace of pistols, plenty of ammunition, and the luxury of a pipe and tobacco, were provided specially for the campaign. Supplies for the mess, which was composed of the commanding general, the officers of his staff, and the writer, were also looked after by the cook.

    The fourteenth of November witnessed a stirring scene at Fort Hays. The day following having been fixed to join the column, already in motion south of the Arkansas, Lebo's company of the 10th Cavalry as escort, Pepoon's (Forsyth's) scouts, the orderlies, Indians, baggage, headquarters train, and extra horses, were ordered to be in readiness to move in advance, First Lieutenant Thomas C. Lebo, commanding. Lebo, with his assorted charge, set out at ten o'clock in the morning. The remainder of the day was well disposed of, by our party at the fort, in making final preparations.

Chapter 15

Arrival at Fort Dodge

By daylight, on the morning of November 15, the officers of the garrison, at Fort Hays, were astir to witness the departure of the commanding general and party for the field. At seven o'clock two ambulances, and a light baggage-wagon, each drawn by four mules, pulled up in front of the general's quarters. The personal baggage, blankets, and buffalo robes, were stowed away in the wagon and started in advance.

An hour later the general, the members of the staff, and the writer took seats in the two ambulances, and after an interchange of farewells with the officers of the post, set out on the journey.

It would have been difficult to have designed a more disagreeable day. It had rained heavily all night. In the morning the air was filled with a heavy penetrating mist. A strong wind was blowing from the north, adding to the driving moisture an almost freezing temperature.

By ten o'clock we reached the Smoky Hill River, twelve miles distant, and by noon the Big Timbers eight miles further. At the latter point Lieutenant Tayler, with the staff horses, and an escort of twenty men, awaited the arrival of the general. Several of the staff finding the ambulances so utterly comfortless, mounted and galloped ahead.

We had still twenty miles further to make before reaching camp. The storm grew more violent. The mist had turned into a heavy rain and aided by the wind, pelted against the ambulances in a nowise encouraging manner. The trails, considerably cut up by the numerous trains which had passed over them, were heavy and soon exhausted the animals. Our "team" showed very evident signs of being "played out." The art of effective mule driving consists, at all times, of a liberal allowance of raw hide, applied with tornadoes of epithets, given with a variety of expression and accent. These usually satisfactory measures were totally inoperative in our case. The driver, a powerful robust man, with an excellent pulmonary development, and a powerful leverage in the whip-hand, gave up in complete despair. He had not only demolished his whip, but also his patience, and by way of peroration gave vent to a *soliloquy* in denunciation of "shave-tails," declaring that they were only "sulky and playing off."

At four o'clock, we were at least three miles in the rear, and no prospect of making camp at a very seasonable hour. To heighten the interest of our situation, the driver reported mounted figures in sight, but several miles off the road. An optical reconnoisance, on our part, confirmed the report of the driver. It was certain the objects were not troops nor passing couriers. Our rifles and pistols were dragged out from under the seats for service, if necessary, and the figures were closely watched; meanwhile the "shave-tails" took their own time, notwithstanding the repeated emphatic and artistic declamations of the driver. The predicament in which we found ourselves was anything but consoling. Night coming on, far in the rear of the rest of the little command, and Indians evidently awaiting a chance to pounce upon us.

Our anxiety was, however, allayed by the arrival of a detachment from the front, sent to our relief. With the assistance of a periodic probing with sabres, executed by troopers galloping abreast each mule, we managed to worry the animals into a run, which was kept up by constant applications of the same argument, and shouting and yelling like so many savages. The Indians at a distance, who appeared to be watching our movements, vanished upon the arrival of the escort.

About an hour after dark, we rejoined the rest of the party on the banks of the north fork of the Pawnee. Owing to the severe weather, the train was overtaken on the road. Upon reaching the site of the camp, great difficulty was experienced in pitching the tents. The wind blew even more violently than during the day, and was now accompanied by a heavy fall of snow. Wood was scarce, and what little was gathered it was impossible to ignite.

Through the entire night the wind howled across the plain, threatening, momentarily, a demolition of our canvass walls. Our situation was decidedly comfortless, and, as introductory to a campaign of indefinite duration, presented anything but the most flattering anticipations of bodily comfort. Our tents had been pitched hastily, and flapped, and groaned, and jerked the livelong night. The ground was wet. The men and animals without shelter were severely tried. There was no sleep in camp that night.

It was with every sense of gratitude that we arose, on the following morning, to find a cloudless sky. The wind was still at its height. The air was cold and bracing, and the roads frozen. Our animals, exhilarated by the freshness of the atmosphere, were in much better spirits than was anticipated, and made good progress. The train, however, moving less rapidly, it was found could not make Fort Dodge the same night. Orders were, accordingly, sent back to divide the march so as to arrive the following morning. The general and party pushed ahead, arriving at Dodge at four o'clock in the afternoon, making over forty miles our day's journey.

At the fort, we were received with unbounded hospitality. The commandant. Major Sheridan, and Lieutenant Read, adjutant, opened their quarters. The courtesy was the more appreciated by way of contrast with our experience the night before.

About ten o'clock the next morning, the train arrived at the fort. Some of the animals were entirely "used up." A few hours were taken for rest, securing fresh mules, and drawing rations, with instructions to be ready to move by one o'clock.

The fort was built upon low ground, immediately upon the banks of the Arkansas. A range of high bluffs completely enveloped it on the land side, while the river, nearly a mile in width, ran in front. Beyond, stretched an expansive plain, and still further on, a range of bald hills. The work was not only badly located, but, in case of attack, would be difficult to defend. Shortly before our arrival, four or five warriors rode directly through the fort, shooting one soldier, and making their exit in safety. The country in the vicinity admitted of a close approach under cover.

The fort was built about the year 1864, but for what object, except for the sake of having a garrison in that region, would be difficult to surmise. There is no wood within miles of the place, and no other recommendation save an excellent variety of building stone.

As we were now about penetrating the country infested by numerous bands of savages, liable, at any moment, to make a dash, our movements were more compact. The advance was led by the Indian guides, who were to act as trailers. Their keen sight and knowledge of the habits of their race admirably adapted them for this service; and, feeling, as they did, that their "hair" would be subject to the same tonsorial manipulation as our own, were they caught, their vigilance was unsparing. The scouts, under Pepoon, acted as advance guard. Next came the train—about twenty wagons—and in the rear, Lebo's company of cavalry. Our route was down the north bank of the Arkansas, for a distance of eight miles, to the ford. The crossing of the river was rendered extremely difficult by quick-sands and floating ice. By doubling teams, however, we made the south side without disaster, and went into camp.

Large fires of "buffalo-chips" were built, and around these we found agreeable entertainment in conversation and comments upon the prospects of the campaign. No person felt in better spirits than the commanding general. With his usual confidence in the success of his plan, and fully realizing the hardships and losses which would necessarily be encountered upon those bleak plains during that inclement season, he inspired in all those around him the same resolution and anticipations of glorious triumph.

General Sully, with the main column, was four days in advance. It was the object of the commanding general, therefore, by making rapid marches and long stages, to overtake him by the time of his arrival "somewhere" on the north fork of the Canadian.

An hour before daylight on the morning of the eighteenth of November, the bugle, sounding reveille, aroused the camp from its slumbers. The air, chilled by autumnal winds, necessitated the exercise of no little effort to induce one to desert his comfortable quarters between several layers of robes and blankets. There was no time, however, for trifling with the sensibilities of the flesh. Shivering limbs and chattering teeth might be expected, from that time forward, as a usual morning entertainment.

Having indulged in a frugal breakfast, by the time the sun shed its first rays upon the plain, tents were struck, and in the wagons, and the column ready to move. The country, for a distance of a mile, along the south bank of the river, was composed of interminable sand-hills. The train experienced much difficulty in getting along, the animals sinking in above their fetlocks, and the wheels of the wagons cutting deep ruts. Upon reaching the summit of the first ridge, the country swept away as far as the eye could reach, a rolling, treeless plain, covered with buffalo-grass, and at intervals broken by deep *cañons*.

After a journey of four hours, the column reached Mulberry Creek, twelve miles on the way. Here we experienced much delay, having lost Sully's main trail. Several of the Indians were sent out to reconnoitre towards the east; meanwhile, a party of scouts were dispatched to look for a crossing. The banks of the creek were very precipitous, and ranging from twenty to fifty feet in height. The water was poor, A few trees skirted the bed of the creek. After an absence of several hours, the Indians appeared upon a "divide" about a mile distant signalling to the column to advance in their direction. Making a journey of not less than eight miles, we struck the main trail which followed the crest of the "divide."

Our route now lay in a south-easterly direction. The "divide" carried us between two tributaries of Bluff Creek. As we approached the creek, the country became exceedingly broken and the descent difficult.

By sunset, we crossed the main stream and camped on a sedgy island covered with a thick growth of cotton-wood, which furnished an ample supply of fuel. The bed of the creek, about two hundred yards wide, indicated the flow of a large volume of water at certain seasons.

The main stream, at the time we visited it, was about thirty feet in width, with sandy bed. At several places, a current of water, about six feet wide, could be traced running beneath the sand, the moisture merely oozing through the surface.

At Bluff Creek, we effected a junction with two companies of the Nineteenth Kansas Volunteers, which had been left by the main column to await the arrival of the commanding general. The evening was spent in writing letters, to be dispatched north the next morning by couriers. This, probably, would be the last chance, for days, to communicate with the outer world. We had now cut loose from home and civilization. The opportunity, therefore, was industriously improved. For half the night, in the dim and uncertain light of the camp-fire, seated on the ground, with a log for a desk, lead-pencils were busily driving thoughts of love and remembrance to those far away enjoying the comforts of the fireside.

CHAPTER 16

Hunting-Parties

At sunrise, on the nineteenth, the column was again in motion. Our force reached nearly three hundred men, exclusive of officers, teamsters, orderlies, Indians, and servants. We were now sufficiently formidable for any attack, except by a very large body of savages. We moved, however, with flankers and *videttes*, who kept a vigilant lookout for lurking war-parties.

On the south side of the creek we ascended the "divide" by a deep and narrow ravine. After reaching the summit and following: it for a distance of five miles, the trail descended into a basin in which we found an abundance of dried grass, from four to six feet in height. A small herd of buffaloes was started and pursued by the Indians and a few scouts.

After crossing a low basin, about a mile and a half in width, the trail led into the valley of Bear Creek. A march of some miles, over rolling prairies, brought us to a gap in a range of sand hills, beyond which lay the Cimmaron. Upon the north bank of the latter stream the column went into camp.

In order to take advantage of the winter pasturage, which was found in the vicinity of this night's camp, all the animals were turned out to graze until sunset. To prevent surprise a strong guard of troops was posted around the herd, and the herders were ready, at a moment's warning, to seize the animals, should a stampede be threatened.

The water of the Cimmaron was strongly affected with alkaline matter, rendering it unpalatable to man. The animals drank it, though with apparent distaste. Considerable inconvenience was experienced from the state of the water. The supply brought in the water-kegs, greatly to our inconvenience, was soon consumed, leaving us but the chance of being able to replenish the stock the next day.

At the usual hour, on the morning of the twentieth, we moved across the Cimmaron flats to the main stream. The ground for miles around had the appearance of a heavy hoar frost, occasioned by the large quantity of gypsum with which the soil was impregnated. The stream of the Cimmaron was about twenty-five yards wide and a foot deep, with a treacherous bottom of shifting sands. Rising from this basin the surface became hard, and a fine trail for the wagons was found tending in a south-easterly direction.

During the afternoon, the chief of the Indian trailers, in the presence of his warriors, formally took the war-path. The column was moving along at a steady gait. The Indians, riding about a mile in advance, suddenly left their position and galloped to the top of a cone-shaped mountain, some distance out of the direction of the trail. Here they dismounted, and after smoking and observing other necessary forms, the chief, who was known as Sam Johnson, gave his own name to the mountain, and assumed the pretentious title of Big Wolf, which was to express the cunning he expected henceforth to display when he encountered any of his red enemies.

This night the column went into camp on an island, in the Beaver River, near the mouth of Trout Creek. Headquarters' tents were pitched beneath the overshadowing branches of an immense cottonwood. The camp furnished an abundant supply of excellent water. In the expansive valley, which spread out from the south side of the Beaver, several small herds of buffaloes were seen grazing apparently unsuspicious of our presence. Hunting-parties were allowed to leave camp in pursuit, in hopes of bringing in a supply of fresh meat, which was very much needed, especially for the men.

As the parties were leaving, the commanding general and the writer strolled about a mile from camp, to a high knoll, from which a fine view could be had of the chase. Under cover of a skirt of timber along the banks of the creek, the hunters succeeded in closely approaching a herd. Suddenly the hunters emerged from the timber and high grass and dashed forward. The buffaloes, bewildered at this unexpected visitation, stood for A moment as if to satisfy themselves, and then set off at a rapid gallop, the tamers in hot chase after them. The race lasted for at least fifteen minutes, when two of the herd were seen to drop behind wounded, and were soon dispatched. While the successful hunters were attending to the "meat" they had taken, the others were to be seen, scattered in all directions, galloping hither and thither, each one bent upon some choice animal he had cut off.

While still observing the graceful evolutions and caracoling of the buffalo hunters, our attention was attracted to the sun, which was about disappearing behind a distant range of low hills. Nowhere, except perhaps within the tropics, is the daily exit of the great luminary characterized by greater splendour than upon the extensive plains of the west. Our position was such as to afford a rare opportunity to take in all the varied changes of beauty, as the effulgent orb descended from its path in space into the apparent bosom of the earth. From the knoll which we occupied, the vast low lands of the Beaver spread around in all directions. The silvery waters of the river, winding in graceful curves, coursed through the valley. Upon its banks the buffalo, the deer, and the wolf found an undisturbed existence. Along the line of the horizon stretched a range of hills, encircling the valley almost completely, while the intermediate gentle undulations broke the monotony of a rigid plain The grasses, robbed of their vitality by the biting frosts of autumn, covered the surface with a carpet of sombre tinge, intermixed here and there with patches of different varieties and varied tints. A few towering trees or a dense underbrush grew now and then along the stream. The pure blue of the great dome of nature spread in sublime expanse overhead.

In the west the sun threw out a parting glare, changing the atmosphere from a colourless waste to a vast ethereal sea of gold. The effect was indescribably grand. All nature seemed to glow with surpassing brightness. The heavens were illuminated with great lines of light, diverging from a common centre on the horizon, completely covering the azure field above, and shedding golden tints of more or less brilliance upon the earth beneath. Immediately surrounding the sun itself were masses of vapour in every form. The evening mists at first slowly gathering, formed in masses from leaden banks to pearly films, A fringe of gold and silver and purple, in graceful and ever-changing outline, bordered the beautiful folds of this vaporous curtain, gradually dropping around the last moments of the vanishing grandeur of day. From golden tints the atmosphere suddenly became of crimson hue, and a moment more the mantle of night covered the face of nature in silent darkness.

Returning to camp before total darkness set in, while crossing the dry bed of one of the channels of the Beaver, we discovered a distinctly defined lodge-pole trail and pony tracks. It was certain these indications were not there when we passed out, and the conclusion was natural that during our absence a small party of Indians had crossed between us and the camp, and under cover of the banks of the stream.

The same night, an hour after retiring, the stillness which prevailed was suddenly disturbed by several shots fired in rapid succession. In a moment the bugles sounded the alarm and called the troopers to arms. The picket reported seeing in the shadow of a tree a mounted figure approaching stealthily, he challenged and received no answer, though the moving figure halted. After a few moments the figure again advanced, and still keeping in the shade was now within twenty-five yards. Instantly the trooper brought his carbine to his shoulder and fired. Bang, came a bullet in reply. The object turned and broke into the moonlight. It was an Indian warrior. As he fled he was followed by two other mounted figures, which dashed out of the bushes nearby. The three savages were evidently stealing up in hopes of cutting the sentinel off quietly and thus get into the midst of the camp without creating alarm.

At the first fire a detachment was sent out to the support of the picket. The savages had fled; several troopers, taking advantage of the moon, examined their tracks. They had evidently been prowling around the camp in search of some vulnerable point, and this, being better covered, was selected for the purpose.

At another point on the picket-line about the same time, as the officer of the guard was approaching one of the posts, he heard, in tolerably good language, a voice in moderate tones: "Are you pickets?" The reply was the cocking of pieces and a discharge of carbines from the picket. A small party, hidden from view by the undergrowth, wheeled and fled, making no little rustling of bushes.

There seemed to be no doubt now about the presence of a war-party in the vicinity, but as to their numbers all was uncertainty. One of the hunting detachments which had been sent out during the afternoon, upon reaching camp about dusk, reported being chased by a few warriors, who followed them within a short distance of camp. The general himself, during the afternoon, while observing the hunting-parties, by means of his glass, remarked seeing a large number of figures moving rapidly about on the crest of the range of hills across the valley. It was then impossible, however, to define whether they were warriors mounted, or buffalo, though their peculiar movements were decidedly in favour of the former.

To be prepared for an emergency an extra officer of the guard was detailed for duty during the night, and a strong reserve was mustered to remain under arms. The officers and men were cautioned to employ the utmost vigilance, especially towards daylight, as the attack, if made at all, would be made then.

The defence of a camp, and particularly a small camp, against even an insignificant party of Indians is a matter of no little difficulty. An Indian warrior invariably approaches his enemy by stealth, sometimes in the guise of an animal. By a sudden blow, or a fatal arrow from his bow, he noiselessly removes the obstacle in his path, and passes on without alarm. It has frequently occurred that warriors have stolen their way into a sleeping camp in this way. Once within the sentinels the wily savage creeps about unpicketing the animals. He now passes out, either taking the animals with him, or, by a preconcerted signal, causing an attack to be made by a war-party, stationed for that purpose, under cover close to the pickets.

At such times, in order to effect a stampede of the stock, an Indian pony, with a buffalo robe dangling at his heels, is started into the camp. During the confusion caused by the presence of the pony, or more particularly his appendage, the alarm soon communicates itself to the other animals, the savage warriors dash about, yelling furiously, adding to the terror of the already terrified brutes. To control the animals at such times is an impossibility, and to oppose them would be attended with serious casualties, Stampeding the stock is usually the first aim of the savage in a fight. If the party be small he then feels sure of securing his prey at his leisure.

At three o'clock the following morning, November 21st, the camp was aroused, tents struck and packed, horses saddled, and troopers under arms. The camp-fires of the night before were smouldering in their ashes, and were allowed to remain so to prevent an undue exposure; but no attack being made at sunrise, the troops resumed their march.

Our course now lay in an easterly direction, following a range of high hills several miles south of Beaver Creek. During the day traces of the recent presence of the advance column indicated that we were not far in the rear. At noon we halted on the banks of a creek, which the night before had been the site of Sully's camp. The fires were still burning, and other indications were visible which set aside all doubts as to the whereabouts of the main body of the troops.

At two o'clock in the afternoon, from a commanding eminence, the smoke of camp-fires was to be seen at a distance of four miles. Hastening our march, shortly after three o'clock we reached Sully's camp, and pitched our tents in a sheltered ravine nearby.

The arrival of the commanding general was formally recognized by the officers of the command calling to pay their respects. After dark, the band of the 7th Cavalry visited headquarters, and performed several popular airs, in honour of the occasion. It was an unusual scene. But a few days before the buffalo and the deer resorted thither to enjoy the rich winter pastures of this fertile and charming valley—the melancholy howl of the wolf alone disturbed the stillness of the night. Now the scene was changed. The former solitudes were broken by the spectacle of war and martial preparation.

Chapter 17

Custer Takes the "War-Path"

We were now in the heart of the chosen hunting-grounds of the hostile bands. "The red man's paradise," as it was frequently designated, in view of the abundance of game, pasture, wood, and water. We were now more than one hundred miles south of the Arkansas River, and two hundred miles away from the railroad. The intervening country was a barren waste, traversed by roaming bands of savages, closely watching every movement of the invaders of their lands, and ready to pounce upon small parties should they leave camp. In his instructions from the commanding general, General Sully had been ordered to proceed south to the Canadian River, and to select a suitable point, which should possess the requisite natural advantages of a depot of supply, with sufficient wood, water, and winter pasturage for a large command—the distance, south of the Arkansas, not to exceed one hundred miles.

As guide, there had been secured the services of an old plainsman of thirty years' experience, familiarly known as Uncle John Smith. Smith had passed much of his life among the Indians then on the war-path, and had the additional recommendation of a Cheyenne squaw as the partner of his isolation from civilization and the world. The site selected was suggested by Uncle John, who claimed to have been the first white man that had visited the country bordering the two Canadians. Acting upon his suggestion. Sully visited the spot, and, after a thorough reconnoissance, found the country to possess all that was claimed for it. On a tongue of land, formed by the junction of Beaver and Wolf Creeks, which formed the North Fork of the Canadian, the army pitched its tents, and began preparations for the building of a fort.

The force now concentrated at the Camp of Supply, as the new post was termed, consisted of eleven companies of the 7th Cavalry, under Custer, and a battalion of infantry, under Major Page, composed of three companies of the 3rd, one company of the 5th, and one company of the 38th regiments of Infantry. This force, with the troops attending the commanding general, formed an aggregate of eleven hundred men. The supplies of the expedition were transported on a train of four hundred and fifty wagons, in charge of Major Inman.

Hardly had the tents at headquarters been pitched, than a violent snowstorm set in, lasting, with but trifling intermission, for three days. At one time, fears were entertained that we were destined to a snow blockade, and thus an end, for some weeks, be put upon active operations. Notwithstanding the storm, Sheridan, with characteristic energy, resolved to send out a column at once, in hopes of striking the savages when he knew their vigilance would naturally relax, and it would be impossible for them to offer any determined resistance. Custer, ever ready to undertake a desperate mission, was to be entrusted with the command; the troops designated for the service were the eleven companies of the 7th Cavalry, numbering about seven hundred men.

The very next day after our arrival at the camp, regardless of snow and wet, a train was made up to convey thirty days' supplies for the expedition. The troops and horses, arms and accoutrements, were inspected. But few tents were allowed. A pair of blankets, strapped to the saddle, and the clothes on their backs constituted the quota of baggage alike for officers and men. By the same night, the command was in condition to move.

At three o'clock, on the morning of the twenty-third of November, the reveille sounded the trooper from his slumbers. The camp of the "Seventh" was now a scene of busy preparation. Horses were groomed and saddled, and the men buckled on their weapons to await orders to mount. By six o'clock the bugle called the troopers to "boots and saddles." The line was formed, and the train started. "By fours, right;" "forward," was borne along the line. The dark forms of horse and rider broke into column, and, led off by their gallant leader, set out on their hazardous mission.

The storm was still at its height. The snow lay upon the ground to the depth of twelve inches; but, with a determination of purpose, the command moved out with cheers and the highest anticipations of inaugurating the campaign by striking a decisive blow.

It was the gray of dawn. The camp was buried in snow. As the column passed through the long line of tents occupied by the infantry, officers and men turned out to say a last word of cheer, and express a pious wish that "they might kill plenty of red devils and have a speedy return."

The column moved out on the plain, followed by the long train of wagons. Through the falling flakes, the dark mass could be traced pressing forward at a tedious pace, braving the elements overhead, and struggling through the soft snow beneath.

The instructions issued for the expedition were brief and simple: "To proceed south, in the direction of the Antelope hills, thence towards the Washita River, the supposed winter seat of the hostile tribes; to destroy their villages and ponies; to kill or hang all warriors, and bring back all women and children." This, in a nutshell, was the Sheridan policy towards refractory savages, not only to break their power, but also to afford them a salutary lesson of "two parties playing at the same game."

The commanding general determined to have on hand a large amount of extra supplies, at the store depot, to be constructed in connection with the new fort, and, notwithstanding the heavy weather, sent a train of over two hundred wagons back to Fort Dodge, with orders to draw from the large stock accumulated there, for store, at the Camp of Supply.

After the return of Sully to the north, to resume command of his district, and the departure of Custer, and the supply train, the force at the new post was materially reduced and scattered over a large space. It became necessary, therefore, in order not to be caught napping, to keep a number of lookouts posted during the day, and at night the guards were strengthened and ordered to fire upon any approaching object without waiting to challenge. Reveille was sounded at four o'clock each morning, at which time, officers and men were required to be fully armed and prepared to repel an attack.

On the morning of the fourth day after our arrival, the sun rose upon a clear sky. The storm had passed, leaving several feet of snow as the evidence of its presence. The first advantage taken of the turn in the weather, was to concentrate the camp into a smaller compass. All tents were now pitched in close vicinity to the site of the fort. As it was expected we would not move for several weeks, the headquarters' tents were heavily banked, and thus rendered quite comfortable. Strong wooden frames were also set inside to strengthen the frail structures in resisting the terrific winter blasts. In the course of a few days, our little canvass dwellings presented quite an appearance of luxury and taste, considering hundreds of miles intervened between us and civilization.

Daring the recent storm, work had been almost entirely suspended upon the fort. The reappearance of sunlight, and the grateful heat, imparted by the welcome luminary, caused the snow to vanish almost as rapidly as it had fallen. The camp, as a consequence, was once more a scene of industry.

The entire work of building the fort was to be accomplished by the troops. In order to perform the duty without confusion, and, at the same time, to be prepared for the emergency of an attack, the infantry of the command was divided into reliefs, each having certain duties assigned to them. A large detail of choppers, under proper officers, were pent into the woods, with no other duty than to fell trees. Mule and ox teams, brought with us for labour, or, in case of emergency, as a reserve commissariat, with the requisite number of teamsters and labourers, were detailed from the train to drag in the logs as they were cut. Another party of troops, under the supervision of officers, was stationed at the fort, to prepare the logs and move them into position in the structure, A strong guard was stationed in the timber and on the adjacent hills, to signal war-parties, or to repel any attack until the working details could be rallied for defence.

The picture presented in our everyday life, in the depths of our wild home, reminded us more of the first steps to the establishment of a pioneer settlement, than the work of the less peaceful pursuit of war. At sunrise on each day, the bugle called the various details to their labours. The choppers with axes and rifles, were marched into the woods under escort of the guard. The teams followed with drag-chains clanking. From morning until night the strokes of the chopper's axe and the shouts of the teamsters rang through the silent wood Immense fires were built for the comfort of the men.

Occasionally, the sharp crack of the hunter's rifle mingled with the hum of industry. At night, after the hours of toil, the troopers returned to camp, generally bringing in with them goodly quantities of buffalo-meat, elk, deer, antelope, wild turkeys, and rabbits, killed by the guard. It was worthy of remark to see the perfect readiness of the troops to engage in pursuits so novel and entirely out of their line of duty. Their interest was certainly heightened at the prospect of more comfortable quarters than the canvass habitations they were then occupying; and a choice supper of game, in the place of salt pork, was all the more ravenously devoured by an appetite sharpened by the day's toil.

The failure of the ten companies of volunteers to make their appearance gave the commanding general some concern. The regiment had left Topeka on the fifth of November. It was now nineteen days since it had been heard from, and was certainly several days overdue. On the afternoon of the twenty-fourth the scouts were ordered out on a reconnoisance, but not to extend further than fourteen miles from camp, in hopes of finding some traces of the regiment. The point at which he proposed establishing his camp was laid down by the commanding general before starting. This was done, too, as we now found, with remarkable accuracy, particularly as it was without any reliable data. By means of the compass, efficient reconnoisances, and guides experienced in the theory of traversing such monotonous regions as the plains, there seemed to be no question of the prompt arrival of the volunteers. It was known, also, that the rations with which they had started were just sufficient to bring them through, and any unusual delay, such as losing the way, would in all probability be attended with scarcity and suffering.

The same evening the scouts returned, having had a fruitless journey, as far as the missing regiment was concerned, but brought in as a sort of compromise twenty-eight wild turkeys, which had been killed at a "roost" in the woods some distance down the North Fork. From all accounts the promiscuous firing which ensued upon the discovery of the turkeys made it as "hot" for man and beast as it was for the turkeys.

One old scout observed, "I've a bin a fittin Injuns an' other critters all my life, an' I never seed sich a time. I was a shootin of turkies one minit an a doggin bullets the other minit, an yit no blood spilt. All I got to say, it was lucky for the men ef it wasn't for the turkies." A monstrous eagle was also brought in, measuring seven feet between the tips of the wings.

Late in the afternoon of the twenty-fifth the lookout gave an alarm. A scouting party was ordered out at once to reconnoitre. The scouts returned at dusk, and with them one of the companies of volunteers that had left Topeka.

The captain halted in front of headquarters, and reported having left the remaining nine companies of the regiment on the Cimmaron two days before, snowed up and entirely out of rations, and hunting buffalo and other game for subsistence. He had been sent ahead in search of the camp of supply and to report the condition of the command. He struck the North Fork some distance below, and in following up discovered a trail in the snow, made by shod horses, which he knew could not be Indians, and pursuing the trail came in sight of the camp.

The next day the volunteers, together with the scouts and a train of wagons with supplies, set out for the regiment on the Cimmaron, and to guide it to our camp.

Had the volunteers arrived when expected two columns instead of one would have been sent out. Custer operating on one line and Crawford upon another, which would have considerably multiplied the chances of striking a demolishing blow at the power of the warlike tribes. This necessary delay, in a portion of the active operations contemplated by the commanding general, was not allowed to waste itself in inactivity. To economize in the use of stores almost every day hunting parties were made up and traversed the woods in all directions in the vicinity of camp in search of game. The general was the crack shot, and usually brought in more than his share of the spoils of the chase. The usual sport was Jack rabbit hunting with hounds. The general had with him his stag hound Cynch, a powerful animal, and well trained, and Juno, less powerful, but more fleet, belonging to one of the officers of the staff, also joined in the sport.

Starting one fine morning with a party of five, we penetrated the low lands and sand hills along the Wolf River. It was here, in the long grass or knotty brush, the rabbit resorted, as much for protection as for food. In the snow innumerable tracks were visible, leading in every direction. As the hounds ran by sight alone our party separated, and advanced over the ground like a line of mounted skirmishers. After proceeding but a short distance a fine animal was started A shout was raised, which put the hounds on the alert. They quickly scanned the ground. In a moment their eyes rested on the rabbit, and in a flash both set out in pursuit, followed by the party galloping rapidly, so as to keep in sight and secure the game.

After a spirited chase of half a mile the hounds overtook the rabbit. Both sides were pretty well exhausted. By a sudden spring old Cynch neatly caught the animal by the back, which finished him almost instantly. As the result of two hours' sport our party succeeded in "bagging" six. The animals were larger than the "Jack Rabbit" proper, and had a close resemblance in size and structure to the English hare.

The twenty-sixth of November, being the day set apart for a National Thanksgiving, the occasion was appropriately celebrated at headquarters in a dinner made up entirely of the productions of the country. We were favoured with a good cook, a burly Teuton, rather slow, but possessed a compensating amount of good nature, which enabled him to overlook a few impetuous observations at times, particularly when his pans and kettles were not ready to be put in the wagon in the morning, or, perhaps, the camp-stove was too "heavy" to be handled just at that moment. However the dinner was not only a novelty, but was worthy of all praise as an exhibition of the culinary art. I will give the bill of fare as I took it down at the time:

Soup—Wild Turkey.
Boiled—Wild Turkey, Buffalo Tongue.
Roast—Buffalo Hump, Wild Turkey, Saddle of Venison.
Red Deer, Common Deer, Antelope, Rabbit.
Entrees—Rabbit Pies, Wings of Grouse, breaded,
    Turkey Giblets.
Broiled—Quails, Pinnatted Grouse.
Vegetables (imported)—Canned Tomatoes, Lima Beans.
    Dessicated Potatoes.
Bread—"Hard Tack," plain and toasted. Army Biscuits.
Desert (imported)—Rice Pudding, Pies and Tarts.
Wines and Liquors—Champagne "Pinetop Whiskey," Ale.

The flavour of the game of the country was remarkably fine. The turkey particularly had a richness about it derived from the hackberry upon which it feeds. The "thanksgiving turkey," which we were so fortunate as to possess, weighed thirty pounds dressed. With its plumage it was truly a magnificent bird. Indeed the camp was overstocked with game. Turkeys, buffalo meat, deer, and all the other varieties during the three first days after our arrival went begging. In fact every one soon became surfeited, and returned to salt meat with an evident relish.

While the work of building the fort was going on those having a surplus of time on their hands were certainly at no loss how to employ it. A good horse and a rifle were the means of a fund of entertainment of which no one grew tired. The temperature had materially moderated, and the snow during midday on the sheltered sides of hills found a potent enemy in the sun's rays. The weather was delightful though cold. Camp life on the Canadian, isolated entirely from the world as we were, was found a happy episode, away from the noise and bustle of human strife, and full of interesting incidents and days of ease and amusement.

CHAPTER 18

The Battle of the Washita

The Sabbath day, on November 29th, broke beautifully clear. The genial sun, soothing the asperities of the chill and damp early morning, was gratefully recognized in repeated exchanges of compliments upon the delightful weather, and speculations upon the probabilities of its duration. The troops had turned out *en masse* to enjoy the pure bright air, and the animals, herded in the neighbouring valleys, seemed to have broken from the depression and signs of drooping spirits, which had noticeably taken possession of them. The mysterious influence of the Sabbath nowhere more deeply touches the mind than in the wild solitudes of primitive nature. That holy and reverential quiet which pervades all creation on that day, there falls upon the religious sentiment of the soul with impressions of mingled sublimity and awe. The great volume, there spread out, opens new fields of meditation and new fountains, from which to draw strange lessons of philosophy.

The primitive woods, sighing in the winds of heaven, the wolfs wild howl, or the mournful note of the raven, brings the mind to reflect upon the ages of silence that have there found no interruption, save from the voices of nature and savage man. The quiet stream, flowing onward to the great ocean, reminded the immaterial being of its onward passage to the vast ocean of eternity. The savage, in all his wildness, the child of nature controlled by instincts and passions unrestrained, presented the type of man before the doctrines of religion and the institution of the Sabbath were sent into the world. This holy inspiration, united with such solemn influences, unmarred by the vanities and anxieties of life, were appropriate and interesting topics of meditation and comparison.

About ten o'clock in the morning the officers at headquarters were surprised by the unexpected arrival of Custer's chief scout, known as

California Joe. "Old Joe" was a veteran pioneer of over thirty years standing. He, exhibiting an altitude of six feet one inch, wore a ponderous mat of flaming red whiskers and a growth of long knotty hair of the same description; as his companions expressed it, he was "brass mounted." Both his hair and whiskers were well powdered with a series of layers of dust, intermingled with stray blades of dry grass, leaves, and chips, reminding the beholder very forcibly of the old fellow's previous night's slumber on the bosom of mother earth.

Joe's manner, upon making his appearance before the general's tent, indicated that he had some agreeable intelligence to communicate. His two diminutive blue orbs flashing on either side of a prodigious nasal formation, confirmed the belief.

"Well, Joe, what brings you back so soon; running away?" said the general.

Joe replied somewhat indignantly in manner at the suggestion of running away. "I've just made that ole critter of mine out thar get up and dust, for the last thirty-six hours, I tell yer it's a big thing, and we just made those red devils git."

"So you have had a fight," said the general.

"Weel, we've had suthin; you may call it fittin, but I call it wipin out the varmints; yes, and sich a one as they wont have agin, I tell you."

While this introductory dialogue was going on, Joe indulged in a preliminary boring of his optics with his knuckles, and having methodically rubbed the rasp-like end of his nose on the corner of a gunny sack, which he carried by way of the necessary refinement of a pocket handkerchief, poked his long fingers into his broad, manly breast, and from it drew a budget of official dispatches from the scene of the fight. The general took the dispatches hastily, and having glanced them over, read them aloud. Our curiosity was satisfied to learn that on the twenty seventh of November the village of the Cheyenne chief, Black Kettle, on the North Fork of the Washita River, was captured. Over one hundred Indians were killed and bodies left on the field, and fifty-three women and children taken prisoners.

An immense amount of property captured and destroyed, consisting of fifty-one lodges, nearly one thousand horses and mules, rifles, ammunition, horse equipments, robes, &c. With this came the sad intelligence that "Captain Louis M. Hamilton was killed in the first charge. Colonel Barnitz was seriously wounded, Major Elliott and eighteen men were missing, and there was no doubt had been killed.

One man of the Seventh was killed and fourteen wounded." The dispatch added, that the Indians, including women and boys, fought with great desperation from the cover of bushes and grass. "Black Kettle, the principal chief, was killed."

This told the story of "Joe's" enthusiasm, which, as the general read the dispatch aloud, so as to be heard by those standing around, found vent at irregular periods in gratuitous observations, less elegant than forcible, and wound up by the old scout impressively wiping his nose on the fur sleeve of his overcoat.

The details of the movement were these. Leaving our camp the column headed in a southerly direction. At the intersection of the Texas boundary line with the main Canadian, and tending in a southeasterly direction, Custer struck a fresh Indian trail of about one hundred warriors. While Elliott kept the trail at a trot, Custer leaving the train and all tents in charge of Lieutenant Mathey, with a guard of eighty men, and taking but a few wagons, containing three days rations, started across the country. Fortunately the general struck Elliott's column. The entire command now hastened forward at the utmost speed the animals could endure. At nine o'clock on the same night, after an unparalleled march, the column was halted, but for a single hour for refreshment and rest. The march was again resumed. In the grateful light of the moon, which made itself apparent through the passing clouds, the column was enabled to move with certainty of retaining the trail.

At half past one, on the morning of the twenty-seventh, one of the Osage trailers returned to the column, reporting an Indian village within less than a mile distant. A solemn stillness reigned. The snarling wolf, and the accustomed wild sounds of the savage surroundings, alone disturbed the silence. The hostile Indian, enjoying a sense of security in the deep snow, which covered the plain, slumbered within his lodge.

When the report of the Osage trailers, of the discovery of the village was announced, Custer, with several officers, crept up stealthily to the crest of a hill overlooking the plain. At first they doubted the authenticity of the Osages' report. The light of the moon was not sufficiently bright to enable them to define the dark objects which they saw before them. At first they remarked they were buffaloes, as it was an extraordinary occurrence to get so close to a village without an alarm being given. Suddenly the distant tingling of a bell broke upon the alert ears of the party. This slight and welcome sound solved the mystery. The Osage chief repeated his words, "heaps ponies." Custer, turning to those with him, said in a whisper, "I am satisfied they are ponies, the herd of the village. Buffaloes are not in the habit of wearing such ornaments as bells in this country." The party now returned, and fearing that the untimely neigh of a horse, or some unusual noise might signal their presence to the sleeping village, the column was withdrawn to a distance. The men were ordered to stand by their horses and not allowed to build fires, or even to stamp their feet, for fear of defeating success. A small detachment of dismounted men were left with instructions to attack immediately should the savages show any signs of suspicion by issuing from their lodges.

Custer now took his principal officers with him to a point, giving an idea of the situation of the village. It lay upon the south bank of the Washita, The Cheyenne lodges were in the centre, the Arrapahoes above, and the Sioux below, all ranging along the banks of the stream. The nature of the ground as it could be indistinctly traced by moonlight, seemed to indicate that the village was accessible from all points.

The general and his officers now retired to a ravine near the impatient troopers, and determined upon the plan of attack. Four columns, composed as follows, were organized to make the assault.

Right column—Companies B and F, Colonel Thompson, commanding; Captain Yates, Lieutenants Wallingford and Gibson, on duty with column.

Right centre column—Lieutenant Colonel Myers, commanding; Captain Brewster and First Lieutenant Johnson, on duty with column.

Centre column—Companies A, D, C, and K, General Custer, commanding; First Lieutenants Moylan and Robbins, Major Bell, Captain West, Captain Hamilton, Lieutenant Colonels Weir and Custer, Captain Berry and Lieutenants Godfrey and Law, on duty with column.

Left column— Companies G, H, and M, Major Elliott, commanding; Lieutenant Smith on duty with column. A detachment of sharpshooters under Lieutenant Colonel Benteen and Lieutenants Hale and Cook, with centre column.

The left column was directed to take position in a timber below the village, the right centre column was to move along the Washita and attack from the timber above. The right column was to attack from the crest of the hill, north of the village, while Custer, with the centre column, determined to make a direct charge from the hills overlooking the village from the left bank of the Washita.

In the dead of night the columns upon different lines of march started. The dawn of day was fixed as the unfailing indication of the moment of attack. As each command reached its appointed position, it halted to await the time designated. So close were some of the troopers that the Indian dogs could be heard barking, as if sensible of the approaching danger. Probably accustomed to these nocturnal demonstrations, the warrior, in his lodge, gave no heed to the noise without.

The bank of the stream towards the village was low, while opposite, it was bold and precipitous. A find belt of timber grew immediately upon its borders. The limped waters of the Washita acted as a defence on the one side, while a range of low hills encircled the valley on the other. The lodges of the village were visible, only as so many dark cone like objects. In their midst was the lodge of the famous chief Black Kettle. As the evidence of rank, his lodge was black and ornamented, on the exterior, in the highest style of Indian art. The stores of the village, the herds and all that appertained to Indian affluence were gathered around.

The welcome moment of action had arrived. Several hours of comfortless delay and deep suspense had quickened the eagerness of the troops to dash into battle. Hardly had the first rays of the approaching day shot up into the heavens, than the solitudes of the Washita were rent by the clarion tones of sounding bugles, the shouts of the troops, and the clamour of charging squadrons. The regimental band from an eminence near the field, joined in the din of battle to the tune of "Garry Owen." From all sides the trooper, led by his proper officer, hastened to the vortex of the fray.

This sudden confusion without, fell upon the ears of the slumbering warriors as their death knell. The attack was simultaneous. The first shout, the heavy tramping of horses, and clanking of sabres inspired all with life. The charging squadrons came. galloping madly from all directions upon the fated village. Black Kettle broke from his bed of robes, and in an instant appeared without his lodge. He had heard the tramping of the horses on the snow. He looked around him, and witnessing the frenzied columns, fired his rifle and gave one wild whoop. Each warrior springing up as if by magic, seized his rifle and responded to the yell of despair which broke from the lips of the chief. Some of the warriors fled to the river and began fighting, at the same time standing waist deep in the water; others took to a ravine nearby. The squaws fled towards the high hills south of the village.

It was as the centre column was charging down the precipitous bluffs to cross the river, and take the village, that Hamilton was killed. Barnitz fell seriously wounded while charging with Elliott's column up the river. As the fight became general, each man picked his antagonist. It was after this mode of fighting had commenced that Elliott, with the sergeant-major of the regiment, and a handful of men started down the river after several fugitives.

In the ravines and underbrush, the warriors took up a position and kept up a deadly fire. The women and children, inspired with the courage of warriors, took up arms and attempted to drive back the angry wave. Amid the fire and smoke of the burning lodges, the crack of the rifle, the whistling of bullets, the whirring of arrows, the wild whoop of the warrior, and the mournful wail of the women, the conflict raged for several hours. To lend additional fierceness to the scene, from the lodges at intervals, the detonations of exploding gun powder could be heard above the general confusion and spreading destruction in every direction.

A number of squaws also participated in the fight, and were seen firing with all the energy and precision of warriors. During the engagement Colonel Benteen made an effort to capture the son of Black Kettle. The young warrior in response, fired several times at the colonel at but a few yards distant. Having killed the Colonel's horse, the young warrior made a rush at the prostrate officer, but was arrested in his murderous design by being summarily dispatched.

Prior to the fight, one of the Osages was in mourning for the murder of his squaw some months before by a party of Cheyennes. Every night and morning he kept up his wail of grief. When the fight began, while all his companions were covered with war paint, and presented more the appearance of so many devils, rather than human beings, the mourning warrior sat mumbling over his grief in solemn strains. He was not painted. As soon as the conflict began in earnest, an Osage warrior, having shot a Cheyenne, rushed upon his fallen foe, and in an instant with his knife severed the head from the body. With a wild whoop, he took the ghastly object to the mourning warrior and threw it before him. The warrior seized the trunkless head and in an instant had the scalp. His "bowl of blood" was full.

As if by magic the face of the sorrowing warrior was bedaubed with war-paint. Starting to his feet he gave one yell, and waving the propitiatory scalp in the air, cast his woes aside and disappeared in the thickest of the fray. A few moments after, the same warrior was seen standing over the lifeless form of a Cheyenne warrior. He had discovered the murderer of his squaw. Stooping, knife in hand, he was about to take the scalp, when he discovered it was gone. Such an expression of fiendish disappointment was probably never exceeded. Frantically gesticulating, he fell upon the body with the ferocity of a beast of prey, and severed the throat from ear to ear. Again he stood erect, his whole frame quivering with rage. Once more he fell upon the lifeless form. Completely severing the head from the trunk, he took his knife between his teeth, clutched the gory object in both hands, and raising it high above him, dashed it upon the ground at his feet with a convulsive imprecation.

After the fight had commenced, a party of Osages discovered the squaws trying to escape. They immediately started in pursuit and seizing switches, gave the fugitives a severe whipping and drove them back. After this exercise of authority, the squaws became exceedingly submissive and made no farther efforts to get away. In return they set up a howl, which was answered from the warriors. Hitherto they had shouted defiance. When they found their families were in possession of the troops, their yells were changed to mourning and they seemed to realize that the star of Black Kettle's band of the Cheyennes had set.

It would be impossible to enumerate the acts of heroism, hairbreadth escapes, and hand to hand encounters, had in the conflict with Black Kettle's warriors. Each savage resolved to sell his life as dearly as possible. Each officer and trooper knew, with him, it was victory or torture and certain death.

During the excitement of the fight the continued absence of Elliot and his party was not observed. Firing was heard in the direction he had taken, but supposed to be Indians signalling. When the conflict with Black Kettle's warriors lulled, the question ran along the line, "where is Elliot? where is Elliot?" No one answered. He had last been seen disappearing over the "divide."

The alarm carried by the fugitives, whom Elliott and his men were pursuing, aroused the warriors of the villages which were situated on the same stream lower down. The fight with Black Kettle's warriors had not ended when a large party of Kiowas and Arrapahoes, under Satanta and Little Raven, came to the assistance of the Cheyennes, This display of force from so unexpected a quarter was a surprise to the troopers and solved at once the fate of Elliott. There was now no doubt that he and his party had struck the approaching Kiowas and Arrapahoes, coming to the rescue of the Cheyennes, and had been cut off by them. There is no question that each man of this ill-fated band parted with his life as dearly as possible, and died at his post. For these unfortunate men, there was no possibility of escape. Their alternative was death by some friendly bullet, or death by the horrible torture which the hellish ingenuity of the savage alone can invent.

The reinforcements from the other villages opened their attack with considerable vigour. In order to keep them at bay, while the troopers were still engaged with Black Kettle, Weir was detached to oppose them. The savages fought with unexampled bravery, in hopes of succouring those of their allies still surviving the fight, but without success. They could not withstand the discipline and bravery of the troopers. Under the supreme impulse of self-preservation, the hostile reinforcements fled, to save themselves, their families, and their possessions from the inevitable doom of the Cheyennes. The detachment of cavalry pursued the retreating Kiowas and Arrapahoes as far as prudence, and the necessity of co-operating with the rest of the troops, would admit.

The victory was complete. One band of the most powerful and relentless of the hostile tribes had been destroyed. The captures were immense. Two white children were released from a fearful bondage. A white woman and a boy, ten years of age, held captive, were killed by the savages when the fight commenced. In the midst of the conflict, the bullets falling around in a perfect shower, a squaw, with demoniac fury, knife in hand, as if looking for an object upon which to revenge the loss of the day, fell upon an innocent captive child, and, with one terrible gash, completely disembowelled it—the warm, smoking entrails falling upon the snow.

Three days had now elapsed since leaving the train. The display of strength made by the Indians, caused a natural anxiety in regard to the safety of the supplies and the inadequate force left to protect them. These considerations fixed the resolution of Custer to hasten back to his wagons.

While all that was left of Black Kettle's village was being destroyed, seven hundred ponies, belonging to the late chief and his warriors, were shot. Two hundred were taken for the captive squaws and children, or brought in as trophies of the victory.

On the return march, no Indians were seen. They were, evidently, in great alarm at the just and terrible punishment meted out to the Cheyennes. Night and morning the captives set up their mourning songs, but received no response from lurking warriors.

At the first camp on the return, according to custom, the Osages hung their scalps outside their tents and fired several volleys over them. All the savages have a superstition that such demonstrations of hostility drive away the spirits of those from whom the scalps were taken, and that, in the event of the neglect of so important a precaution, these spirits would come and rob them of the hard-earned and ghastly evidences of their prowess.

So decisive an achievement as the battle of the Washita, was not without its sacrifices. Like all other deeds in the records of war, victory and defeat alike close up with a melancholy list of dead and suffering. Of the killed, were Elliott and Hamilton, and nineteen enlisted men. Of the wounded, were Barnitz, seriously but not mortally, and thirteen enlisted men.

The loss sustained by the savages, was one hundred and three warriors left on the ground. In property, eight hundred and seventy-five horses, ponies, and mules; two hundred and forty-one saddles, some of very fine and costly workmanship; five hundred and seventy-three buffalo robes; three hundred and ninety buffalo skins for lodges; one hundred and sixty untanned robes; thirty-five revolvers; forty-seven rifles; thirty-five pounds of powder; one thousand and fifty pounds of lead; four thousand arrows and arrow-heads; seventy-five spears; three hundred pounds of bullets; four hundred and seventy blankets; seven hundred pounds of tobacco; besides axes, bullet-moulds, lariats, saddle-bags, &c.

Having no means of transportation, the bulk of these captures were destroyed in the village before leaving. Among the warriors killed, were sixteen chiefs, including Black Kettle and Little Rock, two of the most influential warriors among the Cheyennes, Three squaws and three children, one boy and two girls, were wounded.

The banks of the Washita were silent. The charred remains of the village, and the stark corpses of the warriors, were the only vestiges of Black Kettle's band. The wolf, prowling in the midst of the blackened ruins of the Indian lodge, now alone disturbed the solitary haunts of the once proud and fierce warrior.

CHAPTER 19

Safe Arrival of the Volunteers

A courier having arrived at the camp with the announcement that Custer's column would be in that morning, (Dec, 1,) great preparations were made to give a suitable reception. Everyone was anxious to greet the victors of the Washita, and it was with considerable impatience the appearance of the column was looked for. Shortly after the sun had passed meridian, a cluster of dark objects appearing upon the crest of a hill, about a mile distant, accompanied with shouts and the firing of musketry, announced their approach. The mules and horses, grazing in the valleys nearby, hearing these unusual sounds, stampeded in great alarm from all directions towards camp. On the summit of the hill the head of the column halted for a few moments. Meanwhile, Sheridan, accompanied by his staff and a number of officers of the garrison, took position in the valley. All the officers and soldiers, not on duty, assembled in the vicinity of the fort to witness the warlike pageant.

The troopers now resumed their march, and as they descended the hill, the flashing of sabres and carbines, and the shouts of the men, were in wild counterpart of the dreary surroundings of their departure a week before.

The column was now within a short distance of the Commanding General. The Indians whooped, the band reiterated the stirring tones of "Garry Owen," and the troopers cheered. In response, rounds of huzzas from the troops of the fort shouted welcome and congratulation. In the advance were the Osage Indian trailers. Before leaving camp that morning, they had arrayed and decorated themselves in a manner becoming the importance of the occasion. Their faces were fantastically painted, and about their persons dangled the trophies which they had captured in battle. Spears, upon which were fastened the scalps of their fallen foe, were slung upon their shoulders.

From their own plaited scalp-locks were suspended long trains of silver ornaments and feathers. Over their shoulders hung shields, and bows, and quivers full of arrows, while in their hands they held their trusty rifle. Even the animals, which the Osages bestrode, were decorated with scalps and strips of red and blue blankets. At the head of the band rode Little Beaver, the chief, with a countenance as fixed as stone, yet in his bearing showing indications of an inward self-glorification, which was, apparently, kept stirring and swelling higher and higher by discharged firearms and wild notes of the war-songs, shouted by his warriors. In a moment of enthusiasm, the chief exclaimed, "they call us Americans; we are Osages," to which sentiment went up a responsive yell of approval.

Conspicuous in this party was the young Osage warrior, Koom-la-Manche, (Trotter). It was he, under the impulse of the highest aspiration of Indian valour, who singled out the great chief. Black Kettle, the terror of all the Osages, as his victim. After a severe conflict he reached the crowning point of his efforts and bore away the ghastly scalp of the terrible chief as the trophy attaching to his success. As a mark of special attention, this scalp was carefully and artistically decorated and hung prominently among the most sacred possessions of the young warrior.

At the head of the troops rode Custer, attended by the officers of his staff. Next followed the living evidences of the victory, over fifty squaws and their children, surrounded by a suitable guard, to prevent their escape. These were mounted on their own ponies, seating themselves astride the animals, their persons wrapped in skins and blankets, even their heads and faces being covered, leaving nothing visible but the eyes, The mothers had their offspring mounted behind them, the papoose being visible only by its diminutive head peering over the back of its mother. As many as three were mounted on some of the ponies. Without a sigh, without a glance to the right or to the left, these remnants of the band of the once powerful Black Kettle, followed with all the submission of captors. Next came the brave officers and men of the different squadrons.

The regiment moved up the Beaver, about half a mile from the fort, and there went into camp. The scene, during the remainder of the day, was that of joyous holiday. Officers and men recounted the perils and hardships of the march and the battle, and exhibited the trophies, which had been saved from the burning village. Custer's Sibley-tent raised its cone-like outlines in the centre; on the left, a hundred yards off, were the prisoners, the Osages and scouts, in front the long line of picketed horses, and the wall and shelter tents of officers and men.

On the night after the return of the troops from the Washita, the Indians proposed to celebrate the victory by giving a scalp dance. Shortly after dark a huge log fire was built upon the banks of the Beaver. A number of officers, including the Commanding General, resorted to the spot to witness, in all its wild originality, this triumphal celebration. The savages were seated around the fire, uttering not a word, and looking the personification of the denizens of some infernal region. Notwithstanding the wintry winds sweeping through the valley, they had dispossessed themselves of their blankets, and about their persons wore the trophies taken in the battle.

At a given signal from the chief, the warriors sprang to their feet and set up wild shouts, accompanied by a violent pounding upon an Indian drum. The young men jumped and danced, and distorted their bodies in every conceivable shape, some yelled furiously, while others chanted a song of triumph or recounted the deeds of daring they had performed. They renewed their declarations of hostility towards the Cheyennes and made vows "to be buried deep under the ground before running from their enemies."

During almost the entire night, long after the officers and men, assembled to witness the occasion, had departed, the Indian drum and the shout of the warriors could be heard, borne upon the still air.

During the first few days after their arrival at the Camp of Supply, the captives, taken at the battle of the Washita, manifested evident anxiety. They all expected to be killed in retaliation for the atrocities committed by their people. At first the wounded rebelled against all offers of humanity, in alleviating their sufferings, and would not allow themselves to be separated from their companions, in order to be taken to the hospital, imagining that they were the first singled out for vengeance. Their own camp, for greater safety, being pitched near that of the Seventh Cavalry, and surrounded by a chain of sentinels, farther excited their uncertainty. To add to this, the soldiers talking amongst themselves, not in the mildest or the most euphonious tones, was construed by the captives into a controversy as to how and when they were to be disposed of.

In constant dread of their fate the sister and niece of Black Kettle visited the headquarters of the Commanding General to ask him "when they were all to be killed." On the assurance that such was not the custom of the white people toward women and innocent children, the two squaws departed with light hearts, and their report soon changed the sullen and drooping spirits of the captives into a high degree of contentment and satisfaction at their change of life, and particularly the abundance of food they enjoyed. The squaws busied themselves in a variety of ways about the camp, while the children amused themselves along the banks of the Beaver, throwing arrows and pitching stones,

I was most struck with the remarkable fortitude exhibited by several Indian children, not over eight years of age, and in the hospital, from wounds accidently received in the fight.

From the lips of none of them fell the least audible indication of their sufferings, yet their distorted features, and the delirious glare of the eye, betrayed the physical anguish prevailing within their rigid exterior. During such painful operations as probing and cleansing the wounds the little sufferers placed their hands over their heads and closed their eyes, submitting without a murmur. One little girl, with a bullet-hole through her body on the left side, sat up as if in perfect health. The vigorous condition of their systems assisting nature, as well as human skill, in their efforts, soon found the sufferers able to join their friends in the camp, greatly to the delight of all.

During the fourth of December the troops of the seventh, and a portion of the garrison, were ordered under arms, to perform the last tribute of respect to the gallant young officer, Hamilton, who had fallen at the head of his squadron in the late battle A neat coffin had been made of pine boards, in which the remains, attired in the full uniform of a captain, were placed. The troops formed in the vicinity of the tent in which the body had lain since its arrival at the camp. At two o'clock in the afternoon the roll of muffled drums, the solemn refrain of the band, and the slow step of the pall-bearers, announced that the remains were approaching. The coffin, enveloped in the national colours, was placed in an ambulance. The long line of mourning comrades, in reverse order, broke into column. The squadron of the deceased officer took the advance. Next came the remains, followed by the riderless horse, covered with a mourning sheet and spurs reversed. Then the long column of troops and officers, all moving in measured tread towards the grave.

The site selected for the resting place of Hamilton was beautifully situated on the banks of the Beaver, beneath the over-spreading branches of a few cotton-woods. Here the troops massed, and the body was lowered into the cold and solitary grave. The burial service was read by a brother officer, and amid volleys of musketry the earth closed upon its dead.

The remaining companies of the volunteers by this time had reached camp, and were enjoying an abundance compared with their march. Although the command had left Topeka on the fifth of November incessant storms and an impassible country had so impeded their progress that their supply of rations were exhausted before they had made more than half of their march. The safe arrival of the regiment was a source of relief to the Commanding General; and allowing a few days rest for the entire command it was proposed to set out again on the "war-path."

The troops participating in the campaign were now concentrated in the vicinity of the Supply Camp. The wagon train had returned with additional supplies, and the fort was sufficiently completed. The Commanding General was quick in his resolution as to the next move. He had now an abundance of forage and rations for thirty days, and a sufficient number of extra wagons for transportation. The horses and mules, though numbers had died from exposure and scarcity of subsistence, were in fair condition, and a majority at least were equal to much more hard service. The men were in excellent health. Cases of scurvy, the most dreaded disease during such a campaign, were comparatively rare, and more remarkable than all, colds and inflammations, requiring hospital treatment, were almost without a victim. Under these circumstances everything was favourable to another successful invasion of the regions occupied by the hostile bands.

The seventh of December was the day fixed for the departure of the new expeditionary force. This movement, it was also announced, the Commanding General would attend in person, The objective point was Fort Cobb, to be reached by a circuitous route, in the hopes of striking other Indian villages along the head waters of the Washita.

To interrupt the preparations for the departure of the expedition another violent snow-storm set in, attended by a terrific wind from the north. All the indications were opposed to our getting off by the time appointed. The snow, however, after falling for a single night, disappeared, leaving the ground covered to the depth of eight inches. The wind kept up, drifting it into immense banks, blocking valleys and almost the camp. The air was cold and biting, but the sky was clear.

Late in the afternoon of the sixth the general designated the infantry battalion, composed of companies B, E, F, of the 3rd, K of the 5th, and G of the 38th, as the garrison to remain at the new fort. Lebo's company, of the 10th Cavalry, was also attached for scouting or escort duty Two companies of volunteers were detached to act as escort to the trains moving between the camp and Fort Dodge. Page of the third was assigned to the command of the post.

Before the bugle had sounded "tattoo" the same night the troops were under marching orders. Everything was ready for an early start the following morning.

CHAPTER 20

California Joe

At an early hour on the morning of the seventh of December, the entire command was occupied striking tents and packing the camp equipage in the wagons. The day was clear, but intolerably cold and wintry. To break camp, with its few comforts, and set out on an extensive expedition in such weather was not a subject of agreeable contemplation. But wind and weather were entirely ignored in the catalogue of valid reasons for delay. Accordingly at the appointed hour, ten o'clock in the morning, the long dark lines of troopers and wagons were to be seen stretched across the snow covered plain awaiting the order to advance.

The expedition consisted of the eleven companies of the seventh cavalry, ten companies of the volunteers, Pepoon's scouts, and fifteen Osage and Kaw Indians, making a total of about seventeen hundred men. The supplies for men and animals for thirty days, together with shelter tents, cooking utensils and baggage, were conveyed in three hundred wagons. Three of the Cheyenne squaws were also taken with the expedition, to be used in giving information respecting the country. When all was ready, Sheridan mounted his horse and attended by his staff, rode to the head of the column, and in person gave the order, "Forward." The scouts and Indians took the lead, and were followed by the Seventh in front, the wagon train in the centre, and the Volunteers as a rear guard. From the crest of the last range of hills, many an eye turned for a regretful gaze upon the little fort in the distant plain. The rude expedients, but appreciated comforts found there, passed in quick review before the mind, and then with a last lingering glance all was forgotten in the hardships and perils which lay before. Even the "robber's roost" that resort of mirth and tobacco smoke had to be left behind. Here daily, as regularly as the sun went down, the cam-

The Canadian

paign and the affairs of the nation, about a month behind time, were elaborately discussed. Good natured controversies and singing were used as powerful antidotes for valueless time, and smoking acted as a sort of mental and physical sedative generally. The daytime had been devoted to the building of the fort, or the more exciting occupation of the scout or the chase. Thus though hundreds of miles away from the comforts and attractions of society, our busy little world, buried in the depths of a vast bleak surrounding wilderness, was not the last place for contentment.

The column as it moved through the drifting snow, ascending the low range of hills nearby, and stretching out along the bank of the Wolf River, presented a novel appearance. In the lead as a sort of figure head to the muffled and motley objects which followed, was California Joe with a crew of light hearted reckless fellows around him. Joe was, in the first place, mounted on a horse of that vigorous stripe of energy and constitution over which it seemed nature had abandoned all control. The skin of the hide bound quadruped was drawn tighter than a drum head, over the numerous sharp corners and projections which here and there displayed themselves. By way of personal comfort, Joe wore on his head a dilapidated *sombrero*, with a rim so wide that it served as a covering for his ears.

This duplex purpose was effected by a rope brought down over the top of the head and under the chin. This peculiar affair, taken from a side glance, gave Joe's head the appearance of a huge scoop. In front it suggested, a gigantic telescope on a pivot. Around his neck Joe wore a strip of red strouding, which looked very much as if it had originally served an Indian for a breech-clout. He wore a cavalry overcoat, the tail of which was well singed. He wore on his heels a pair of monstrous Mexican spurs. His companions were arrayed in a variety of styles, coon-skin caps, buffalo leggins, blankets, in fact anything or everything, which would aid in keeping out the shivering cold.

Next in the column, came the Indian trailers. Their general appearance belied their historic as well as poetical hardihood. The red man, when he consults his own inclinations, is emphatically fond of the fires of the lodge and the society of his squaws and papooses, particularly as compared with the war-path in winter. The warriors with us presented a disconsolate look. They closely hugged their blankets and buffalo-robes. They sat upon their horses gazing rigidly at the glistening snow, as if afraid to turn in their seats lest some new aperture for the ingress of fresh currents of blood-chilling air might be opened. Hard Rope, the counsellor of the nation, remarked, before starting, "that he was an old man, and it was bad for old men to be alone in cold weather. He would capture a Cheyenne squaw to keep his back warm." The old man, judging from his shrivelled and shaking form, should have been supplied with a bed-warmer and a footbath for the campaign.

Next came the scouts and troops, rigged up in every conceivable manner. The weather had dissipated all attempts or disposition to preserve a uniformity of dress, and it was decidedly amusing to observe the ingenuity of some in their inventions, especially to keep up the comfort of the extremities, such as the nose, fingers, and toes.

Everything was cold and cheerless. The sun sparkled upon the far-extending plain of snow and ice. The wind swept violently from the north. The streams were blocked. The troops and wagons moved slowly and tediously.

The first day's march, was up the north bank of the Wolf River, over a high, rolling country. At a distance of eight miles from camp, we crossed the stream, though with great difficulty, owing to the shifting sands in its bed, and pitched our tents on the south side.

The journey of the clay, in consequence of the snow and roughness of the weather, told severely upon the animals. Thirteen teams were already used up, and others were in little better condition. A detachment was dispatched back to the Supply Camp, with orders to bring up fresh teams to replace those which had given out. The Commanding General had determined to start fresh, no matter what might be his condition when he got through the march.

The site of the camp, was upon a level plain, surrounded by a range of high hills. The Wolf River ran at our back, and, beyond, the plain was broken into numerous sand-hills. The headquarters' tents were pitched in a cluster of cotton-wood trees of enormous size, and immediately upon the banks of the river. A large fire was built in front of the general's quarters, which threw a bright light over a large surrounding space, and cast a brilliant glare high up into the heavens.

This matter of large fires in a country inhabited by skulking savages, reminds me of an opinion on one occasion expressed on the subject by an old chief. Approaching a fire, at which a number of officers were seated, for some moments the chief appeared engaged in profound meditation. Suddenly lifting his eyes, in a sort of soliloquizing manner observed, "Big fool! white man big fool! Big chief, me, fire so," (stooping, and representing a very small fire), "no one see him; white man so," (extending his arms to show the extent of conflagration), "everybody see him. Many sleeps off and come and shoot him."

This evidence of the precautions observed by the warrior in preventing his presence being discovered, was thrown in the shade by a philosophical savage, who, noticing an immense fire, said, "Red man build little fire, and sit around to warm his body; white man build big fire, and can't get near it." Any reader, experienced in camp life, can appreciate the force of the Indian's observation. On the night in question, a circuit of four or five yards was considered the most convenient scorching distance.

During this halt the camp was disturbed, the entire night, by the distribution and equalization of the supplies for transportation. The wagons had been badly packed, and most of the work, therefore, had to be done over. At three o'clock on the morning of the eighth of December, the fresh teams arrived from Camp Supply, and those broken down were sent back under escort.

In starting fairly upon the march, the Commanding General issued orders that reveille be sounded every morning at four o'clock, and the column in motion by six, or by the dawn of day. This order had a double importance. An early start was always desirable, and was in our case no less so as a measure of precaution. Sunrise and sunset, or when coming out of or going into camp, were known to be the favourite opportunities for an Indian attack. Although the utmost vigilance was exacted from the *videttes*, particularly in keeping a sharp lookout, extra precautions were observed at the times mentioned.

At the hour designated the teams were in harness and the troopers mounted. Some minutes before the sun rose from behind the eastern waves of rolling highlands the column was "stretched out" on the plain, and toiling along into the depths of the surrounding wilderness. For greater security the wagons were moved in four columns; abreast the right flank of the train, at a distance of two hundred yards, moving in a parallel line, was the seventh. In the same position, abreast the left flank, were the volunteers, both regiments in column by fours. A squadron moved in front to oppose any demonstration in that direction, and a similar force brought up the rear to repel attack, and with instructions to shoot all animals that might give out on the march, and could not be driven with the column. A line of flankers rode at a distance of a quarter of a mile off to signal the appearance of war-parties.

These measures of precaution, considering the character of the enemy, were even more important than in civilized war. Ambuscades and sudden dashes were possible at any moment. When least expected, aa army of warriors might spring up as if from the depths of the earth. With their light equipments, swift and fresh ponies, expert horsemanship, and rapid evolutions, the better part of valour in our case was to be always ready for an emergency. Far more dreaded than an attack was a stampede of the stock, a piece of strategy always resorted to by the savages.

I had once the experience of being with a wagontrain in which the animals took fright from some unknown cause. The alarm seemed to communicate itself in an instant. It spread like wildfire. Mule teams, with drivers, and without, dashed in all directions over the plain at a dead run. Every effort to check the tide only seemed to increase it. The animals were perfectly frantic and beyond control. No obstacle could stay them, and to be anywhere in front of the terrific wave was certain death. The alarm kept up until the animals could run no longer. The wagons were gathered and formed into a corral, in which the animals were placed to allow the excitement to pass off. A stampede of a large train is frequently attended with loss of life. To prevent any such calamity as this befalling our own column every measure of safety was adopted, and strict injunctions were placed upon teamsters never to leave their posts.

Our course during the day was over a high rolling plain, very similar to the country to the northward. At one stage of the journey we struck a remarkably peculiar section, the plain being covered with a number of hummocks of red earth and gravel, without any apparent connection or system. During the morning we moved through forests of miniature oaks. These diminutive types of the giant specimens were perfect as regarded structure, and bore an abundance of acorns. The tree, for such it was, ranged from six to twelve inches in height. These forests were found upon the sides of the higher ranges, and frequently covered as much as twenty and thirty acres. For hours the column, like so many mighty monsters, marched over the tops of forests of oak.

About noon a small herd of buffaloes was chased by a party sent out, and the meat of two fine animals was secured. After a march of thirty miles the column went into camp on Hackberry Creek, so named by the Commanding General on account of that tree predominating on its banks. The stream was insignificant in itself, but important as the only desirable camping-place between the Wolf and Main Canadian Rivers. At several points on the stream recent traces of Indians were discovered, and a "lodge-pole trail" was seen leading off towards the south.

Travelling on the plains bears the relation to railway travel, that navigation on the broad ocean does to that on rivers. A vast sea of earth, its waves rise into great swells and sink into deep troughs. To an inexperienced eye there is a dull monotony, a sameness, and an expanse of vision which seldom varies. For days the "direction" lies apparently over the same ground. No roads, rarely a stream, and a painful scarcity of timber. The startled game sometimes creates a transient ripple, but this vanishes as suddenly as it comes.

The plains have few streams, particularly in summer, but the configuration is wisely provided for purposes of drainage by means of valleys and ravines, all of which form part of a regular system, leading into the main water courses. The swell in the surface, which constitutes the main water shed, is termed the "divide." To know the "divide," and how to follow it, constitutes the highest art of the guide. Here the best footing is found, and the broken ground in the ravines is avoided. It is wonderful to observe how the guides in a new country, by a sort of intuition, will distinguish one "divide" from another, and select that which is most desirable for the line of direction.

All travelling parties on the plains use the compass. Except with a perfect knowledge of keeping the points by astronomical objects it would be as impossible to traverse them, except by some unerring guide, as to navigate the ocean without the needle. There are no roads. The trail of the buffalo the war-party, or the village, are the roads of the country. At points wagon-trails have been opened for the use of emigrant and supply trains from the verge of eastern civilization to the advancing tide from the west, but blank spaces of hundreds of miles intervene. Under such circumstances the perplexities of moving a column of nearly two thousand mounted men, and nearly four thousand animals, may be imagined.

Breaking camp at Hackberry Creek at the usual hour, the column headed towards the Canadian. In the night a "norther" had set in, and now swept over the plain with the force of a tornado. The train found great difficulty in making any progress whatever. The temperature figured at 10° to 15° Fahrenheit. The men suffered severely from their feet and hands, although a pair of stout buffalo shoes and a pair of substantial gloves had been provided each before starting on the campaign. During most of the day's march the cold was so excessive that the troopers dismounted and led their horses.

The country, on the line of march this day, presented an entirely new and novel appearance. Immense quantities of gypsum were visible in all directions, cropping out at the surface, frequently resembling at a distance, extensive banks of snow and ice. Specimens were picked up by the way exhibiting every stage of crystallization. A delicate selenite, composed of transparent crystals or crystalline masses, easily splitting, with the assistance of a knife, into thin transparent plates, was found in great abundance. Several varieties of an earthy nature were gathered, and again specimens of a smoky hue or more beautifully coloured with tints, from a pale pink to a deep crimson. Other varieties closely resembling alabaster were met with. In some forms the gypsum was easily crushed with the fingers, and presented a pulverized mass of minute sparkling crystals, while in other conditions, it possessed the hardness of the most durable stone.

The entire region between the Cimmaron and the Main Canadian, a distance of nearly a hundred miles was of the same character. The water in all the streams met with, had an extremely bitter and unpalatable taste. In traversing this section it was necessary to transport a supply of water, taken from the smaller streams, which were found to be less impregnated than the rivers.

The beds or layers generally made their appearance on the face of high bluffs, or upon the sides of the loftier "divide." The position of the veins indicated upheaval from a considerable depth, and were universally found in extensive fields of red earth and shale. An experiment made in camp, by burning a small quantity, produced an excellent quality of the Plaster of Paris known to commerce. Small deposits of gypsum have been discovered in Wisconsin and Iowa. Also on some of the western slopes of the Cordilleras,

The configuration of the country as we approached the Main Canadian increased in the vastness of its proportions, to the degree of sublimity. Bald hills rose on all sides, towering high over the plain, while the intermediate valleys could be followed away in the distance until the powers of vision failed to define the line of demarcation between the earth and the heavens. From some lofty eminence, gazing upon the extensive landscape, chaos and desolation alone conveyed the spirit and the reality of the scene. Countless hummocks of red gravel and rocks in every conceivable shape, from perfect cones to jagged boulders, covered the surface of the low grounds in every direction. Not a sign of animal life was visible, not a sound broke the awful stillness which prevailed. Vegetation was sparse. The hardy buffalo grass grew in bunches, between which seams of barren red earth stared forth a perfect type of sterility. Owing to the lack of every inducement as a place of abode, the tribes of the plains knew the country as the "bad ground."

After a tedious march of ten hours, in which time making but fifteen miles, the column went into camp on the north bank of the Main Canadian. As might be expected in such a region, the advantages for camping were not very inviting. Timber was scarce and water barely palatable. The "norther" which had impeded our progress during the day, showed no signs of being "blowed out." The thermometer had fallen several degrees. During the day a number of animals overcome with exhaustion were shot, and left a rich feast for the half starved wolf.

From the summit of a hill in the rear of our camp, the valley of the Canadian presented the same scene of desolation witnessed throughout the day. On the north side, the "divide" descended abruptly into a plain several hundred yards in width, extending to the river. On the opposite bank, the country rose at once into high bluffs of red clay furrowed by deep arroyos.

"The camp on the Canadian" will long be remembered by all who participated in the campaign of 1868—69. The wintry blast swept mercilessly through the valley, demolishing tents and extinguishing the few fires built against the intense cold. The night was intolerably dark. The troopers unable to keep warm, could be heard through the long hours tramping up and down, within the limits of the camp, afraid to lie down for fear of freezing to death. The animals without covering or protection from the wind suffered intensely. All night shivering at the picket-rope the poor brutes uttered melancholy moans, but it was beyond the power of man to alleviate their sufferings. At headquarters it was no better. Fires were out, tents were either down or flapping in the wind.

It was with a feeling of relief and satisfaction that the reveille sounded. The camp had long been astir, for there was no rest taken that night. The intense cold occasioned a material delay in getting started the following morning. The animals almost paralyzed by the cold, refused to move except by beating. The teamsters half frozen were almost powerless to perform their accustomed duties.

About an hour after daylight, the column left camp moving down the Canadian a distance of about a mile to a suitable place for crossing. The thermometer stood near zero, (Fahr.) The wind blew more violently then ever. A dense smothering cloud of sand, started from the dry bed of the stream, rushed furiously by. The current of the river was about a half a mile in width. It was now frozen from shore to shore, but not sufficiently to bear up the train or even the animals. To effect a crossing against such obstacles, for a time considerably exercised the wits of the engineers.

After some discussion of the best plans for crossing, it was proposed to cut a passage. A large detail of troops was sent to the front and with axes broke the ice in a number of places so as to weaken its resistance. A squadron of cavalry was next ordered in and with great difficulty floundered across. The legs of the animals were badly lacerated in the undertaking. Several of the horses, riders and all, stumbled into the water, but were dragged out in time to prevent any loss of life. The advance party built large fires, of "buffalo chips" gathered on the neighbouring hills, for the accommodation of the men as they crossed, particularly those who found an inhospitable bath in the freezing waters of the Canadian.

The crossing of the river occupied five hours and was effected without the loss of a single wagon, notwithstanding several were frozen fast while delayed in the stream and had to be cut out.

The ascent from the Canadian to the high grounds on its southern bank was a labour of excessive difficulty, owing to precipitous bluffs and yawning gorges. After reaching the elevated lands, the column progressed slowly. The temperature kept at the same degree of cold, and the wind displayed no signs of moderation.

During the afternoon we came in sight of the Antelope hills. These hills consisted of several lofty peaks, perfectly barren of trees, and presenting a very peculiar appearance. Rising out of a high table-land, they were visible at a great distance, and have always been used by the Indians as landmarks. The country, in the vicinity, was always a favourite resort for the wild Indian tribes on account of game.

Before striking the Washita, we entered a vast basin, as sterile as that encountered north of the Canadian. The whole country was covered with hillocks, shooting out of the even surface, to a height of fifty and sixty feet. The carcasses of a number of buffaloes, recently killed, were found, together with other unmistakable signs of the presence of the savages within a few days.

At four o'clock in the afternoon, having made eighteen miles, the column went into camp on the north side of the Washita.

To old Joe, the expedition was a source of great perplexity. The old scout was specially "demoralized," and naturally complained more than ever. The cold weather was particularly a source of doleful repinings. To cap the climax, his horse had given out, which subjected him to the humiliating necessity of "footing it." Reflecting upon his former experience, doubtless, he never lost an opportunity to observe "that it was an infarnal country that could'nt farnish a feller a horse when he had need on one." After trudging along for a day or two, the old worthy presented himself astride an old mule, which had been abandoned. While belabouring the poor brute with the heavy end of a quirk, he did not fail to extol the remarkable patience and pluck of his new acquisition, and swore if he could ever get the mule "in," he would make out of it the finest animal in all the country.

Sheridan and Joe were warm and old friends. Ten or fifteen years before, while the general was in a subordinate command in Oregon, Joe revelled in all the power and importance of affluence, in such a shape as the country afforded. In speaking of those days, the old scout would reiterate an inventory of his worldly goods then, which consisted of ox and mule trains, "the finest in those parts." He was then, withal, a "gay gambolier," as he expressed it, and after a long chapter of vicissitudes, at the hands of fickle fortune, "trying to mend," he came down "ka-wollup." Financially flat on his back, he struggled along, and finally resolved to leave the scenes of so much of frontier experience on the Pacific coast. He came back to civilization, tried a new mode of life for several weeks, got into a series of rows, and was almost constantly entertained by the servants of the law. The despotism of society was too much for him, so he returned to his native clement, the frontier, bound in the course of his wanderings to Texas. From his reckless and solitary sorties through the country, the chances were ten to one that some "red devil" would suddenly divert his route into probably a worse region than Texas.

The fact of old Joe having known the general "on the slope," speaking a little Chenook, and having, in his days of prosperity, "done much teaming for him," the old fellow had additional privileges at headquarters. These he never failed regularly to enjoy, usually calling after dark, and seating himself, in due form, on the ground by the camp fire, lighting an old cob or mud pipe, domestic manufacture, and in profound meditation, apparently, awaiting an introductory observation from the general.

After reaching camp on the Washita, Joe made his appearance, as usual. He had been missing for several days, and a curiosity to learn what the old fellow had been doing, induced the general to make a few inquiries. "Joe," said the general, "you have not been around, these few days. Busy looking after those red friends of yours."

"No friends of mine, good evening, General," remarked Joe by way of response and salutation.

"Well, what is going on? you are always posted," said the general.

"Nothin, except I've bin havin a infarnal chronicle cough, that's been nigh scuttlin me this two days, an I've been a thinkin that I cotched the glanders, an' they might as well shoot a feller to onct as to have that bothering him."

The general hereupon produced a small flask of brandy, and handed to the old scout a good "swig," in a tin cup.

"Well, it won't do any harm," said, Joe, with well-feigned diffidence, "but it's been so long since I see anything like that, it's mighty sure to surprise a feller's in'ards."

The old scout took his drink, without farther reflection, and after a relishing smack of his lips, became doubly voluble, occasionally throwing in a little Chenook, by way of reminiscence.

Several hours after every one had retired to his blankets, Joe still sat by the fire, narrating his experiences and telling of his former opulence, to an imaginary audience.

Chapter 21

Fiendish Mutilation

We had now reached the chosen resort of the wild tribes occupying the country between the Arkansas and the Red Rivers. The extraordinary fertility, the abundance of timber and game, rendered the valley of the Washita an inviting spot for the savage warrior and his kindred during the inhospitable season of snow and rain. The almost impassable nature of the extensive country to the north was in itself considered a sufficient barrier against encroachment at almost any period of the year, and especially in winter. Until the present year innumerable herds of buffaloes, driven by the severe weather and scarcity of pasturage, to the lower latitudes, roamed through the country in ready access, and hunting-parties were daily employed in bringing in meat for the winter store and hides for barter with the Indian trader. The military operations for the preceding few months had driven back the buffalo to the north, while the recent visit of Custer had alarmed the savages themselves to such an extent that the country had been abandoned, and the chiefs with their people had either moved in the direction of Fort Cobb, to take advantage of the intercession of the officers there, or fled to the Wachita Mountains, as they supposed, out of danger.

Our camp was but eight miles from the scene of the then recent fight with Black Kettle's band. The anxiety felt in regard to the fate of Elliott and his men, who had not been heard of since their disappearance in the battle, and hoping to find some trace of the missing party, Sheridan directed that the column should remain in camp one day.

On the night of the tenth of December a small expedition was made up to visit the battle-ground, and to scout the country adjacent. By eight o'clock on the next morning the expedition was ready to start. The party consisted of the Commanding General, Custer, several of the staff, and four or five officers, and the writer. The escorting squadron was composed detachments of each of the companies of the seventh, commanded by Lieutenant Colonel Custer, Captain Yates, and Lieutenant Weston. Several Osage and Kaw Indians were also sent in advance as scouts.

The morning was clear but cold. Animal and rider felt little disposition to tarry by the way. A sharp, biting wind blew in our faces, and it was with rapid movements we hastened to our destination. Our line of march was along the north side of the stream. A heavy growth of timber and underbrush skirted the bank, from which in passing we started several deer and large droves of turkeys. Away from the river the country rose abruptly into high ranges, broken here and there by a number of bald red hills.

A ride of an hour and a half brought us to the immediate vicinity of the battle-ground. At a distance, looking down from a "divide," which the column was crossing to avoid a large bend in the river, the scene was one of most intense solitude. The sunlight glistening upon the heavy frost, which had not yet disappeared from the trees and long grass of the lowlands, lent the only charm to the landscape. The barren hills, the wild and silent valley, the leafless and lifeless vegetation, formed the picture of desolation.

We had now reached the line of formation taken by the left centre column in the fight. The horses' tracks were still visible. It was here Elliott in the darkness formed his squadron, and awaited the first finger of dawn to hurl his troopers upon the fated village. Beyond this we entered the late field of strife.

The foot prints of the charging squadrons could be followed in one extended front through tangled brush. As we moved closer to the immediate site of the village, our approach breaking upon the quiet surroundings of the scene of death, and alarmed from their sense of security and enjoyment, fled innumerable beasts and birds of prey. Suddenly lifting from the ground could be seen thousands of ravens and crows, disturbed in their carrion feast. The dense black mass, evidently gorged, rose heavily, and passing overhead, as if to take revenge for the molestation, set up the greatest confusion of noises. The cowardly wolves started from their abundant repast on human flesh, reluctantly left the spot, and while slowly getting out of reach of danger often stopped to take a wishful look behind. Retiring to the summit of the nearest hills, they seated themselves on their haunches and watched every movement of the intruders,

A few yards in advance of the first position taken by Elliott an object having the appearance of a bundle of blankets laid up against a tree was discovered. A large quantity of underbrush had been gathered and deposited around to prevent disturbance or molestation. Upon examining the mysterious bundle it was found to be a warrior killed in the fight, and whose friends returning had given him part of the rites of an Indian burial. As we moved along these evidences of the severity of the conflict became more numerous. Thirty bodies were found on one part of the field alone.

It was very evident that the rest of the tribe, and their allies occupying the villages lower down on the same stream, visited the battle-ground after the troops had departed. Many of the warriors left on the field were carefully tied up in two or three thicknesses of blankets. Some were laid in the branches of trees, out of the reach of the hungry wolf, while others were deposited under protections made of bushes. The most important men of the village were dragged off and buried, doubtless at a distance, in some remote and hidden *cañon*, where man nor beast would ever disturb their bones. Several bodies with *lariats* about them, which were evidently in the act of being dragged off, were subsequently found abandoned on the hills adjacent.

Entering the space lately occupied by the Indian lodges, on all sides were scattered the charred remains of Black Kettle's village. The conflagration started by the troops had done its work effectively. Scarcely anything of a combustible character escaped.

From the village, the Commanding General, attended by several officers and a small escort, rode to the top of a neighbouring ridge, from which there was an excellent view of the battle-ground. The positions of the Indian lodges could be distinctly traced by the circular rows of pins and the rude fire-holes in the centre. On the right of the village, at a distance of less than two hundred yards, were strewn the carcasses of the ponies of the village, which had been shot by the troops. The bodies numbered not less than seven hundred, and covered an area of several acres.

After the battle was perfectly understood and the ground well surveyed, Sheridan and Custer, accompanied by Lieutenant Hale, the writer, and a small detachment of troopers, moved down the south bank of the Washita, over the route taken by Elliott and the missing men, in hopes of recovering the bodies. The remainder of the party spent some time longer in the village, and subsequently moved down the bed of the valley of the river.

We crossed the stream and proceeded down the south bank until we ascended a high "divide," from which an extensive view could be had of the surrounding country. Descending on the other side, the party had not proceeded but a hundred yards, when the body of a white man was found, perfectly naked, and covered with arrow and bullet holes. The head presented the appearance of having been beaten with a war-club. The top of the skull was broken into a number of pieces, and the brain was lying partly in the skull and partly on the ground. At first, it was supposed that the body was that of Elliott, but, upon minute examination, this was found not to be the case; but it was one of his men.

Marking the spot where this body was found, we continued moving down stream. Crossing, with some difficulty, a small ravine, about the centre of an extensive plain, at a distance of two hundred yards farther on, objects were seen lying in the grass, and were supposed to be bodies. Our attention attracted in this direction, we rode to the spot at a gallop. A scene was now witnessed sufficient to appal the bravest heart. Within an area of not more than fifteen yards, lay sixteen human bodies—all that remained of Elliott and his party! The winter air swept across the plain, and its cold blasts had added to the ghastliness of death the additional spectacle of sixteen naked corpses frozen as solidly as stone. There was not a single body that did not exhibit evidences of fearful mutilation. They were all lying with their faces down, and in close proximity to each other. Bullet and arrow wounds covered the back of each; the throats of a number were cut, and several were beheaded. The body of one of the horses only, which the men had ridden out, was lying at a distance of fifty-yards The other animals had evidently escaped and were taken by the savages when the party found themselves hemmed in and obliged to fight on foot. All the bodies were carefully examined, but it was with great difficulty that any of them were recognized, owing to the terrible atrocities to which they had been subjected.

Judging from the nature of the ground and the location, it was concluded that Elliott started under the impression that the village the column had struck constituted all in that section of country. Three warriors, the only fugitives, had left, on the first alarm, to arouse the bands below. Elliott, seeing them break through his lines, started in pursuit. According to the Indian account, which I subsequently obtained, two of the three were killed, but the third gained the nearest village with tidings of the attack on Black Kettle's people. The warriors of the neighbouring bands hastily mounted their war ponies, and set out for the scene of the fight.

Elliott was several miles from the column when the Indian allies, from the lower villages, struck him. The savages began an immediate assault, and were in such overwhelming numbers, that he retired rapidly, in hopes of making good his retreat. Crossing the second "divide," before he had time to pass the valley, the ravine between him and the column was occupied by warriors, who opened fire as he and his men approached. There was now no alternative but to dismount and take a stand and prolong the fight, in hopes of being rescued, or if the worst came, to die together. Elliott gathered his men around him. The Indians now appeared on all sides, and with wild shouts gave vent to their savage determination. An Arrapahoe warrior, braver than the rest, in hopes of inspiring his people with courage, led off at a gallop, with the intention of riding down the party. As he came near, followed by one other warrior, a volley from the troops finished both.

Confronted by the whole force of the Arrapahoes, and a large number of Kiowas, and having abandoned their horses, the party on foot made an effort to force their way down to the river and seek protection behind the trees, under cover of which Elliott, probably, hoped to fight his way back. Here, again, the savage warriors intercepted him. When all hope of rescue or escape was given up, the gallant band, evidently, determined to sacrifice their lives as dearly as possible. The grass, where they lay, was much trodden, and numbers of cartridge-shells, scattered on the ground, testified to the valour of the defence, until some friendly, fatal bullet, afforded the only alternative of escape from the terrible torture awaiting them, if taken alive. It is not likely that the entire party were killed before overpowered, but whether any, and who were thus taken, and the trying and terrible moments which followed, will always remain a mystery. All the missing bodies were found. Not one was left to narrate the fearful story. The last act of humanity—a proper burial—was all that remained.

Although the savages, with whom I afterwards conversed upon the subject, readily spoke of their first knowledge of the attack, upon the closing scenes attending Elliott's party, they were remarkably reticent. Every one disclaimed any participation in the killing of the soldiers, declaring that they merely went up to see the fight.

After the troops, under Custer, had withdrawn, the savages must have returned to wreak their vengeance upon the dead bodies of the brave little band. The horrible work was too effectively done to have been accomplished in a short time. The savages admitted that they lost many braves before they "killed the white men."

It is considered "good medicine" for each warrior, who participates in a fight, to put a bullet or an arrow into the body of his enemy or to commit some other atrocity, even more hellish. In this instance, there was no exception. In order to furnish an idea of the nature and extent of these mutilations, I will give an extract from the official report of Dr. Henry Lippincott, Assistant Surgeon United States Army, with the Seventh.

Major Joel H. Elliott, one bullet hole in left cheek, two bullets in head, throat cut, right foot cut off, left foot almost cut off, calves of legs very much cut, groin ripped open and otherwise mutilated.

Walter Kennedy, sergeant-major, bullet hole in right temple, head partly cut off, seventeen bullet holes in back, and two in legs,

Harry Mercer, corporal company E, bullet hole in right axilla, one in region of heart, three in back, eight arrow wounds in back, right ear cut off, head scalped, and skull fractured, deep gashes in both legs, and throat cut.

Thomas Christie, company E, bullet hole in head, right foot cut off, bullet hole in abdomen, and throat cut.

William Carrick, corporal company H, bullet hole in right parietal bone, both feet cut off, throat cut, left arm broken, and otherwise mutilated.

Eugene Clover, company H, head cut off, arrow wound in right side, both legs terribly mutilated,

William Milligan, company H, bullet hole in left side of head, deep gashes in right leg, left arm deeply gashed, head scalped, throat cut, and otherwise mutilated.

James F. Williams, corporal company I, bullet hole in back, head and arms cut off, many and deep cuts in back, and otherwise mutilated.

Thomas Downey, company I, arrow hole in region of stomach, throat cut open, head cut off, and right shoulder cut by a tomahawk,

Thomas Fitzpatrick, farrier, company M, scalped, two arrow and several bullet holes in back, and throat cut.

Ferdinand Linebach, company M, bullet hole in right parietal bone, head scalped, one arm broken, throat cut, and otherwise mutilated.

John Myers, company M, several bullet holes in head, scalped, scull extensively fractured, several arrow and bullet holes in back, deep gashes in face, and throat cut.

Carson D. J. Myers, company M, several bullet holes in head, scalped, nineteen bullet holes in body, throat cut, and otherwise mutilated.

Cal. Sharp, company M, two bullet holes in left side, throat cut, one bullet hole in left side of head, one arrow hole in left side, left arm broken, and otherwise mutilated.

Unknown, head cut off, body partly devoured by wolves.

Unknown, head and right hand cut off, three bullet and nine arrow holes in back, and otherwise mutilated.

Unknown, scalped, skull fractured, six bullet and thirteen arrow holes in back, and three bullet holes in chest.

The discovery of the bodies having been made, and all doubt as to the fate of Elliott and his comrades having been settled, we set out on our return to camp, to send back wagons to bring in the bodies. Near the scene of this struggle the bodies of several dead warriors were found, probably killed by Elliott's men. After a short ride of several miles the remains of the villages of the Arrapahoes and Kiowas, who came to the support of the Cheyennes, were found. It was evident that both these nations cleared out with their families as hastily as their means of locomotion would allow. Camp-kettles, coffee-pots, cups, powder-kegs (empty), several rifles, hundreds of untanned robes, hundreds of lodge-poles, and a variety of other articles, were left behind. Orders were given to destroy everything found. It was not long before a stream of consuming fire and smoke could be described following the line of the Washita for a distance of six or seven miles, all the way to camp. Not less than one thousand lodges occupied this stretch of country at the time of the fight.

Although the fate of Elliott's party would appear as a gross abandonment by Custer, particularly for not even recovering the bodies, or making some effort to learn what had become of them, when found missing, after the fight, the circumstances of the event were of such a character, that while no attempt was made with that view, the conduct of Custer in ordering a withdrawal was justifiable according to the laws of war. He struck the upper flank of a long range of villages, numbering several thousand warriors. His own force was small, and without supplies.

In going into the fight the troopers had divested themselves of overcoats and all unnecessary trappings, leaving them near the field. These fell into the hands of the savage allies. The men, consequently, were without the proper protection, while the weather was cold and wintry. The wagontrain containing the subsistence stores and tents of the entire column, which had been left miles away, had not yet come up. The guard consisted of but eighty men. Custer, after the fight commenced, seeing such an extraordinary display of force, felt a natural anxiety to look after his wagons, for their destruction would involve the loss of the entire command, and probably defeat the whole campaign. He therefore set out for the train, and was hastened by experiencing greater opposition than was anticipated.

It will be seen that there were reasons, the second, particularly, which would warrant the abandonment of the field, and there being hardly a doubt of the fate of Elliott, when found missing, the safety of the command was certainly more to be considered than the loss of a small fraction of it. The pursuit of the fugitives, by Elliott, was entirely exceptional, as he had his own squadron of attack to look after, this fact has led to the opinion that his horse ran away with him, and seeing him pass, a number of troopers, not actually engaged in the fight, joined him and were the companions of his sad end. Major Elliott was an efficient and much esteemed officer, and his loss was deeply deplored by his associates.

During the journey to the battlefield, a. detachment, moving close along the banks of the river, found, near the remains of the Kiowa camp, the bodies of a white woman and child. The bodies were brought into camp and examined. Two bullet holes, penetrating the brain, were found, also the back of the skull was fearfully crushed, as if by a hatchet. There were no marks on the child except a bruise on the cheek. This fact led to the conclusion that the child had been seized by the feet and dashed against a tree. When brought in, the body of the woman was recognized as Mrs. Blynn. This woman was captured by Satanta, chief of the Kiowas, near Fort Lyon, while on her way to her home in the "States." At the time of her capture she was in a wagon, in the centre of a civilian train. The men with the train, it appears, fled, and left Mrs, Blynn and her child to fall into savage hands.

Satanta kept her as his captive until the time of the fight of the Kiowas, when she was ruthlessly murdered. The body was dressed in the ordinary garments of a white woman; on the feet were a pair of leather gaiters, comparatively new. Upon the breast was found a piece of corn-cake, and the position of the hands indicated that the woman was eating when she, unexpectedly, received the fatal blow. The body presented the appearance of a woman of more than ordinary beauty, small in figure, and not more than twenty-two years of age. These bodies, and that of Major Elliott, were brought in on horseback by our party, to be conveyed to Fort Arbuckle for interment.

By three o'clock in the afternoon we reached camp. Immediately several wagons were detailed, under Lieutenant Hale, with an escort, to bring in the rest of the corpses. It was nine o'clock at night before the wagons returned with their load of stark and ghastly dead. During the afternoon a trench had been dug on the crest of a beautiful knoll, overlooking the valley of the Washita. Large fires were built at night to enable the burial party to perform their sad work. Each body was examined, and several men from each of the companies, to which the deceased soldiers belonged, were present to identify the remains. Each corpse was now wrapped in a blanket and laid in the trench. At the hour of midnight, the solemn duty was consummated. The usual military honours were dispensed with. The death-like darkness and the mournful wintry wind, the low tones of the working party was their requiem. The spot was marked, and the bodies left alone in that howling wilderness, away from the tender solicitude of friends for the last tenements of loved ones.

After returning to camp, the situation of the various Indian villages, between our position at the time, and the scene of the fight, was satisfactorily explained by the squaws with the column. From our own observation, during the day, there was no exaggeration in fixing the aggregate number of lodges at one thousand, and the estimate was confirmed by the squaws, as near as their primitive ideas of numbers could convey. According to their statements, the village of Black Kettle's band of Cheyennes was the highest up the river. Next, in descending, were the Arrapahoes, under Little Raven, next the Kiowas, under Satanta and Lone Wolf; next the Cheyennes and Arrapahoes, then several bands of the Comanches, and lowest down the Apaches, (Lipans).

CHAPTER 22

The Flight of the Savages

At daylight on the morning of the twelfth of December, the column again broke camp. In resuming the march, our route lay along the course of the Washita, following the trail, the fugitive Indians had taken in hastening for Fort Cobb. The remaining bands of the Cheyennes and Arrapahoes were traced in an opposite direction, leaving the valley and tending towards the head waters of the Red River.

Owing to the configuration of the country on the north side, the column crossed the Washita near camp. The stream was about thirty feet in width, with almost perpendicular banks from fifteen to twenty feet in height. From the river, the column ascended the "divide," which afforded good travelling and an extensive view of the surrounding country. The morning had been threatening, and the moderated temperature was a sure indication of a storm.

Towards noon the heavy fog which had prevailed for several hours was changed to snow. The wind sprung up with violent force, adding greatly to our embarrassment. By noon the atmosphere had become so dense with snow and sleet, and the wind drove so furiously in our faces that the column was compelled to halt. It was impossible to see fifty yards in any direction. To go forward was likely to result in losing the river, upon which we had to rely for camping, as well as our guide to our destination. To remain in our present position exposed to the full force of the wind, and having the benefit of an extra dose of snow, would be attended with suffering and probably loss of men and animals. The Commanding General, consequently, gave orders to head the column in the direction in which the river was last seen, and attempt to reach it before dark.

There being constant danger of detached parties losing themselves, or the column becoming separated and not getting in together, the troops and wagons were obliged to keep up close. The descent of the "divide" was difficult in consequence of the ravines which furrowed its sides in all directions. To avoid these was impossible.

Late in the afternoon, the advance struck the valley of the river and following it for a short distance, led the column into a fine bottom covered with tall dry grass and an abundance of timber, Here we went into camp. In the short space of four hours, the snow had fallen to the depth of twelve inches. The mildness of the temperature, however, promised to carry it off as rapidly as it had come upon us.

The camp this night was wet and disagreeable. In order to pitch the tents, it was necessary to brush away the snow which, however, had little effect to improve the comforts of sleeping on the ground. Immediately after reaching camp, a large detail of troops was sent into the woods to fell cotton-wood trees of which we here found a great abundance. It was known that the young branches of these trees were used by the savages as food for their ponies, when the depth of snow prevented them from getting to the dry grass. Large quantities were brought in and strewn among the horses. The animals half starved as they were, vigorously applied themselves to this novel forage, and ate it with an air of satisfaction at least.

During the night, the weather made a decided change. The morning dawned clear and cold. It was with great difficulty the tents could be struck and loaded on the wagons. Everything was frozen. After daylight the column again got in motion. The course taken instead of following the "divide" was now along the bed of the river, pursuing the trail of the savages in their flight down the valley. The three Cheyenne squaws brought with the column, in passing over the ground so recently occupied by their people, seemed to be very indignant at the cowardice shown by the neighbouring tribes in not coming to their assistance. The sister of Black Kettle, an old squaw, while riding along in the ambulance noticed the signs of haste with which the villages had fled. This was a fact as well apparent to the most inexperienced eye. She observed "The Kiowas and Arrapahoes, our friends, run like dogs. They were worse cowards than women, Black Kettle was killed because they were afraid of the white man. They killed Black Kettle and our braves. If the white man fights the Kiowas and Arrapahoes, I want a knife and will fight too, and kill all their papooses." All the squaws more or less excited, frequently exhibited their hatred of the Kiowas and Arrapahoes.

On the night of the fifteenth, upon the column going into camp in a heavy timber on the river, it was discovered that we were in the midst of a favourite roost of immense numbers of wild turkeys. The traces were everywhere visible, and some lively sport was anticipated when the droves returned from their rambles after food. Towards sunset, about fifty fine birds, beaded, as usual, by a noble cock, appeared on the bluff overlooking the camp. With an air of surprise at the intrusion, the flock gathered in full view, apparently holding an inspection, and resolving what to do. At this moment, another immense flock came floating down from another direction, and lit in the trees within the lines of the camp. In an instant about fifty shots were fired, killing several.

As the daylight drew nearer to a close, the turkeys, having failed to look out for other accommodations, were bent upon taking possession of their customary haunts. The numbers also increased. It was now impossible to cast the eye anywhere along the heavens without getting a glimpse of turkeys sailing about in the air. One drove entered the camp, running amongst the tents and wagons. It was decidedly amusing to witness the scene which ensued. Soldiers, teamsters, and dogs joined in the pursuit. One moment dashing under a wagon, and the next amongst the horses and mules. In the early part of the race, the turkeys had the best, but, bewildered and headed off, soon became exhausted. A number were caught in this way.

While this exciting chase was going on, a party of soldiers occupied themselves with shooting at the birds as they settled in the trees, or as they approached the ground. During this fusillade, one of the volunteers, tying his horse to the picket, was somewhat astounded to find the animal jerk away from him and instantly fall to the earth. A stray bullet had finished him. Considering all the firing and confusion, it was a matter of great surprise that no other casualties occurred.

That night there was a feast in camp. The fragrance of turkey, boiling or roasting, pervaded the atmosphere, with a grateful variation of the customary vapours of fat pork and fried bacon.

On the morning of the seventeenth, while the pioneers were engaged in the advance, cutting a crossing for the train, word came in that a number of Indians were in front, signalling with a white flag. One of the party was seen advancing alone. Upon reaching our lines, it was discovered to be a courier bearing a dispatch from General Hazen, Military Superintendent of the Southern Indians, and dated on the sixteenth, at Fort Cobb.

The dispatch was addressed to the "Commanding Officer of the

United States Forces," and stated that information had been received that a column of troops was within twenty miles, and declared that all the Indians between the column and Fort Cobb were disposed to be friendly. As an indication of this friendly spirit, however, the two couriers, who had left Fort Cobb the night before, had been captured by a party of Kiowa warriors, and were taken to their camp, A council of warriors was held as to what disposition to make of the two white men. At first the determination was to put them to death instantly. Several chiefs of influence proposed to allow one of them to go to the soldiers' camp and deliver the letter, and return. His companion was to be kept as a hostage for the fulfilment of the wishes of the council. This plan prevailed, and the courier was escorted by the band of warriors within several miles of our advance.

While the pioneers were still working on the crossing, Custer, accompanied by several officers, the writer, and an escort of fifty men of Pepoon's scouts, rode out to meet the flag. A gallop of three miles brought us within six hundred yards of the savages, who stood in the broad valley in front. Among the trees along the banks of the Washita a number of warriors, mounted, could be seen, stationed as a reserve. On the hills beyond, five hundred warriors, in battle array, dashed about, brandishing their spears, and assuming various menacing attitudes.

The warriors with the flag made signs of a parley. Two interpreters answered the signs, and advanced. Two of the savages imitated the movement, until the parties came within speaking distance. The two Indians were Satanta and Lone Wolf, the head chiefs of the Kiowas. They professed friendship, and asked to speak with the "Big White Chief." A sign was given, when Custer, Crosby, and the writer, joined the interpreters. It was not certain whether the Indians meant war or peace, and every man of our party had his pistol and rifle ready, and kept mounted, prepared for emergency, should any hostile demonstrations be made.

When we came up to them, the Indians opened negotiations. Satanta rode up, and with an air of arrogance exclaimed "*how*," simultaneously extending his hand. This civility, Crosby, to whom it was extended, refused to receive. The Indian drew back in anger, exclaiming "me Kiowa," striking his breast, and was about to signal his warriors, when noticing more troops approaching on a hill about a mile distant hesitated. Then advancing to Custer he offered his hand. The general said through the interpreter: "I never shake hands with any one unless

I know him to be a friend." After some *parley* Satanta and Lone Wolf, and a Comanche, joined the column. During the day about sixty warriors also came in.

It was evident that the Kiowa warriors at first came out with hostile intention, supposing us to be weak in numbers, but when they saw the unusual array of force they professed the warmest friendship. Their faces bedaubed with war paint, their persons attired in all the panoply of war, their weapons ready for use, told a different tale. At nightfall the warriors, except Satanta and Lone Wolf, disappeared. About noon the next day Satanta was allowed to leave the column to communicate with his warriors. About three o'clock he returned with his son, a fine boy, about eighteen years of age, and attired in the highest style of Indian costume.

While riding along a short distance from the column the old chief put spurs to his pony. His intention was evidently to escape, but in a moment several officers, each of whom had fleet horses, and were nearby at the time, dashed after the fugitive. There was a lively race for half a mile, when his Indian highness, finding himself overtaken, checked his pony, folded his arms across his breast, and made several exclamations. After this adventure a guard of soldiers was at once placed over both Satanta and Lone Wolf. The prisoners were brought in and held as hostages for the fulfilment of their promises.

Just before going into camp the same night about a hundred of the warriors who had accompanied the column during the day assembled on a knoll near the line of march. Their highly caparisoned war ponies stood nearby, the warriors were lying upon blankets spread on the ground, or lounging cross-legged in their saddles. They were constantly talking among themselves. As the writer rode past a formidable warrior approached, waving his hand with a motion to halt. At the time I was riding a beautiful black Cheyenne war-pony. The warrior examined the animal as if he recognized it. It was taken from the Cheyenne herd at the battle of the Washita. The warrior said: "Gude pony, *Bueno* big chief—you swap, how much?"

From his manner the animal before it fell into our possession was the property of a prominent personage in the Cheyenne village. With the merits of the pony he seemed to be familiar; and asking to "swap "was the Indian fashion of asking "what will you take." As I had already learned to appreciate the value of the pony the Indian discovered that it was "no swap," and went off.

Some of the warriors as the column was passing occupied themselves in trying to count the soldiers, but their primitive system of calculation was totally inadequate, so that in order to express our force one chief told another in the presence of the interpreter that he had tried to count the soldiers, and after keeping on for a long time, thinking the end would soon come, he got tired, and when he stopped he was not half done. During the same day the column drew in sight of the Wichita Mountains, at a distance of between forty and fifty miles The range resembled a dense black cloud upon the heavens. The fogs gathered about the summits of the peaks gave a peculiar and an ever-changing outline to the higher elevations, at times resembling broad table lands supported by innumerable columns, and again huge boulders rising high into the air. Perfect spires at times shot up into the heavens, which again changed to craggy cliffs.

Our last day's march before reaching Fort Cobb brought us into an extensive open country, presenting the most enlarged and fertile valleys we had yet encountered. The country now exhibited a material change for the better. The luxuriant grasses which covered the soil far and wide presented an unmistakable argument that at no distant time that entire country would be converted into vast pasture lands. At noon, while the animals, very much exhausted by the soft and slippery condition of the surface, owing to a heavy thaw, were moving ahead at a slow and laborious gait, one of the Indian captives pointed out the site of Fort Cobb by a lone tree which stood upon a hill at a distance of at least ten miles. This piece of information was decidedly gratifying. For two days before we had anticipated camping at Fort Cobb the same night. The country was entirely new to everyone attached to the command, and therefore from day to day we only had to move ahead and trust to the chances of making our destination sometime before our thirty days' supplies were out.

Our proximity to Fort Cobb was communicated to the commanding officer at that point by an officer and escort who camped with us the night before our arrival, and preceded us on the following morning.

The same afternoon, about three o'clock, the advance being a mile from the post, General Hazen, and Captain Rife, sixth infantry, met the column, and with the General and officers exchanged the warmest greetings. The troops poured over the hill, and descending into the valley went into camp on Pond Creek, about half a mile from the post.

The physical features of the valley of the Washita, for a distance of over a hundred miles, followed by the column, presented altogether the finest section we had met with during the entire campaign up to that time. The soil in the bed of the valley was a rich black loom, producing a luxuriant growth of grass frequently six feet in height. In descending the stream the arable soil of the valley widened, and the adjacent country had a less sterile appearance. Everywhere along the stream there was an abundance of wood, cotton-wood, burr oak, elm, black walnut, ash, hackberry, box elder, Osage orange, and some locust. In the *cañons*, away from the river, quantities of cedar were met with.

The main stream we found fed by numerous tributaries, in many of which the water was of excellent quality, while again others were strongly impregnated with alkaline matter. The hills for miles away from the river grew an excellent variety of "bunch" grass. At different points the country was considerably cut by ravines with perpendicular banks. In many of these could be seen traces of gypsum. Along the march we met with hard sandy loam, red loam, gravel, disintegrated limestone, sandstone in a variety of forms, gypsum, selenite, and a variety of alabaster.

The valley was alive with game, such as several varieties of deer, antelope, wild turkeys, pinnated grouse, and quails. It had also been in previous years a favourite resort of the buffalo, though there were very few to be found during our march through the country, the herds having been driven off by the movements of the. army and Indian war-parties.

In our march we made from depot of supplies to the Canadian, 55 miles 1,487 yards; from Canadian River to the Washita, 18 miles; from camp on Washita to Pond Creek, 113 miles 1,438 yards.

CHAPTER 23

Arrogance of the Savages

The arrival of Sheridan at Fort Cobb, was as unexpected to the garrison there as it was to the Indians, in the valley of the Washita. The principal object to be accomplished by this transfer of the centre of operations, was more ready access to all parts of the country inhabited by the hostile tribes.

Fort Cobb was situated on Pond Creek, about a mile from its junction with the Washita River. The name of the post was more in remembrance of what it had been, than what it was at the time of our visit. The site had been selected some years before as a cavalry station, from which to watch the movements of the southern wild bands. It was, however, soon after abandoned, and the few mud huts, which had been constructed, were destroyed by the savages. The position, in a defensible point of view, amounted to literally nothing, and were it not for the fine water, abundance of timber, and winter grass, it might, quite naturally, be concluded that the person who selected the site never visited the spot. The buildings, constituting the old post, were constructed in a valley on an arm of Pond Creek. A high hill commanded one side, a low plateau swept the other, while a thick underbrush concealed the approach of an enemy along the stream.

The conduct of the savages in violating their pledges to Sheridan, at Forts Dodge and Larned, compelled General Hazen to reach Fort Cobb by way of Fort Gibson. Before his arrival, Rife's company of the 6th Infantry, and Alvord's company of the 10th Cavalry, were detached from Fort Arbuckle to take possession of the post. It was not until November 8, 1868, that Hazen arrived. This officer had been sent out by General Sherman, then commanding the Military Division of the Missouri, to represent him under the provisions of the law, appropriating a large sum of money to carry out the various treaties which the government had made with the southern bands.

It was not until November that the Indians, who were parties to the agreements, on the Arkansas were heard from. It was now discovered that, instead of returning to Forts Dodge and Larned, all the bands took a share in the predatory expeditions which followed. The Yamparicko Comanches made a raid into the Cherokee country, killing a half-breed and stealing a number of horses. The Kiowas came south and established a camp about sixty miles above Cobb, on the Washita River. From this point a large number of the warriors of the tribe, led by Kicking Bird, a chief of remarkable ability, began depredations across the Red River in the south into Texas, after which, some of the bands reported at Fort Cobb.

The delicate relations existing between all the southern tribes, as well as the additional fuel, added to the flame by the battle of the Washita, necessitated an increase of military strength at Cobb. Kidd, with Walsh's, Gray's, and Robinson's companies of the 10th Cavalry, occupied the post early in December. Up to the arrival of the troops, under Sheridan, the officers at Cobb were in constant anticipation of an attack. Double guards were on duty at night, and a vigilant watch was kept during the day. A stockade fort was erected on the hill to cover the defences in the valley, and to be used as a place of refuge in case of emergency. Satanta and Lone Wolf, backed by their warriors, were insulting in the highest degree.

This conduct led to the order for reinforcements from Fort Arbuckle, making the garrison to consist of one company of the 6th Infantry and three companies of the 10th Cavalry. When the additional companies were on the way, a band of warriors, with Satanta at their head, told the officers they should not come any farther, The officer commanding informed their savage majesties that he had been ordered to go to Fort Cobb, and there be would go. The savages threatened, but their couriers, at this timely moment, reporting the presence of troops in the north, probably had the influence of suppressing any bloody schemes of revenge. the officers gave their experience with these vagabond savages as the most humiliating of their lives. Threats and insults were of constant occurrence, and it was necessary to accede to the most arrogant demands for the sole purpose of preventing an immediate massacre of the garrison.

The arrival of the column, consequently, was a welcome event. To the credit of at least one of the bands in the valley, the Peneteghtka Comanches, it must be said, remained faithful. When their people threatened to destroy all the whites at Cobb, the Peneteghtkas moved their village close to the post and declared themselves the friends of the whites, and anyone who attacked must fight them also.

There were at this time but three hundred lodges at the post, principally Comanches and Apaches, (Lipans). The Cheyennes and Arrapahoes had taken to the Wichita mountains, about forty miles distant. the Kiowas, as we have seen, had promised to keep with the column. After waiting several days, and still no signs of the Kiowa villages arriving, a scout up the valley developed the fact that they had also disappeared towards the mountains.

When this was discovered, the two chiefs, in the guard-house, were accused of their rascality. They were informed that if their people did not get in the next day they would be hanged to the nearest tree. Both the chiefs were completely unnerved by this exhibition of decision. They begged earnestly for more time. Their entreaties were of no avail. They delegated an old chief, who was voluntarily sharing their captivity, to overtake the fleeing villages and turn them back. As the old Apache and his companions left the prison lodge, the chiefs motioned them emphatically to hasten, accompanying their gestures with the words, "*hudeldy, hudeldy.*"

Late the same night, a delegation from the tribe came in and offered themselves as hostages, that their families would join them the next day. This expeditious work alone saved the wily chiefs from a short rounding off of their career of blood and treachery. The families of all, except Kicking Bird's band, came in during the next few days, and established their villages on the north bank of the Washita, about a mile below our camp.

The Indians who had thus surrendered remained quietly in their villages, except during times of drawing rations. Frequently fifty or a hundred chiefs and warriors entered our camp to visit the captives, or to hold a talk and lounge about. Sheridan would have nothing to say to any of them, notwithstanding their repeated importunities by messenger, or by seating themselves, for hours at a time, in front of his quarters. The trouble with the Indians had been that they had been consulted too much.

In order to secure constant and reliable information of the movements of the hostile tribes, and to keep a strict watch upon the doubtful bands, as early as the end of October preceding, Sheridan addressed a letter of instructions to Fort Arbuckle, "to take the necessary steps to employ scouts to operate from Fort Cobb, for the purpose of ascertaining the location of the families and stock of hostile Indians south of the Arkansas, to be reported semi-weekly to department headquarters." A number of Peneteghtka Comanches were employed to act as scouts. The Peneteghtkas were originally the most southern band of the southern Comanches. They were of the same origin and spoke the same language. They had, for some years, been friendly towards the whites, and had, in a great measure, given up their nomadic habits. All these considerations admirably adapted these people for the duty proposed; and their reputation among the other bands for bravery, gave them the additional recommendation of fearing no danger in carrying out any mission that might be entrusted to them.

The head of the corps was Tosawi, (Silver Brooch), the civil chief of the band. As he was an old man, little was expected of him, except to go the rounds of the villages and gossip with the old squaws—for this is a common pastime with a certain class among Indians, as well as whites. Essahavit, (Milky Way), was a middle-aged Indian of powerful frame and remarkable shrewdness. He was the war-chief of the Peneteghtkas, and had active supervision of the Indian scouts. As many warriors of the band as were needed were furnished, and, for the time they were employed, were paid, at an established rate, in goods.

From this source the Commanding General learned, upon reaching Fort Cobb, the locality of nearly every Indian band between the Washita and the Red Rivers. This knowledge subsequently proved invaluable.

The condition of our little army, after its long march, was anything but flattering. Exposure and hardship already told severely upon men and animals, but particularly upon the latter. Several hundred horses had given out entirely, and were shot The rest of the animals were in a fearfully weakened and reduced condition. Our forage was nearly exhausted, and the extra supply expected at the fort had not yet arrived. The animals, guarded by strong parties of herders, were turned loose upon the neighbouring hills where they were compelled to eke out a miserable sustenance on dry grass.

Our camp lay in an expansive valley, bordering Pond Creek. The men, anticipating some stay in that locality, began to exercise their ingenuity in contriving such additions to the limited space allowed by their "dog" tents as would not only increase their accommodations, but materially improve their personal comfort. In some cases, square pits, three or four feet in depth, were dug, and the tents set over them. Fireplaces were also built, which were very grateful accessions. In the course of a week, the camp had the appearance of a regular winter cantonment. The weather was inexplicable, It was one of two things—either very wet or very cold. It rained in torrents one day, and blew and froze the next.

During our delay at Cobb, I took opportunity, in company with Jones, the interpreter, to visit the Indian villages near our camp. Jones was a Texan, and, notwithstanding his long life on the frontiers, was a man of agreeable manners. He was one of those intensely patient individuals rarely met with, yet an admirable trait, especially in an interpreter. He was unobtrusive, and never was so well satisfied as when let alone. Unlike interpreters generally, he had a gentlemanly modesty about him, and a fund of information, which made him an acceptable companion under all circumstances. He seemed to little concern himself in the affairs of the world. As long as he had a few yards of canvas to protect him from the dews and the pelting rain, plenty of buffalo-meat and game for home consumption, and a private soldier's outfit in clothes, he was in a state of mental quiescence and unconcern truly wonderful. Jones had knocked about a great deal, and had seen much of the world—that meant the plains.

He was, however, constitutionally opposed to a change of locality. For ten years he had not left the banks of the Washita. In fact, that was the nearest he had ever been to civilization. A fact that impressed me with a sort of reverence for him, was that he, a creature of the nineteenth century, had never seen a railroad, a locomotive, nor a telegraph. What greater proof than this of his equanimity of temperament and settled habits. Nor was he in any hurry to satisfy even an infinitesimally small amount of curiosity in the matter. He observed, one day, that "if the brutes of savages did not lift his hair, in his pirouetting around with everybody, he thought he would go sometime to Riley, and see what those machines called railroads looked like."

Essahavit's lodge

Chapter 24

Christmas Day

After tarrying for a short time on the way, watching some juvenile sports, we continued our journey. Our advent was duly announced by a drove of snarling, snapping curs, of all sizes, colours and conditions. Two great clubs with which we had provided ourselves beforehand alone prevented a complete route before this canine demonstration. Our movements, however, were most cautiously performed by backing in the direction we wished to proceed and thus preventing a dash on our heels. The noise of our approach as developed by the dogs, started a few old squaws who came out of their lodges, and by giving vent to a few gutturals completely silenced the growling storm, and we continued to the lodge of the chief without farther interruption or molestation.

There were about seventy lodges in this village, about the same number of warriors, and twice that number of women.

We proceeded at once to the lodge of Essahavit, the war-chief of the band. This exalted hero of the savage community heard of our coming and was ready to greet us. He politely waved us an invitation to enter. We complied by crowding through an aperture made by the meeting of the two extremities of the outer covering of the lodge, about three feet in height, and covered with a piece of buffalo hide dried, and as stiff as a board.

Upon entering the lodge we were invited to a seat on a fine buffalo robe spread upon the ground, for the accommodation of visitors.

Having seated ourselves, the interpreter opened a conversation. The war-chief was a man of about forty-five years of age, heavy muscular frame, and a broad face. The latter was specially illuminated with a coating of vermilion. He wore a brown shirt, and about his waist a broad belt supporting a breech-clout, his lower limbs were bare, with the exception of a pair of beautifully worked *moccasins* on his feet. Both ears were fearfully disfigured by large incisions which had been made in them for the accommodation of a profusion and variety of earrings.

Like most men of deeds, Essahavit soon began to narrate his warlike performances against the Utes and Navajoes, the ancient and mortal enemies of the Peneteghtkas. His fierce black eyes while thus talking, soon flashed up, indicating the chief's fire of temper and no ordinary intelligence. He was reclining, his coarse raven hair streaming over his shoulders. His couch consisted of a number of rushes ingeniously piled together, pinned and held down with small thongs. It was elevated at the head. and over the top was spread a royal buffalo robe, the shaggy mane forming a pillow.

Near the couch, and within arm's length, stood a forked stick, upon which were suspended the chief's trappings for war and the chase, his head gear and ornaments, and shell and silver breast decorations; his silver mounted bridle and highly adorned saddle; which had evidently in former years been the property of some luckless *alcalde* in far off Mexico. Opposite the chief on our right, lay several very fine robes and *parfleshes* finely painted. On our left, lay the rude cooking utensils of the lodge. In the centre, a hole sunk about six inches, contained a small fire burning brightly, and emitting a pleasant heat.

At the head of the couch, lay a squaw incorrigibly ugly and emaciated. We were early informed by herself that she was sick "a heap." Nearby were a medicine drum and other necessary instruments in the savage art of expelling maladies by physical force, and unearthly noises. At the foot of the couch sat the favourite squaw, young, pretty, and unusually cleanly in appearance.

During our entire presence this one of the female members of the family was busily occupied in finishing a beautiful buffalo robe which she had just tanned. Occasionally from her work in response to some words from the chief, she would lift a pair of fine black eyes, and with a pleasantness of expression respond in striking contrast, with the old hag cuddled up in the corner.

The extent of Essahavit's conjugal bliss, was three squaws and four or five *papooses*. The chief was a thrifty savage, and kept a watchful eye upon his extensive herds of ponies. His lodge was the finest that Indian art could produce, his equipments and decorations were of the most expensive character, and his squaws wore new and bright red blankets. The youngest as a mark of special favour, wore a belt covered with large silver plates, and by her side an awl and paint pouch very elaborately worked with beads. Her moccasins were in keeping with the rest of her attire.

The chief was certainly pleased with our visit, and did everything to show his hospitality. The interpreter and himself kept up a lively conversation. I usually took part when the laugh came in, by way of imitation to let it be seen that I fully appreciated all that was said. The chief with great pride took down his otter quiver and bow case. It was without question the finest I had ever seen.

While showing the quiver and admiring it, pointing to his pretty squaw, for so I must distinguish her, he remarked *"squaw me bueno, heap bueno,"* meaning that his favourite had made it for him and it was very good. This "outfit" to use a common expression, was for occasions of state and ceremony.

After pulling out the arrows and commenting upon each one having a particular history and value, the chief handed everything over to his squaw, remarking "squaw work, put away me no." The squaw took the hint.

After we had been in the lodge about half an hour, one of the interesting household handed around water in a *calabash*. After partaking of this, she also distributed a few Indian cakes about the size of walnuts and as hard as bullets. By way of courtesy I contrived to dispose of my first. The second I slipped into my pocket to preserve as a curiosity, a fact I, subsequently, found was much more satisfactory to the digestion than the use to which I had put the other.

Essahavit observed with unfeigned regret that the "white men had all the fire water and drank it all himself." He said also, "he was very poor" a piece of information an Indian is never at a loss nor diffident about conveying.

The rest of the time passed at the village, we occupied in strolling around amongst the lodges. A retinue of dogs escorted us about, occasionally making an offensive flourish which was usually counterbalanced by a rap over the head of the most audacious brute.

The woman about the village were occupied in most of the daily outdoor employments of their sex. Some were driving in the herds of ponies, others fleshing buffalo hides, others carrying water and fire wood. In this last occupation I was amazed at the wonderful strength of the women. I saw one old squaw, not less than sixty years of age, with an enormous bundle of wood on her back held together by strips of raw hide. What she carried at the time could not have weighed less than three hundred pounds, and I was even told that for a short distance it was not uncommon for squaws to carry six hundred pounds in the same manner.

Out of curiosity we entered another lodge of less pretentions than that of the war-chief. The interior had not in any comparison that air of comfort, was less spacious and filled with all sorts of rubbish, jerked buffalo-meat, bones, robes and skins. Three squaws were seated around the little fire in the centre, and a warrior was lounging on a pile of untanned buffalo-skins. As we went in, the usual form of Indian ceremony being to enter without any preliminary manoeuvres, the warrior exclaimed "*how!*" to which we responded more emphatically using the same salutatory observation.

While I was watching and admiring the bead-work of the squaws in the lodge, with the vocal assistance of the interpreter I secured the promise of a beautiful awl-case nearly finished, for four cups of brown sugar. Sugar was a favourite commodity with the squaws. The next day I went over to the village, but found my red friend had very capriciously resolved not to part with her work, saying it was not hers, it belonged to her cousin. Determined to get one, after scouring the village from one end to the other, I was successful, and obtained a better one at an advance of one cup of sugar.

Christmas Day, with its associations of home and winter recreation, was duly celebrated in camp. Milk punch, concocted of the condensed material, sugar, and Texas "spirits," was the popular beverage. With their usual facility of discovering everything that is going on, the leading warriors in the vicinity of camp in some way or other found out that the day was more than an ordinary affair. Resolved to convince themselves of the fact several delegations, painted and plumed, and mounted on their best war ponies, set out for the various headquarters. At the time at Hazen's tent a number of officers were present. As the warriors came up, and heard the conversation within, they probably felt reassured that something was going on.

The chief of the party dismounted, and poking his head through the entrance of the tent, cast one hasty glance at the crowd of officers. The chief exclaimed "*how?*" and grinned invitingly. A chorus of "*hows*" were returned, but nothing further was said, notwithstanding the chief kept his feathered head in sight for some minutes.

Alter withdrawing his regal pate a half dozen other warriors got down from their ponies and gratified their curiosity by taking a peep. Essahavit, war-chief of the Peneteghtkas, soon came along, and, bolder than the rest, entered the tent. A number of the other warriors followed him, and squatted in one corner, assuming their usual stolidity of countenance. Probably twenty minutes had elapsed, and all the officers except one or two had gone. Essahavit, unable to withstand the temptation, very methodically walked up to the improvised punch bowl—a horse-bucket. He observed to the general, "*bueno*," at the same time evidently awaiting an invitation. After repeating this suggestion several times the old chief found his hints were not appreciated and left. The other warriors left also, observing as they filed out of the tent "white man no *bueno*."

In the afternoon Sheridan gave a Christmas dinner, which, however, was not so bountifully supplied with the game of the country as the feast of Thanksgiving-day at Camp Supply.

Saturday of each week was the ration day of all the villages in the vicinity of Fort Cobb. It was a great occasion at the post. From sunrise to sunset the squaws, with their papooses strapped on their back, and mounted on ponies, and sometimes a few warriors, could be seen descending from every hill. The squaw's duty was to receive the Government rations, which consisted of flour and meat. The women of each tribe seated themselves cross-legged on the ground, with their papooses around them. Outside of the circle the dogs collected, each group behind its owner, and impatiently smacking their lips and curiously gazing within over the shoulders of the women. The head civil chief, aided by several old men of the tribe, received the rations and distributed them to the various families, calling them by name, whereupon the head squaw of each came forward and received her allowance. It was observable that the savage chief was not unlike more civilized functionaries. He always went away with a decided increase of his pile, a surplus which he managed to secure to himself by short measurement.

The beef was generally killed by the young warriors, who for that purpose would visit the large herds of Texas cattle near the post. This kind of sport precisely suited the young men. After the necessary permission from the officer in charge was obtained several of the savages with bows strung would ride into the midst of the herd. The cattle seemed to know what was going on, and the moment a warrior put his eye upon one, the "spotted" bovine took to his heels as hard as he could travel. The warriors dashed after, and coming up alongside launched an arrow into the side of the terrified brute. Having dispatched the animal several squaws would set to work with knives and axes skinning and dividing the carcass according to the number of families entitled to it. As might be supposed there was always some dispute and dissatisfaction. Some complaining they did not get their share. A strong guard was always ready to put down any serious difficulty.

A crowd of several hundred squaws, it may be imagined, was not a bad place for forming some notions of Indian beauty. The better class always presented themselves at these gatherings in their best "outfits." The hard lot of the squaw is not conducive to beauty or freshness, though examples are found of both. There is no doubt but that the hard life is in a majority of instances the chief reason for the intense ugliness of the women of the southern wild tribes. The affiliated bands are less harsh, and present finer women and better developed men than any of the wild tribes. A Witchita, or a Caddo, in feature, and many points of dress, is more suggestive of an Italian brigand than a plaints savage.

The women of both these bands dress with unsparing extravagance. Their *moccasins* and leggins are covered with plates of silver, made of Mexican dollars hammered out. Their buckskin shirts are elaborately decorated with bead-work, their blankets are unusually new and clean, about their person they carry a profusion of beads and shell and silver ornaments. The men dress as well as the women, and wear a puritanic peaked hat, decorated with great streamers of blue and red ribbon, and when mounted on their fleet ponies present a very picturesque appearance.

The weather after our arrival at Fort Cobb became wet and stormy. Incessant rains poured upon the earth, deluging our camp, and raising the streams until they were entirely impassable. Such weather at this time was particularly embarrassing, as the supplies were rapidly disappearing, and it was almost impossible to move the trains for more. The troops who had constructed pits for their accommodation were compelled to seek other quarters. Everywhere the mud was of that peculiar pasty nature that it required more than an ordinary amount of physical exertion to manipulate a pedestrian tour about camp. Everything was topsy-turvy; stores piled on hill sides under canvas. Officers sat upon their bunks in order to keep out of the wet.

Hunting and other amusements were entirely suspended. The whole camp was thus subjected to a sort of water embargo, which was infinitely worse than snow or cold. Our march had now brought us down to a latitude where, though snow was not a rare occurrence, it was an exception. The prevailing meteorological displays were rain, with an incidental "norther," and winding up with a variation of sleet and ice, trying both to men and animals.

CHAPTER 25

The Occupants of the Country

I purpose here devoting several chapters to the traditions, localities, manners, and customs of the wild Indians, against whom the operations of the campaign were directed. In the same connection, it will be necessary, in order briefly to introduce the subject, to say something concerning our own knowledge of the discovery and exploration of the country.

Owing mainly to the remoteness and inaccessibility of the plains, until the beginning of the present century, this section was comparatively unknown. We are indebted to Spanish dominion in Mexico for our first accounts. Having planted their flag upon the halls of the Montezumas, the daring soldiers of Spain, in search of mountains of gold and silver, fields of gems and precious stones, fountains of everlasting youth, and under the impulse of other notions, equally as extravagant, fitted out expeditions into all parts of the adjacent countries.

From the narratives of such often long and toilsome journeys, history has frequently gleaned a ray of light, and making due allowance for the magnified intellectual vision of these pioneer travellers, much that is reliable is to be gathered. The first description we have of the country, answering to that of which I have been speaking, is contained in an early Spanish work, subsequently translated into French, and entitled *Relation du voyage de Cibola entrepris en 1540, ou l'on traite de toutes les peuplades qui habitent cette coutree, des liurs moeurs et coutumes par Pedro de Castaneda de Nagera.* The work contains an account of the journey of Francisco Vasquenz Coronado, from Cicuyé, New Mexico, in search of the "golden city" of Quivera.

Some days after leaving Cicuyé, the expedition arrived at a large river, which was also very deep. Here they built a bridge, which consumed four days. The writer, with the expedition, then proceeds: "Ten days after, we discovered some huts inhabited by Indians, who lived as the Arabs, and we named them Quereches. We had seen their traces for ten days. These Indians live in tents of the skin of bison, tanned, and live by the chase." Marching in a north-easterly direction, the expedition encountered "such a multitude of bison, that it appeared almost a thing incredible." They found numerous villages. "The country was very flat." The people had great numbers of dogs. They had no horses, but used dogs for packing. Castaneda closes by saying, "the Spanish were well treated, and the journey, though it cost many days of fatigue, and was profitless in lands abounding in wealth, there was much knowledge gained of the country."

It is probable, from other evidences gathered, in descriptions of localities, met with in the narrative alluded to, that the travels of the party extended to the stream now known as the Red river, if they did not cross it. The accounts answer for that section. The country along its banks is a favourite resort for innumerable bison or buffaloes. The people, too, answer in every respect. They still live in huts or lodges, made of the skin of the bison, and possess numerous dogs. Their traditions, also, show that an early day there were no horses, and dogs were used instead for transporting all the effects of the village.

Accepting this testimony, we must accede to the Spanish adventurers of Mexico, over three centuries ago, the honour of first laying eyes upon the country of which we are now speaking. About the same time that De Soto, from the east, was traversing the extensive country of the present states of Florida, Georgia, Alabama, and Mississippi, overcoming numerous and powerful armies of warriors, climbing mountains, penetrating trackless forests, crossing rivers, wading interminable swamps, and crowning his work by the discovery of the great river of the continent, Coronado, from the golden lands of Mexico, crossed pathless, treeless wastes, under parching heats, and gave to the world the first knowledge of that vast region, the American plains.

Whatever may have been their motives, to such daring adventurers as De Soto and Coronado, we must, at least, offer a passing tribute of admiration for their courage, their perseverance, and their success as explorers.

In the early years of French dominion, on the lower waters of the Mississippi, a party was sent out under the auspices of the imperial government, to explore the Red river regions. Meeting with numerous hindrances in the hostility of the people, and the impassable nature of the country, and having reached the present town of Natchitoches, in Louisiana, they returned after a fruitless expenditure of time, energy, and money. In 1806, the Territory of Louisiana, having become a portion of the United States, Captain Sparks, Lieutenant Humphrey, a Dr. Curtis, Mr. Freeman, and seventeen soldiers, started from near Natchez to ascend the Red River. The expedition was known as the exploring party of the Red River. They had proceeded but a short distance above the great "raft," when they were confronted by a force of Spanish, probably on the same mission. Being refused passage through the country, and unable to insist, the party retraced their steps.

In the same year, another government exploring expedition set out under Lieutenant Pike. The instructions were to ascend the Arkansas to its source, thence to strike across the country to the head waters of the Red River, and return down that stream. After a toilsome journey, attended with numerous privations and great suffering, they reached the head waters of the Arkansas. From this point they marched across country until arriving at a stream flowing east. Taking this to be the Red, they commenced its descent. Subsequent events showed it to be the Rio Grande. They were taken prisoners by the Spanish and Bent to the governor of New Mexico, by whom they were held for some time.

In the summer of 1820, Major Long conducted an exploration along the Canadian river, the middle stream between the Arkansas and the Red. Thirty years later, Captain, (now General) R. B. Marcy, accompanied by Captain, (General) George B. McClellan, Lieutenant J. Updegraff, Dr. R. G. Shurnard, and fifty-five men of company D, 5th Infantry, were detailed to make an exploration of the Red River and country adjacent from the mouth of Cache Creek. The party having laid in a stock of provisions at Fort Belknap, on the Brazos River, in Texas, got started early in the spring. On May 9, 1852, they were at the mouth of Cache Creek. The explorations were very thorough. Up to this time the section set apart as the field of their labours was entirely unknown. They returned laden with stores of information of the character of the country, its topography, its soil, and its productions. In later years, other expeditions have been sent out, each of which has contributed its share to the general stock of geographical knowledge.

The plains, according to the unsatisfactory and indefinite assertions of Indian legends and traditions have, for ages, been the home of various tribes of Indians. The peculiar physical features of the country, soon had an effect upon their habits, thoughts, and superstitions. Whatever may have been their characteristic development previously, a long occupation of the country unquestionably, not primitively, inhabited by the present representatives of the race, produced a type of the American Indian, distinct in his mode of living, tribal, and individual relations, superstitions, religion, government, and war.

By the wild Indians, I mean those still following the habits, customs, and mode of life inherited from their ancestors, unmodified by the least step towards changing their condition—the enemy to progress, and the implacable foe to civilization.

These tribes, in the south, are the Kiowas, Comanches, Cheyennes, Arrapahoes, and Apaches, (Lepans). Although several bands of Sioux frequently move south of the Platte, and hunt along the head waters of the Republican, mingling with the northern bands of Cheyennes and Arrapahoes, properly they belong to the plain country northward, in Nebraska and Dakota.

Midway between the Platte and Red Rivers, flows the Arkansas, having its fountain sources in the heart of the Rocky Mountains of Colorado, following a general easterly direction almost the entire width of the plains, and dividing them into two almost equal divisions. The stretch of territory south of the Arkansas is not only the home of the largest Indian population of any section of equal area, but also constitutes the chosen hunting-grounds over which the wild tribes roam.

None of these tribes claim this country as the primitive seat of their people; but the more powerful nations, in their migrations, taking possession by force, the weaker were pushed along in search of new abodes, and, in turn, also displaced an earlier population.

From a comparison of the respective claims of the wild tribes, upon the authority of tradition and the recollections of the oldest men, the Comanches, as they are improperly designated, were the first of the present occupants to make their appearance in the country, in general terms, these people say that they came from the south, and, within the memory of their living men occupied the immense and fertile region bordering on the Brazos and the Colorado, and thence extended in the direction of the Rio Grande and the Rio Pecos, now embraced in western Texas. The Brazos was the seat of their council-fires, and from this section, remote from pursuit, for years these renowned horsemen and warriors of the plains kept up a state of unrelenting hostility against the Mexicans. Their war-parties penetrated beyond the Rio Grande, into Chihuahua and Sonora, and even down into the heart of old Mexico, spreading terror and devastation almost to the very gates of the capital. Cities and towns were taken, and the *alcaldes* and chief men, upon their knees, tune and again, implored clemency at the hands of the savage conquerors. Even to this day, large war-parties fit out, and, from their present distant seats, carry on predatory wars across the Rio Grande. In these forays, they follow what is familiar to the frontiersman as the Grand Comanche War-trail, crossing the Pecos and the Rio Grande, and the Horse-head hills.

There seems to be little doubt, that, several centuries ago, the Comanches were a portion of the primitive Mexican population, and lived upon the frontiers of a nation of people possessing a superior civilization. It is easy to trace out the circumstances which would conduce lo their present savage condition. Their mode of life, their isolation and indolence, relying principally upon the success of marauding expeditions, and the chase, as the means of gratifying their spirit of adventure, all tended to that end.

The name "Comanche," by which these people are known, is a term of Mexican origin, meaning "wild men." In their own language, applied to their nation, the Comanches call themselves "*Neum*" "our people." When speaking of others of their race, they say "*Ab-ta-witche*," meaning a "different people." When they see human figures at a distance and are unable to distinguish them from their own people, they use the expression "*No-hinne-neum*," meaning "people we do not know." But when they discern them to be of their own nation, they say "*Neum*," "our people."

The occupation of Texas by the whites, and the wars which led to the acquisition of that region by the United States, forced the largest bodies of the Comanches to fall back, and ultimately they occupied the country north of the Red River, while some settled in the Llano, Estacado, or Staked plains, north of the Pecos.

Of late years, the Comanches have, from various causes, become divided into a number of bands, more or less powerful, and known by different names, suggested by some characteristic. All these fragments of the original people recognize an identity of origin. They exhibit no marked dissimilarity of customs and habits. Still there is no other union than that natural feeling of relationship inspired by the ties of blood. These bands are influenced by no common interest; and, while they generally have maintained peace, as parts of the same parent stock, each band generally follows its own impulses.

There now exist five different bands of Comanches, roaming over the same country. Although they claim a division of eight, three of this number have lost their distinct character; and, while they have their chiefs and head men, the people have divided up, and have incorporated themselves into the other bands.

The largest subdivision of the Comanches, is the Qua-ha-de-de-chatz-kennes, or Antelope Users. This band inhabits the *Llano Estacado*, or Staked Plains, and keeps up a continual series of raids into Texas and northern Mexico. This branch has maintained an exclusion from all intercourse with the government, and the barren, unexplored, and inaccessible nature of their haunts, has given them, thus far, complete assurance of security for their families.

The *Llano Estacado*, or Staked Plains, a desolate waste, was so named, many years ago, by a party of Mexicans, who for the convenience of intercourse with the tribes to the north, and for the purpose of communicating with the American settlements, marked out a route across that sterile section by planting stakes.

The remaining bands of the Comanches, are the Cost-cheteght-kas, or Buffalo Eaters; Yamparikos, or Root Diggers; Peneteghtkas, or Honey Eaters; and No-ko-nees, or Wanderers, The three bands broken up, are the Moochas, or Crooked Mountain band; Ten-na-was, or Liver Eaters; and Tea-chatzkennas, or Servers. These bands roam over the country bordering on the head waters of the Red River, and as far as the Canadian.

About twenty-five years ago, these people were cut up into three grand divisions—northern, middle, and southern Comanches—designated by the names, Ten-na-was, Yamparikos, and Comanches proper. Each of these divisions was subdivided into bands. The southern Comanches at that time roamed in Texas, extending their movements from the Red River to the Colorado, and wintered on the Colorado and Brazos. The northern Comanches followed the migrations of the buffalo from the Red River to the Arkansas. The middle Comanches occupied the region intervening. The No-co-nees and Ten-na-was then wintered in north-western Texas, and in the summer season moved north, establishing themselves sometimes as far as the Red, sometimes to the Canadian, and even visited as far north as the Arkansas.

Their superior character and intelligence, as well as their bravery in war and expert horsemanship, gives the Comanche the precedence in influence among the tribes of the southern plains.

CHAPTER 26

The Apache (Lipans)

Next in point of character and importance are the Kiowas. These people today hold a kind of medium of intercourse between the Comanches and other wild tribes and the Government. They are shrewd in diplomacy, and have frequently, to use their own expression, successfully "played wolf with Washington." The latter being the name by which the commissioners of the Government are known. Kiowa and Comanche warriors are often found together on the same warpath, pursue their hostilities against the Navajoes in the mountains of New Mexico, or divide the rich spoils taken from the heavily laden wagon-trains *en route* to the far western settlements.

The Kiowas claim that their primitive country was in the far north. That other tribes coming upon them, a long and sanguinary war ensued, in which both parties were nearly used up. Seeing their condition, and still too proud to offer or to accept terms of peace, both withdrew. After remaining for a while in their old country, continually harassed by their enemies, their hunters brought back stories of extensive regions to the south, and inhabited by a people much weakened by wars. The entire tribe resolved to drive out these prior occupants, and take possession of these new lands. The families were collected and the removal commenced. Their affects were carried on dogs, or sledges drawn by that animal. From the north they reached a river, now the south forth of the Platte. Their residence upon the borders of this stream is within the recollection of the old men of the tribe.

Not satisfied with the Platte country, they moved on across the Republican and Smoky Hill until they reached the Arkansas. Thence they moved upon the head waters of the Cimmaron. Here they permanently located their council fire, and after much fighting secured control of all the country south of the Arkansas, and north of the

Witchita mountains and head waters of the Red River.

There are many evidences in the names of tributary streams on the Upper Missouri indicating that the Kiowas at one time were in that vicinity. Kiowa pride would not descend to an admission that the tribe was compelled to leave. But that such was the case is hardly to be doubted, as the later occupants for years past have proved an equally brave people, and have exceeded the Kiowas in many of the fiercer qualities of warriors. It is also quite satisfactory that an Indian has rarely been known to desert the hunting-ground of his fathers unless compelled to do so by some extraordinary circumstance. It is equally certain in their removal the Kiowas were not influenced by considerations of climate or country, as in neither respect is the Arkansas preferable to the regions beyond the Platte. The Cheyennes and Arrapahoes claim some years ago, to have had severe wars with the Kiowas, and that they whipped them to such an extent that they left the country. There still seems to exist a latent hostility between the conquerors and the conquered.

The Kiowas preserve a tribal union, rather remarkable in a region where such a variety of considerations combine to defeat the concentration of large numbers into a single body. They possess in form no central council for purposes of a general government, still, in fact, the superior authority of some chief gives the tribe nominally a central influence, respected alike by all the subordinate bands. This controlling rank has frequently resulted in very threatening misunderstandings between rival aspirants for the honour of being head chief, and it is only due to the family ties, which in an Indian are singularly strong, that more serious divisions have not long ago occurred. The requisites needed to hold this high rank are principally wisdom in council and bravery in war. For several years Satanta has filled the office of head chief. A peculiar dash of manner, a grin equal to all occasions, a remarkable shrewdness exhibited in managing affairs between the different tribes with which his people come in contact, or their intercourse with the National Government, have won for him a prestige which he has very well maintained.

Satanta, when I met him, was a man of about fifty years of age. He rose first through prowess on the war-path, and afterwards through skill in council and diplomacy. He had an intelligent face, and was large in frame, and of muscular development, exhibiting also a tendency to obesity. Lately Satanta had found a threatening rival in Lone Wolf, the war-chief of the tribe. While he still holds his own with the old men, Lone Wolf, a middle aged Indian, was the choice of the young. In the latter the young warriors found plenty of encouragement and opportunity to win renown. Their restless spirits, craving the excitement of the war-path, and the acquisition of scalps, naturally sided with one who gave way to their instinctive thirst for blood.

The Kiowas, for convenience of subsistence, are divided up into smaller parties, led by a chief of prominence. These divisions are generally composed of, and influenced by, the relatives of the chief, and follow him more as a leader of the family than for purposes of independent action. The principal bands thus constituted, and in the order of their importance, are those of Satanta, Lone Wolf, Timbered Mountain, Kicking Bird, and Stumbling Bear. Big Bow, with his band, during the recent troubles, went over to the Cheyennes, influenced by jealousy of his rivals and hostility to the Government. In their general arrangements the voice of the tribe directs any measure in which the whole people are interested. Upon certain occasions, also, all the bands are concentrated in the same vicinity to participate in the important and solemn ceremony of making "big medicine" for the year.

As the result of a sort of community of interest, the Cheyennes and Arrapahoes have for some years been united in a band of alliance for war or peace. Both these tribes reached the plains country from the north. Their presence south of the Arkansas is within the memory of their people. Anterior to their habitation upon the Platte, whence they came last, they have no definite ideas, merely alluding to their coming there as the result of their wanderings in search of more desirable hunting-grounds. They allude to the Kiowas as preceding them, compelling them to leave the country and push farther south. Upon moving below the Platte, about thirty years ago, the Cheyennes occupied the country from the mouth of Beaver Creek to the head waters of the Platte, and between the Republican and the Smoky Hill Rivers, also away towards the south-west, along the north side of the Arkansas, west of the Dry Fork, and now embraced in southern Nebraska, the northern half of Kansas and north-eastern Colorado.

This extensive region was the favourite range of the buffalo. The multitudes of this animal, almost countless even at the present day, existed then in larger numbers. A successful traffic in robes, and an abundance of food raised the pride and excited the martial spirit of the Cheyennes, until they became the terror of all their enemies whether red or white. In the chase, and on the war-path, they early became associated with the Arrapahoes who ranged more particularly upon the western border of the country conquered by the Cheyennes. Thus by degrees, the one emulating the conduct of the other, the two people were led to a unity of purpose which renders them today practically one. The fine country beyond the Platte and the intermarriage of some of the Cheyennes with the Sioux, tended to a division of the tribe. The separation, however, was accomplished peaceably, the withdrawing faction leaving about the year 1848, under its chiefs. Standing Water and White Cow, and occupying the regions towards the north, living with the Sioux between the head waters of the Missouri and the Platte.

The main bands now confined their wanderings more towards the Arkansas. Reaching that stream, the warriors frequently come in contact with the Kiowas, who were living on the south. The Kiowas, probably, still bearing in mind their ancient wars with the strangers, were not in a spirit to make the proximity of the Cheyennes, the cause of a renewal of hostilities. The Cheyenne could still muster a formidable array of warriors, and Kiowa prudence suggested the wisdom of giving the new comers a hospitable greeting. This amicable course averted a fresh outbreak of the enmity which existed between the earlier representatives of their tribes, and stayed a war which would inevitably have broken the power, had it not effaced the name of the conquered.

The Arrapahoes during this division among the Cheyennes, stood aloof and remained with the main tribe. The Arrapahoes, however, in turn experienced also a division, but of a less peaceful nature. Soon after the separation of the Cheyenne bands, an Arrapahoe chief named Nam-e-sum, Cut Nose, in a fit of intoxication offered some indignity to a rival. The warriors on the spot took sides, and a free-fight resulted in which Cut Nose was killed. The warriors of his faction deserted the main band and went north, while the remainder continued with the southern branch of the Cheyennes.

This division of the Cheyennes and Arrapahoes conduced to a permanent separation of the two tribes, now known by distinct names. The two divisions are generally designated the northern and southern Cheyennes and Arrapahoes, They, however, have their own terms of distinction. In the case of the Cheyennes, the northern tribe is called the Shell band, from Mene-e-er-yah, which means shell, the Indian name for the Platte (Shell) River near which they lived. They are also known as the Mission or Eater's band. The southern tribe is known as the Flint band, from *Mutesohue*, meaning flint, the Indian name for the Arkansas (Flint) River, the largest stream near which they roamed. They are also known as the Ha-vahtan-ye or Hairy band.

The Cheyennes having been first in the country, and the ruling tribe, were entitled to the names suggested by the location of their council fires. The Arrapahoes assumed names indicating the former identity of the two parts of the tribe. The conquering portion which remained with the Cheyennes, took the name of Teneveu, Father, or Suck-breast band. The other Nam-e-sum, or Cut Nose band. It is asserted by some facetious individual, that this latter appellation was figurative in allusion to that principal of vulgar philosophy known to ourselves in the homely illustration of *cutting off the nose to spite the face*. It would certainly be a very emphatic manner of recognizing the folly which induced the warriors to engage in hostility upon so slight a pretence. Another and more plausible explanation is that the seceded band got its name from the refractory chief whose cause it espoused, the chief having obtained his peculiar cognomen, some years before, as a perpetuation of a series of brawls, in one of which he carried off a "Cut Nose" as a memorial of the occasion.

In the wanderings of the Cheyennes as they increased in numbers, the tribe was subject to another division. This third branch under Long Chin and Little Grey Head, seated themselves more particularly upon the head waters of the Republican River, thence south towards the Smoky Hill, and north towards the Platte. These are now known as the Ho-tam-e-tanyer or Dog Soldiers. How this name originated is not mentioned. It has been asserted that the warriors are composed of outlaws from the other two branches of the parent stock and hence call "dog soldiers," but this is denied by the warriors themselves, as well as by the fact of the friendly relations preserved with the remainder of the tribe. Nor is it from the fact that they specially consume dogs, as this is a peculiarity of taste in all of the Cheyennes.

Thus we discover the Cheyennes divided into three branches, the northern inhabiting beyond the Platte, the "Dog Soldiers" south of the Platte, and the Southern band south of the Arkansas. These different divisions, though broken into smaller bodies, and following different leaders, preserved a rigid union.

The word Cheyenne is, unquestionably, a term of designation applied in earlier days by the *voyageurs*, from Canada, who resorted to the plains country in the far west. The Cheyennes are particularly fond of dogs, served up in the various methods known to their rude art of cooking. In the absence of a knowledge of the language, or to distinguish them from other Indians, not so intensely ungrateful towards the most faithful brute companion of the human race, the *voyageurs* designated these people tersely "*Chiens*." From this, not knowing the word originally to have been French, the American pronunciation, as well as orthography, would naturally suggest "Cheyennes." These people call themselves His-ta-e-yet. This term of designation, and Arrapahoe, have no meaning in our own tongue. The Comanches call the Arrapahoes, Sayre-teghtka, or Dog-eaters.

Though the fight for dominion has now been forgotten between the rival factions of the Arrapahoes, the two bands keep up the old division as regards locality. In the war with the government, all the Cheyennes and Arrapahoes took the war-path, and parties of warriors from the northern bands were known to have moved from their remote seats to assist their southern relatives upon the Washita and the Red.

The fifth and least important of the wild tribes, south of the Arkansas, is the Lipans. These people are improperly known as Apaches, and so called in the official documents of the government. They say of themselves that they are not Apaches, that the Apaches live away to the west. As an additional evidence of the truth of this, the tribe speaks a language of its own, distinct from that used by the Mescelero and Jacarillo, or true Apaches of New Mexico. Some years ago the Lipans lived in western Texas, and have always been on friendly terms with the Comanches, their neighbours. At that time they could gather a formidable force of warriors, but owing to feuds and wars with the whites, they became divided in power and depleted in numbers. A separation took place, one branch seeking refuge in old Mexico, where they are now living, the other moved north towards the Red River, and form the small band found on the plains, and improperly called the Apaches. It is understood that the Mexican wing of the tribe have left that country, and are on their way to join the band on the southern plains in north-western Texas and the Indian territories.

There is a tradition among the Lipans, that many years ago they occupied the region known as the "bad ground," an exceedingly desolate and broken country between the head waters of the Missouri and the Platte, and from here they wandered south until they reached Texas. There is no other authority for this than their own story.

The relations existing amongst the five wild tribes are of a friendly character, for the common object of marauding upon the settlements. The Comanche excels in horsemanship, the Kiowa in duplicity, and the Cheyennes and Arrapahoes in the more decisive qualities of warriors. The Apaches (Lipans), are few in numbers and weak in influence. In their movements they are swayed by the wishes of the Comanches and Kiowas.

In the organization of war-parties, composed of warriors of the different tribes, certain ceremonies of negotiation are observed. Any band wishing to go to war sends messengers, asking its friends to furnish warriors for an expedition. This mission bears with it the council pipe, and is accompanied by ponies as presents, to encourage the favourable consideration of the proposition. A council is held in which the whole matter is fully discussed. If the band accepts the pipe and smokes, the request is granted, and the warriors of the band, or rather such as choose, extend their co-operation. After this ceremony, warriors from all the bands rendezvous at a given point, and start upon their errand of atrocity and spoliation. To decline acceding to the proposition to take the war-path, frequently occurs from policy or necessity. The band seeking for assistance, if not successful in gathering a sufficient number of warriors to make up the necessary strength, abandons its project.

CHAPTER 27

Justice

From the earliest times of which we have any record, the plains have been a common battle-ground. From time immemorial, there has existed a particularly fierce and unyielding hostility between the mountain and the plains Indians. The mountain-tribes, a more hardy and bolder type of the race, have generally proved too much for the warriors of the open country. The leaders in these incursions were the Utes and the Navajoes, who still make occasional descents from their mountain fastnesses, spreading terror far and wide among the plains bands. Their warlike expeditions form an important chapter in the traditions of the Kiowas and Comanches especially. Time and again the warriors of both these tribes have been routed, and the mountain warrior has returned to his retreats laden with scalps to attest his prowess in battle, and large herds of ponies and many squaws as the fruits of victory.

The plains Indians are not known ever to have retaliated by pursuing their enemies on their own grounds. It is true, that, at certain seasons, they still send their bravest men into the mountains to cut lodge-poles; but, upon nearing the dangerous country of their terrible adversaries, they move cautiously, and well examine their path before venturing too far. Having secured their lodge-poles, they usually retreat with the utmost dispatch until out of reach of pursuit.

Many of the tribes seated on reservations near the settlements are also in the habit of visiting the plains annually to kill buffalo. These expeditions, fraught with dangers at the hands of the vigilant wild tribes, are organized with the same ceremonies that attend the gathering of a war-party. Though for the special object of the chase, they adopt the precaution of making every preparation to repel attacks, and, while engaged in killing buffalo, detachments of warriors are constantly employed, scouring the plain, on the lookout for the approach of hostile Indians. The tribes possessing, or rather occupying, the country, jealous of these intrusions, are constantly on the watch; and it rarely happens that a hunting-party returns without a fight, or, at least, being pursued.

In addition to the many distinctions, in regard to manners and customs, between the mountain and the plains Indians, we find a still more marked difference of habits, caused, in a great measure, by the use of the horse, or, more particularly, the smaller and hardier variety of the species, known as the Indian pony. Natural history informs us that the horse is not a native of the American continent. We are informed that the horse first makes his appearance in America, in connection with the Spanish adventurers, and first landed on the southwestern portion of the continent with Cortez and his followers. The terror at first inspired by the presence of this noble animal, went far towards overcoming the primitive Aztecs, in the romantic and daring conquest of Cortez, The constant shock of battle soon familiarized the inhabitants of Mexico with the submissive and subordinate nature of the horse.

Forgetting his supposed preternatural origin, they preserved those taken from their enemies; and the species was still more rapidly disseminated by the subsequent establishment of Spanish dominion m the country. We find the animal soon taking part with the natives in domestic industry, public ceremony, and war. The intercourse between the progenitors of the modern Comanches and the Mexicans, soon put the former in possession of so valuable an assistance in prosecuting their predatory incursions beyond the Rio Grande. The nature of the country, and the indolence of the savage, conduced to a high appreciation of the usefulness of the horse. The plains of Texas, with their fine streams of water and luxuriant pasturage, were well adapted to the habits of the animal. In the lapse of years, each band had its herds, and the maximum of Indian wealth was the possession of numerous ponies.

Changes of climate and other circumstances, led to an almost new creation, which we meet today in the Indian pony. This new type of the species, not only differs in stature and is more tractable and full of endurance, but is more generally adapted to the purpose and condition of the Indian of the plains than the highly developed parent species would be.

The Indian pony enables the savage warrior to scour the expanse from the Missouri to the mountains westward, and from the southern verge of civilization to the distant limits of Dakota. It enables him to transport his villages, his squaws, and his papooses, wherever his nomadic instincts prompt; and the same food which subsists the countless buffaloes suffices to keep the strength of the Indian pony. It is, therefore, not surprising nor unnatural that the warrior's first ambition should be the possession of this valuable animal. With his shield to defend him from the feathered shafts of his enemies, with his bow and arrow as a means to vindicate his prowess, and scalps to reward his triumph, with his pony to carry him through the dangers of battle and to assist him in the acquisition of spoils, the young warrior mounts his way to eminence and influence, emulating the great and brave, and frequently rivalling them in deeds to be handed down in tradition.

In the use of the horse, taking the term in its generic sense, the plains Indians more particularly differ from those of the mountains. The latter conduct their war operations on foot, march long distances, and engage their enemies from behind trees and rocks, or depend upon the irregularities of surface as a defence. They excel in muscular development and cunning. Their capacity of endurance is greater, and mode of living more rude. Their sphere of warlike operations is necessarily limited; but their fights are attended with greater determination, courage, and personal exertion. Some of the mountain tribes, bordering the plains, possess a few horses, captured by their war-parties to the open country. These they use, when they have them, more for speedy transportation and convenience, than as an actual necessity.

On the other hand, the plains Indian is entirely governed by the use of the pony. To such an extent has it become part of his everyday life, that, without it, he would be compelled to make a radical change in his habits and ideas, The warrior of the plains takes pride in his horsemanship—sometimes dignified, again reckless, and often novel. Depending upon his mount, he displays less of true courage, striving to terrify by well-concerted demonstrations and bold dashes. He fears a dismounted adversary, and takes to flight rather than engage, except with overwhelming numbers in his favour.

The Comanches boast of having been the first Indians to use the horse, and, with a wonderful degree of self importance, claim to have introduced that valuable animal to the whites, as well as to others of their own race. In fact the horse, according to themselves, was, originally, specially created by the Great Spirit for their use. The old men say that they recollect when the Kiowas were poor, and used squaws, dogs, and sledges to move their villages, and their warriors went on foot, but now they were rich, and had more ponies than the Comanches.

The plains warrior exhibits less muscular development than those of his race occupying the mountain districts, although his wild and independent life would seem to induce the most perfect specimens of manly form. The fact is almost the reverse. He is tall, but his limbs are small and badly shaped, showing more sinew than muscle. His chest, however, is deep and square His bearing is erect, with legs considerably bowed, the effect of constant use of the saddle. His hair is long and black, and worn at full length, streaming over his shoulders. The scalp-lock, or hair growing on a diameter of two inches on the vertex of the skull, is artistically plaited. His beard, moustache, and eyebrows he plucks out. The object of this mutilation of nature is nothing more than the gratification of a singular phase of vanity. The practice has a tendency to produce a feminine appearance.

In physiognomy we find in the plains Indian a greater diversity than would be supposed. Some have features perfectly Caucasian, while others closely resemble the narrow-faced Malay, or the oval-countenanced Mongolian, and with the different shades of colour, from a dark reddish brown to a perfect olive.

For the purpose of arguing the origin of the race, as far as the plains Indians are concerned, judging from their resemblance to any particular people of the old world, a sufficient variety of facial angles could be found to support any theory. The expansive flat face, high and receding forehead, sharp and small black eyes, thin lips, well arched mouth, high cheek-bones, nose more or less beaked, or Roman, and rather flat across the bridge, but thinning out towards the point, ears large, well formed, and setting well upon the head, represents the type most commonly met with. Specimens are often seen bearing close resemblance to the subjects of several European nations. We have seen one baud, except in colour, perfect Italians, a few resembling the Germans, and quite a number the Jews of today.

These varieties, in connection with the general type, appear in all the five wild tribes. The Cheyennes and Arrapahoes are more purely Indian, and the finest models. The Kiowas and Lipans stand next. The Comanche in numerous instances is adulterated with the blood of the Mexican, either by capture or intermarriage.

The women of the plains tribes, though smaller in stature, show a much more perfect development. The relations between the sexes is the same in nearly all cases—that is, they are the servants or slaves. All the labour performed in an Indian village, taking down or setting up the lodges, packing for transportation, saddling the ponies, cooking, tanning robes, making *moccasins*, doing bead-work, providing covering for the body out of the skins brought in by the warrior, and the raising of children, fall to the lot of the women. The sphere of the men is to hunt and to supply the lodge with game and skins, and to take scalps from their enemies wherever they find them.

The general characteristics of the sexes are in the man a boasting spirit, no moral and little animal courage, consummate indolence, and intolerable pride, and a fiendish thirst for blood. In the women we find patience, a degree of tenderness, industry, devotion, and ingenuity. They are particularly timid, and frequently set off in a regular stampede from some imaginary or real cause. On these occasions it is useless for the men to attempt to use their authority. The usual argument administered towards refractory squaws, such as kicks, cuffs, and violent floggings, are at such times perfectly powerless, so the men, or a portion of them, go with the mass, rather to regulate than to control their movements. Condemned to a sphere of drudgery and domestic oppression, it would naturally be supposed that the women would be gross and hideous.

Although beauty in its higher sense is rare, many winning faces will be seen in the Indian village. The children are uncommonly good looking. The old women are perfect frights. Although the young and middle aged are generally well formed, with full development of bust, well defined lines, and limbs of beautiful proportion, the points of special attraction are their diminutive hands and feet. Encased in a beautifully ornamented and well-fitted *moccasin*, and leggins of buckskin, tightly laced, the foot and ankle are set off to advantage, and not unlike the more refined of their sex of the white race, are as much objects of pride on the part of their possessors as they are the subject of silent and frequently outspoken admiration with that curious creature called man.

The actual dress of the plains Indian is excessively primitive, consisting in summer of a breech-clout, *moccasins*, and leggins. In winter this attire is reinforced by a buffalo robe, worn with the hair inside, and wrapped the whole length of the body, with a sufficient allowance to cover the head. The robe is held in place by a belt around the waist. On milder days the portion of the robe above the belt is allowed to fall back, which leaves the upper part of the body perfectly bare, while around the legs it makes a sort of shirt, with the hair both inside and outside. Sometimes a blanket is used instead of a robe.

The dress of the women in general appearance is the same as the men. In the men the leggins are cut to fit very tight, and with a flap on the outside of each leg. In the women they fit closely, but in place of the flap have a row of small brass buttons, silver ornaments, or beadwork. The men wear their leggins high up above the knee, supported by a strap fastened to the waist-belt, used with the breech-clout. The women fasten their leggins below the knee, and turned over at the top. The Kiowa women wear an ornamented flap, attached to the top and rear part of the leggins, which trails at the heels. The leggins in both cases are made of buckskin. The men frequently wear leggins of strouding. The *moccasins*, are made with buckskin feet and rawhide soles. Instead of a breech-clout the women wear a skirt of buckskin, calico, or strouding, extending from the waist to the top of the leggins, and supported by a belt. Mothers wear their buffalo robes very full at the back, above the belt, thus giving a comfortable and convenient place in which to carry the *papoose*. The children dress like adults, according to sex.

Although this constitutes the only covering used as a protection for the body during all seasons, it is the least portion of the wardrobe complete. The plains Indians, inheriting the peculiarity of their race, exhibit an excessive fondness for gaudy colours and glittering ornaments. This love of extravagant dress is probably a ruling passion. The use of paint is the most common practice in vogue, for the adornment of the face and body. Although there are no particular devices required for certain occasions of public or private ceremony, the colours vary as the warrior desires to appear brilliant or hideous. The ordinary use of vermillion, artistically applied to the cheeks and forehead, and polished, so that the colour fairly sparkles in the sunlight, is the common, everyday toilet of warrior and squaw. In the war or scalp-dances, streaks of ochre, charcoal, and Indian blue, painted across the face from the forehead to the chin, upon a ground of vermillion are added, giving a peculiarly savage appearance. Frequently upon the chest are painted figures of ferocious animals. Tattooing is also common, both with the men and women.

The decorations used consist of shells and ear-rings, made of brass wire. Frequently five or six of these are worn in a single ear, and from which brass chains, and other ornaments, are suspended. *Wampum* necklaces, silver armlets, six or eight brass wire bracelets on each arm, silver ornaments, with crescents dangling from an ingeniously contrived covering for the breast, made of Iroquois shells, hair pipe, *wampum*, and beads, the whole suspended from the neck, are also popular. The most elaborate ornaments consist of a train, three, four, and five feet in length, composed of silver plates fastened upon a strip of rawhide and attached to the scalp-lock, the plates diminishing in size from three inches to one inch in diameter, and frequently very picturesque head-dresses of eagle feathers, and leggins, often beautifully adorned with beads. The women wear belts of silver plates, suspended from which are an awl-case and paint-pouch worked in beads, brass wire bracelets, and immense silver finger-rings. The women wear no head trappings, nor earrings. Nose ornaments are now seldom used in either sex.

The nomadic life led by the plains tribes, and the scarcity of subsistence, which frequently occurs when the hunter fails to secure game, exerts a remarkable influence in the mode of living. Their abodes, though called villages, are strictly nothing more than camps, easily set up and readily moved, as the emergencies of scarcity of subsistence, war, or superstition may dictate. Owing to the precarious character of their daily supply of food, in time of peace the movements of the buffalo principally regulate the location of the Indian camps. For this reason it is also impossible for large numbers to congregate in the same vicinity. The band is the unit of organization, and the harmony which exists between those of a common ancestry, is merely the natural and instinctive friendship of kindred towards each other.

The division into bands is a matter, personal with its members, but having once become attached to one band, permission is necessary before the person can transfer permanently to another. The members of each are generally relatives, descended from the same father to the fifth degree. Intermarriages with and from other bands infuses sufficient foreign blood to keep up the stock. Cousins call each other brothers and sisters, and aunts are called mothers. The ruler of the band is the chief, though the real power is vested in the council, composed of the old men, and the young men on questions involving war. In civil matters the civil-chief, who is generally an old man, presides. In subjects of war, the war-chief, who is the principal leader of all expeditions, takes the seat of authority with the civil chief.

The office of chief is elective, when awarded in due form. It frequently occurs, however, that an informal recognition of the qualifications of a rival in wisdom or prowess, is equivalent to a suspension entirely of the functions of the legitimate chief. Although the object is the elevation of one specially wise, in the case of the civil chief, who is the first in rank, the warrior, with the most relatives, has an advantage. The war-chief is frequently changed. The men of the band are divided into old men to stay at home and sit with the squaws, and young men to go to war and to hunt the buffalo.

The government of the band is strictly a matter of custom, regulated by superstition. In the absence of a precedent the council act as judge and jury. The chief has merely an advisory right. The enforcement of the penalty is left to the sufferer, who, in addition to accomplishing the savage idea of justice, also gets his personal revenge. Murder is punished by the relative or friend of the victim, killing the murderer. In hunting the buffalo, if one leaves the party without authority any one is at liberty to shoot the pony of the insubordinate. Most crimes have their price in ponies, and this convenient and peaceable method is resorted to in a majority of cases, in order to propitiate the injured party.

Considering that the authority of the chief is recognized or not, as most agreeable, the different members of an Indian community get along with wonderful harmony. Personal quarrels are exceedingly rare. The Indians certainly display the most perfect contentment in their low condition, and it is a problem, yet to be solved, whether civilization will not supplant their present contentment for a life of squalid poverty, intoxication, immorality, disease, and inevitable extermination.

Indians on the move

CHAPTER 28

On the Move

In the selection of the site of his villages, the Indian consults the elements above and the conveniences afforded by surrounding nature. The lodges or dwellings of the wandering tribes, will almost invariably be found located in a sequestered valley, sheltered from the blasts of the storm and hidden as much as possible from view. The villages are located also with regard to their defence in event of attack, and to afford the conveniences of water, wood, and pasture.

The unsettled habits of the plains tribes, from various causes, renders it necessary that the village should be easily transported from one point to another An Indian village on the move is a novel sight. Everything is carried on ponies. The lodge skin is folded and lashed upon the animals back, while the lodge poles having holes in one end for the purpose, are strung on a strip of raw hide and fastened on either side, while the other ends trail on the ground. Across these poles, immediately behind the pony, frequently a light wicker-basket is constructed and used for carrying the sick, decrepit dogs and *papooses*, or anything else as occasion may require. The lodge-poles being light and springy, and about fifteen feet in length, transportation in this shape is quiet convenient. The utensils and all things connected with the domestic uses of the village are strapped on other ponies, which the women frequently also ride. Sometimes, however, they have separate animals, and assisted by the younger boys, drive the herds and packponies, or else on foot lead them. There is no order observed in moving except the lodge and effects of the first "soldiers" takes the lead, after that the rest fall in promiscuously and as the result of constant training follow their leaders.

The warriors always ride in advance or on the flanks to keep a vigilant lookout and to give timely notice of the approach of an enemy. At no time are the Indians so powerless to repel an attack as while moving their villages. At the first alarm the women desert their posts, and leaving the herds and effects of the village to look out for themselves, take to flight. In event of a stampede, a part of the warriors surround the moving village, and beat or slay any squaw who attempts to leave. Someone at the head of the drove starts off at a gallop, to direct the movements of the flight. The rest of the warriors take up a position confronting the enemy, and resort to every artifice, such as burning the dry grass and feints. Meanwhile the village is getting out of the way as rapidly as possible. A warrior is never more determined in his ferocity and courage than in defence of his village.

The fugitive village while thus in movement, is, naturally, a scene of confusion and uproar. Shouting and shrieking engage the women, while the papooses take the contagion, and in divers keynotes give vent to their alarm in piteous cries, dogs howl, warriors whoop, and the whole mass thunders along to the tread of ponies, raising clouds of dust, dropping utensils, lodge skins, buffalo robes, everything and anything as the flight grows in velocity. The whole movement is a general and disorderly stampede, which keeps up night and day, occasionally taking fresh ponies from the driven herd, until a courier from the fighting party announces that the enemy has gone.

An Indian village will move about fifteen miles a day as a regular journey, but twice that distance can be travelled over in case of flight or emergency.

When there is no prospect of alarm, a small party of warriors with the chief, ride ahead and select the site of the village. As soon as this is done, they plant their spears on the ground chosen. They then ride to the highest eminence nearby, where they sit and smoke, and keep a vigilant lookout while the band is coming up and the squaws are putting up the lodges. An Indian *wigwam*, lodge or *tepee*, as it is sometimes called, has a neatness of finish and an air of elegance about it, which is not generally presented by the abodes of wild men. Its structure consists of buffalo hides, with the hair shared off, tanned on both sides, by a peculiar process, and whitened. The number of skins thus prepared, necessary to a lodge of liberal dimensions, is from fifteen to twenty. They are neatly fitted, and sewed together strongly with sinews, and are water-tight.

The frame of the lodge consists of a number of long thin poles, usually cedar, sometimes fifteen to eighteen feet in length. These poles are set with the heavier ends on the ground, on the periphery of a circle, while the upper ends are brought together and held by a raw hide strap. Over this frame, the skin is drawn and the two ends meeting, are held together by thongs. The appearance of the lodge when completed is that of a cone, with an aperture at the top where the poles unite and cross, allowing a space for ventilation and the egress of smoke. The entrance which must always face the rising sun is at the lower end, where the skin meets.

The origin of the peculiar structure in which the plains Indian dwells, and which is now universal in that section, is said to be Comanche. Upon what grounds cannot now be known, though Coronada in his expedition from Old Mexico in 1540, alludes to the people living in tents made of the skin of the Bison. This referred to the tribes living about the Red river. The Comanches at that time according to their traditions lived beyond the Brazos south, and within the original limits of Old Mexico. Without specially crediting any tribe with the invention of the Bison skin lodge, one fact must be admitted that it is of very ancient origin.

The number of occupants of a lodge varies. Sometimes it shelters as many as ten and twelve human beings and half a dozen dogs. According to the official returns of the Indian department, the average is seven person. The number of fighting men, estimated, is two to a lodge. Each lodge has also attached to it a small shelter which stands at a distance of eight or ten feet, and is generally occupied at night by the head of the family.

The order of arranging a village is to place the lodge of the chief in the centre and those of his warriors around him according to rank.

The selection or the abandonment of the site of a village is subject to numerous contingencies of "good and bad medicine," Upon this point the savages are excessively superstitious. On the slightest grounds they will change their abode. If any member of the tribe dies, the village is moved, because the ghost of the departed will haunt the spot and be of ill omen in the future. A village attacked by an enemy is looked upon as very "bad medicine," and that locality becomes cursed ground.

Under ordinary circumstances, before moving the village, a council is held. The civil-chief presides. After considerable talk it is left to the warriors to decide. If favourable to removal the women take down the lodges and pack the ponies. At the word of the chief the squaw of the head warrior leads off, the rest of the motley crowd follow.

In times of scarcity, to prevent the band from breaking up, the most trusty warriors surround the village to keep its members together, while the hunting-parties are out securing game. The immense droves of dogs, usually found in every band, form a sort of reserve commissariat. Almost every year, during an unusually long period of snow or rain, when it is impossible for the hunters to be out, it happens that this reserve fund of subsistence is quite convenient.

In strolling through a village, it will be observed that every warrior, not on the war-path, has a tripod erected in the rear of his lodge, and upon this hangs his shield, with a covering of skin thrown over it to keep off the weather. In the morning this skin is removed and the face of the shield is exposed to the rising sun. The superstition in regard to the shield, as mentioned by the Indians themselves, is, that by placing it outside it drives away intruding evil spirits, and acts as a safeguard against their enemies.

Everything about an Indian village is characteristic of a life of unrestrained freedom, irresponsibility, and indolence. As the disposition moves them, the warriors mount their fleet ponies and gallop over the neighbouring plain. Should a buffalo appear in sight, a chase may ensue, more for the excitement and sport than to secure the game. The regular hunt, as the taking of the war-path, is a matter of great preliminary ceremony. Sanitary regulations have no part in the domestic arrangements of either the lodge or the village. Filth seems to be the normal condition of the savage.

Two things in life actuate the Indian to unusual exertion. The struggle against starvation and his mortal hatred of his enemies. The improvidence of the race is so remarkable, that in the face of inevitable suffering, they gorge and waste without a solitary thought of the future. Food in an Indian village is generally in common, particularly as far as the poor and sick are concerned. In seasons of the regular hunts, the whole village will move to the vicinity of the hunting-grounds and there locate, conveniently accessible to the hunter and his game. In times of scarcity of game, small parties set out in all directions. Upon this slender thread often hangs the lives of whole villages Should these parties fail in their desperate mission, suffering is certain to ensue, and the dog reserve is drawn upon.

Hunting-parties frequently leave the village more in the nature of amusement than actual necessity. The main object of these is to secure fine buffalo hides for tanning. These parties are composed of young and gallant warriors. An equal number of young squaws attend them to secure the skins of the buffalo killed, and to see to their transportation. On these occasions at night, the party construct shelters made of reeds. This framework is covered with blankets or robes. These parties are frequently gone for a week or two at a time, and generally return well laden with meat and hides. In fact, in every Indian hunting-party is a certain number of squaws to take care of the game, that being too menial a duty for warriors accustomed to handling deadly weapons.

The culinary art is not any farther advanced than with the kindred of the race elsewhere. In some particulars their preparation of certain food is not at all objectionable. Their best attainment in this branch is in cooking the meat of the buffalo. This is done by cutting the meat in strips and running a green stick through each strip lengthwise. The one end is then inserted securely in the ground and arranged by inclining towards the fire, so as to bring the raw flesh fairly in the heat and free from the smoke. It is a great art, properly, to build a fire for this purpose. Strips of buffalo rump, cooked in this manner, are delicious, and at our own mess we not unfrequently imitated this primitive, but certainly excellent, mode of preparing the meat which we had ourselves taken during the day's march.

During the great hunts in storing up the winter supply, the meat of the buffalo is jerked and laid away in raw-hide packing cases, in which it is free from an extra supply of dirt, and can be conveniently transported. In summer the buffalo meat is dried by hanging it in the sun. It is a remarkable fact, that meat thus exposed to the air will keep days without becoming tainted. The wonderful purity of the atmosphere of the plains is in no instance better illustrated. This simple means is also resorted to by the troops on outpost duty.

A dainty dish among the savages, and which is decidedly agreeable, even to an enlightened taste, is the marrow-bones of the buffalo. After having taken off all the meat, the bones are laid near the fire until sufficiently well done. They are then broken, and from the interior oozes a rich cream-colored marrow.

A less inviting repast are the entrails of the buffalo. These constitute a favourite dish, eaten either raw or roasted over the fire. The most revolting of their articles of diet is the foetus of the buffalo. This embryo, and of other animals the same, when boiled, forms a sort of glutinous soup, which an Indian family will consume with the utmost eagerness. Indeed, there are few parts of the buffalo for which the savages have not found some use. The buffalo on the plains, in the animal kingdom, bears the same relation to the red man in his domestic concerns, that the cocoa-nut tree, in the vegetable kingdom, does in the same sphere of uses to the inhabitants of the tropics. His hide tanned as robes, affords protection against the weather. The hide shorn of its hairy covering and tanned, constitutes the covering of his lodge. In the shape of rawhide, it is used for bridles, quirks, saddle coverings, and for an endless variety of purposes. The brain is valuable for tanning, and the flesh furnishes food.

Dogs are not only an article of diet, in reserve, but on occasions of great ceremony are always done up in the most systematic manner. After being killed the carcass is held over the fire, and turned and twisted about until all the hair is singed off. An economical, labour-saving, method of accomplishing the removal of this hirsute growth. His canineship is then artistically dressed, and impaled upon a stout stick, by way of a skewer, which is inserted down the much-abused animal's throat. The ends of the skewer are then supported on two forked sticks, which brings the victim of the savage gourmands immediately over the centre of the fire. Here the roasting favourite of the lodge spits and crackles, followed in all its varying stages by the eyes of a troop of savages sitting around in anxious expectation.

It is a remarkable fact that, notwithstanding the abundance of other large game, as long as the buffalo is to be had, the buffalo-hunting savages will touch no other animal food. Venison, antelope, elk, or bear, is never used except in times of great scarcity. Nor wild turkey, and the other feathered game, do they touch under ordinary circumstances. Every sort of this class of game met with on the plains, distant from access by the white man, shows this to be true by their want of fear. In my experience this fact afforded a valuable lesson in regard to the relation between man and the lower animals—that fear was not of man, as a superior or formidable being, but because of his aggressive spirit—his natural impulse to destroy.

While crossing the basin of the Canadian, where probably no one had ever visited, save the savage, a short distance from the column, we ran into a fine large flock of pinnated grouse. They stood and looked at us with curiosity, but not alarmed at our presence, and even resumed feeding. We had approached so close that we could almost reach them with the muzzles of our rifles. Three were killed before they took flight. It was very evident that the birds, in the first instance, had no more fear of us than of the animals which they were constantly accustomed to meet in their morning and evening feedings.

Vegetable food is little used, mainly because the country affords only in certain places, widely separated, that variety of diet. There is a white root, a sort of potato, and also a yam, which is held in high esteem. Wild pumpkins and beans are sometimes gathered for use. The pumpkins are cut and dried, and prepared by baking in the ashes, or boiling. Wild fruit and berries, where found, are consumed as a great luxury. It is not unusual for bands living near a large growth of wild cherries to gather the fruit at the proper season. They preserve it by pounding with a mixture of marrow-grease. This composition is put up in cakes, which, when thoroughly dried, are laid away for future consumption. Pecan-nuts, which grow plentifully along some of the streams, are also used as food.

Amid all the pressure of scarcity of game, and absolute starvation staring them in the face, cannibalism has never been known, or even hinted at, in any of the five wild tribes. The Tonkaways, who inhabited the country many years ago, and a few of whose descendants are still living, are said, with some corroboration, to have been in the habit of roasting and devouring their prisoners, and in time of suffering the weak ones of their own flesh and blood had to give up to afford sustenance for their voracious kinsfolk.

Of late years the native food of the savages has been materially assisted by a liberal contribution of beef, corn-meal, flour, sugar, a little coffee, and a very small allowance of extras. The corn-meal very frequently finds a voracious consumer in a favourite pony. Five days' rations of each of the other articles are generally astonishingly well stowed away in one.

Not always possessed of the convenience of "white man's fire," though the use of lucifers, when to be obtained, is one of the modern innovations, the Indian finds a ready means of producing combustion by a rag soaked in a solution of ashes, (corncob it is said,) and ignited by means of flints, rubbed rapidly against each other, a flint and steel, and frequently by the simple rubbing of two sticks. This, however, is often found a difficult and tedious process.

The culinary utensils of a *wigwam*, it may be imagined, are exceedingly primitive. Skewers of green sticks, hot stones, a battered iron kettle, captured probably in a raiding expedition upon the frontier settlements, spoons made out of buffalo horn, worked into shape by the use of grease and heat, *calabash* cups and bowls, mud vessels of various kinds, stone mortars and pestles, corn-crackers, sheath-knives, which also answers the purpose of scalping, composes the whole list. Roasting is done by embalming the meat in a thick coating of clay mud.

Chapter 29
War

In social matters, the Indian is controlled entirely by motives of convenience or expediency, custom or superstition. The rule, in every phase of intercourse, preserves the same unvarying adherence to old forms. Marriage has no responsibility, except that inspired by terror of the male. The wife is the servant of the husband. To this sphere of degradation the women submit without complaint. In return, the men, apart from the position which custom has given her, show towards the woman, when obedient, a degree of kindness and toleration, which would indicate that their savage natures were capable of some of the softer qualities of the heart.

The young women are no exception to the same class in civilized life. They exert an influence of decided weight over the young men, and, through them, over the entire village, The young warrior dwells with pride upon the smiles of the Indian maiden. In hopes of winning her esteem, he seeks the glories of the war-path; and, enriched by ponies captured, or returning with scalps as the tokens of his bravery, he expects to advance himself in the favour and admiration of the object of his savage love.

The young women laud heroism, and the warrior who has taken the most scalps, captured the most ponies, and has the greatest deeds to recount, is sure to win the heart of any maiden of the village.

The time of marriage, in the woman, is twelve or beyond. The man is at liberty to marry as soon as he can support a wife. The usual form is to ask the mother and father, or, if they are not living, the nearest relative. The maiden, generally, is not consulted until after her parent's consent. If matters are satisfactory, the brother of the young warrior makes a present to the brother of the maiden, if she have a brother, or to the parents. Generally a pony is given to the person thus having the disposition of the maiden, and, when the arrangement is perfected, he sends back a pony with the bride. The ceremony of marriage is completed by transferring the bride to the lodge of the bridegroom. The friends of the family throng around the lodge with presents, and the affair terminates in a general feast. The assertion that the savage secures his squaw by purchase, probably originates in this exchange of presents, at least in regard to the southern tribes. Captive squaws are only to be purchased.

In regard to morality, among themselves, the savages exercise, in many cases, the utmost accountability. Woman, having no position except that voluntarily accorded to her, is often the object of inflexible severity. Infidelity in her marital relations is punishable with the greatest harshness. The usual practice is to clip off the end of the offender's nose, and drive her from the lodge. Instances of the application of this mode of treatment are to be seen in almost all of the wild tribes, but the cases are not common. Sometimes an ear is cut off. In the man, the hair is shorn. It is very rare that human life is sacrificed upon such grounds. Kidnapping another warrior's squaw is an offence which generally results in the death of the offending savage, if caught. When in contact with the whites, such a thing as morality does not exist. Polygamy is a common practice. In times of childbirth, it is the custom, in some of the tribes, to drive the women out of the lodge into the woods, or upon the plain. This is supposed to harden the offspring; or, rather, only the hardy ones are expected to survive such harsh, or literally savage, treatment.

With all his ferocity, the Indian exhibits towards the children of his blood a wonderful degree of attachment. The mutual exchange of parental and filial affection, is probably the most redeeming features of his character. This trait is probably more fully developed than any other, unless it be a thirst for the blood of his enemies.

In speaking on this subject, the savages compare the white man to the buffalo. An old Indian once remarked to the writer, that he "did not like the white man's way. It was like the buffalo. When the calf grew up, he went out into the herd, and forgot his father and mother. White children went away, and were gone for many years, and forgot their parents, like the buffalo. The red man wept when he had no parents, or when he had no children to take care of him when he grew old." Indian parents, I have found, also, make a strong distinction in the treatment of their offspring. The boys, who are to become braves, are never punished, whatever may be their offence. It is considered beneath the pride of even a prospective warrior to subject him to the humiliation of bodily indignity for misconduct. The very young are remarkably tractable, and the older boys, imitating the qualities of the warrior, naturally become as serene and inflexible in their general behaviour as old men.

In regard to names, the savages have peculiar notions. Boys receive theirs, generally, in consequence of some amusing action or characteristic. It is the custom to apply to the young warrior, during his first participation on the war-path, a name suggested by some specialty of bravery or cunning exhibited, by which he will always thereafter be known. For instance, if he creeps up and looks over a hill, and there watches the enemy, he might be called "The Wolf that Looks Over the Hill." Sometimes names are suggested by marked physical peculiarities, and, more frequently, by objects in nature, particularly mountains and the larger animals, such as "Iron Mountain," "Big Buffalo-head," &c.

It also frequently happens, when the young warrior has grown to manhood, and has shown a daring spirit, while the old brave, his father, is no longer strong and active enough to endure the fatigue and exposure of the war-path, the paternal brave gives his name to the son, to perpetuate it and incite an imitation of his example. On such occasions of transfer, the father gives a feast, and gives away a pony. Little Raven, the first, was a warrior greatly distinguished. The father, after giving his own name and the memory of his deeds to his son, the present chief of that cognomen, took the name of "Mares Lodge."

The women are named in recognition of their personal charms or defects—such as "Pretty Face," "Bright Eye," "Wall Eye," "Big Mouth," "Marrow Greese," &c.; and very rarely and only in commemoration of some remarkable act, after animals. The "Young Grass that Shoots in Spring," (Mon-e-setah), was the name of the niece of Black Kettle, the chief of the Cheyennes. This poetical form is often adopted in the families of chiefs and braves of importance.

The council of old men, presided over by the head civil-chief, has the administration of everything of a civil character belonging to the village. On the question of war, the young men are invited to attend and sit in an outer circle, and the war-chief sits with the civil-chief. The young men take no part in the discussion, but have a voice in determining action. It frequently happens that young men will take the war-path without the permission of the council, but this is an act of individual responsibility.

The habits of life of the Indian are such, and his spirit of that restless nature, that he never remains quiet where there is excitement in his path. Naturally, in matters about the village, he is indolent and utterly worthless. The thrilling scenes of the war-path and the chase, seem to alter his entire nature. He now rises to a wonderful degree of energy and resolution. Blood and depredation are irresistible incentives to the most remarkable exhibitions of fortitude and perseverance.

An Indian never makes a present without expecting one in return, consequently among themselves these interchanges of civility do not frequently occur. It would be unnecessary to say, in his tastes, the Indian figures in the lowest sphere of depravity. His life, naturally, creates such a tendency. His love of strong drink is inordinate, and a very small quantity will arouse the most diabolical exhibitions of frenzied and untrammelled passion. He seems, under such influences, to be entirely lost to reason, and dances and shouts like an emissary of the infernal regions. Personal encounters are almost certain, and blood is the only propitiatory sacrifice before the heated brain of the drunken savage.

War and the chase are the two leading occupations of savage life. The war-path is considered the highest use to which the powers of manhood can be applied. It is the way to eminence. The number of reeking scalps, attesting the prowess of the warrior, he exposes himself to every bodily danger, in order to secure these fiendish souvenir's of death by his bloody hand. Taking the war-path is always the occasion of great preliminary ceremony, making medicine, or the formal invocation of the powers of good, always takes place before a tomahawk is raised. This important ceremony is performed by the "medicine men," or doctors of the tribe.

Like the impostors of all other heathen people, they are a very shrewd set, and are well posted in all the arts of delusion, fraud, and deception, A large circular space is marked out with stones. A lodge is erected. In this lodge the "medicine men" take themselves apart from the impious gaze of the rest of the tribe. Here they consult the oracles and go through a series of boisterous performances, chanting a monotonous refrain. If this consultation of the great spirit prove favourable to success, the warriors, awaiting in suspense outside, armed, equipped, and hideously painted, are so informed. The war-dance follows.

War-parties sometimes consist of whole tribes, and more frequently of adventurous young warriors from several tribes, wishing to have an opportunity to murder and pillage, and bring home scalps and ponies, in order to give them character among their fellow-warriors. On these expeditions, a chief, of their own selection, is chosen, and for the time being exercises supreme control. Mounted on his pony and equipped for war, the American savage is the type of martial bearing. His dress is simple. *Moccasins*, sometimes elaborately worked with beads, buck-skin logging, a breech-clout, and on the journey a buffalo robe drawn about his shoulders. On his person are the customary decorations. His beardless face is painted hideously, to suit the infernal and bloody mission he has in view.

On his left arm he carries his raw-hide shield, painted and ornamented with feathers. Over his shoulder and across his back hangs his quiver, filled with arrows, and his bow-case, from one end of which, projecting, may be seen a powerful bow, his spear be carries suspended vertically, by a loop drawn up over the arm and resting on the shoulder, his rifle in his hand, with the necessary accoutrements about his body. His head is bare, his raven hair streaming over his shoulders. Even his pony is decorated with feathers and strips of red flannel plaited in his tail and mane.

In all his expeditions the savage carries little or no supply of food, depending upon the game he may find on the way. In a general war the villages are established at some secluded spot, in a deep *cañon*, or on the banks of a well protected stream. The war-parties then issue forth from this retreat, and commit their depredations unembarrassed by their families.

In their military enterprises the details are governed by the will of the soldiers, and in the fight everyone seems to rely upon his own exertions, without reference to his comrades. From this fact in Indian tactics there is no harmony of action, which gives organized troops a decided superiority. On the war-path they generally ride in single or Indian file. The "medicine arrow," in possession of the first soldier, always goes ahead, the warriors following according to their recognized merits or known deeds. While the main party is pursuing its course *videttes* are thrown out in all directions, scouring the country with a vigilant eye. In camping the most retired spots are selected, fires are built as only an Indian can build them. When the camp is asleep one Indian always remains on watch near the fire.

The most remarkable power exhibited by the plains Indian is their wonderful strength of vision. Their acuteness of hearing always struck me with astonishment, but their faculty of discerning objects at long distances was even more surprising. Whether they reveal the nature of remote figures by their actual outline, or by their peculiar motion, they are at a loss to explain. A still object, darkening the horizon, they contrive to make out as readily as one in motion. They can tell the difference between a buffalo, an Indian, or a soldier, when to an untrained eye they look the same. Our Osage guides, at the head of the column of troops, scanned the country for miles in advance, and reported every figure that appeared, when our own organs of sight were not only unable to see anything, but at first invariably reflected upon Osage veracity.

In their movements, in addition to *videttes*, stationed upon almost every commanding eminence, the savages use a code of signals, which enables them to communicate with each other at long distances. The waving of a buffalo robe, or a quiver, communicates certain actions of the enemy, gives the alarm, directs the course of the main war-party in any direction, halts them, or signifies in what manner they shall move. Smoke by day and fires by night are more intricate and tedious methods resorted to, but with almost equal detail and success. The colour of the smoke, either light or heavy, its volume, the diameter of the column, from a thin thread to a broad dense black mass, are all intelligible to the warrior. The varying brilliancy of a flame can also be interpreted.

The secret of these signals is jealously guarded by every tribe, that the knowledge of their meaning may not escape, and thus be used against them in event of hostility. Their use is indispensable in a country the configuration of which opens long ranges of vision, and in their absence would limit the sphere of warlike operations, or hunting-parties, to a very small scope of territory. In the style of tactics employed, it will be seen, the savages have eminently adapted themselves mainly to the open country they inhabit.

The herd is always divided into two classes of animals, war and squaw-ponies, the latter being also used for carrying burdens. The war-pony is selected from the best stock, is fearless, quick in his movements, and of great strength and endurance. These valuable qualities are recognized by clipping the pony's ears, or otherwise marking him. This being done he is relieved from all other labour than to carry the warrior upon the war-path. A warrior usually has several of these selected animals, one of which, even in time of peace, is always *lariated* near his lodge, ready to be mounted at a moment's notice. These war-ponies are really fine animals, and frequently are very fleet. In action they exhibit remarkable courage, and manoeuvre either to the voice or gesture.

CHAPTER 30

Intellectual Development of the Savage

Following the war-party upon a hostile expedition, we find each warrior not only frequently casting a quick, uneasy glance along the horizon, but also closely observing almost every foot of the ground over which he treads. The track of a pony—the footprint of a *moccasin*—occasions a halt and a minute examination.

In moving forward, preserving the same vigilance, the appearance of the enemy is followed by wild whoops and terrific gesticulations at each other. A desultory firing begins; the warriors, on both sides, dash about, and perform many remarkable feats of horsemanship. In the excitement of the contest, a charge is sometimes made by a few warriors engaging, probably, in single combat. The contest is usually brief. In a majority of cases, one or the other gives way before much harm is done. Occasionally the prestige of one party will be too much for the moral courage of the other, in which case the weaker breaks and runs at first sight.

A favourite mode of tactics is to draw the enemy into an ambuscade. A small party in advance will engage and fall back, apparently discomfited. The pursuing party, intent upon overtaking the fugitives, dash unconsciously onward, until they find themselves confronted by a strong force. Almost instantly a cloud of whooping and yelling savages rise on all sides. The contest now becomes desperate, and the invested party must fight its way out, or expect to meet the almost inevitable fate of disaster. In all cases, it may fairly be said, as the exceptions are so rare, prisoners find no quarter. Every mode of torture, if taken alive, is applied to them. To be burnt to death, or punctured liberally with spears and arrows—a part usually enacted by the squaws—is the most ordinary mode.

If pressed, the sufferings of the victims are mitigated by instant death with the tomahawk or bullet. The scalp is the trophy, always necessary to victory. Without scalps, the wonderful stories told by the savage warrior to his admiring squaw and affrighted *papooses*, upon his return to the village, are regarded with incredulity. The scalp is, therefore, absolutely a necessary feature of a successful war-party, by way of a voucher for the bravery of its proprietor. The scalp is carefully preserved, and retained for a certain time, when it is deposited in the "medicine lodge."

The mutilation of dead bodies, after a fight, is a common practice, and to put an arrow or a bullet into the lifeless form of the victim, is considered "good medicine."

Having triumphed over their enemies, the war-party returns to the village. Their approach is generally announced by a courier sent in advance. The old men, women, and children, gather to witness the arrival. As the warriors get near, they begin to sing and recount their deeds, and discharge volleys from their firearms. Reaching the village, they break up and go to their lodges. The scalps are immediately suspended on poles, and at night the usual practice of firing volleys of bullets or arrows is complied with.

The return of the war-party is followed by the scalp-dance, in all its fiendish finery and discordant noise. The families of warriors killed, nightly chant a requiem for the dead. The most marvellous stories, supported by a scalp or two, are now listened to with interest by all the members of the village. Each tries to outdo his comrade, in an effective narration of remarkable performances, until even the credulous squaw is slow to believe. Boasting is a characteristic eminently belonging to the red-man. Even a defeated war-party, returning, has its own story, and the lucky possession of a selection from the *pate* of an enemy is sufficient ground upon which to make a great victory. If Indian stories were to be believed, a defeat would never be heard of. Even the warriors lost in a disastrous conflict would be accounted for, and immortalized in legend.

The natural intellectual force of the Indian has evinced itself on so many occasions during the several centuries of contact with the whites, that the question can hardly be considered worthy of controversy. The speeches uttered by the more brilliant minds of the race, are master-pieces of feeling and oratorical effect. The American Indian is by nature an orator. The wild independence of his spirit is conducive to that lively flight of mental vision, which resolves itself into ideas and images, burning with the warmth of eloquence.

On all ceremonies of a public or private nature, great state and formal proceedings is observed. The chief, presiding in the council, the head men and braves of the tribe, each speak in turn until all, having a desire, have expressed their views. This form of procedure is eminently adapted to the development of the power of expression and persuasion, for in every case the action of the tribe is influenced more or less by the effect of the speeches of the warriors.

The Indian, away from his family and his native hunting- grounds, appears as a dignified, repulsive being, constantly contemplating some horrible scheme of massacre. There are times when the expression of his face and his rigidity of manner are inflexible. There are moments, also, when he relaxes. With the warriors of the village he often tells his stories, jokes, laughs, and smokes, with as light a heart as a country wag.

The languages of the five wild tribes are entirely different from each other, though in some there is a resemblance with the dialects of a few of the northern and north-western tribes. For instance, the Arrapahoes and the Gros Ventres family of Sioux speak about the same language, evidently emanating from the same parent stock. The Black Feet also speak the same language. The Comanches and Snake Indians can converse with each other. The Comanche is also very much adulterated with Mexican-Spanish. The Kiowa tongue does not show any particular affinity with any of the other languages, and those people seem to have forgotten whether they ever could hold verbal intercourse with other tribes. The Kiowa and Sioux speak a different language, or perhaps different dialects of the same language. The two tribes, in early years, were close neighbours.

It is here unnecessary to speak of the dialects of the five wild tribes, philologically. Indeed, such an undertaking would prove almost a hopeless task. Having no literature, the language of the red man is subject to constant change, corruption, and adulteration. In this respect, we see no more forcible example than in the dialects of the southern tribes, that for years past have been in frequent contact with the Mexican. The majority of sentences appear to have no regular form of construction. Words, in many instances, are arbitrary sounds. In their speeches, however, the warriors of oratorical power show a delicate sensibility of figure and strong force of expression. They speak more from objects in nature than from absolute metaphysical forms and reasoning. The language is mainly guttural. Some of the sounds, however, are mellow and smooth.

The infinite variety of dialects which exist, it would naturally be supposed, would prevent or at least obstruct intercourse. Appreciating this inconvenience, and frequently thrown together through a community of interest and friendship, the plains tribes have, by long practice, instituted a language of signs which enables them to communicate with each other with ease and rapidity. This sign language is the most remarkable of all the peculiarities of these strange people. It would seem to be a development of their system of signals for personal intercourse. So widely diffused are these signs, that a Sioux, from the remote banks of the Yellowstone, can communicate with the Comanche of the Pecos and the Red.

Each tribe, to begin with, has its name in sign. A Comanche Indian, for instance, marks out with his finger the movements of a snake, that being the sign of his people on account of the stealth they practice towards their enemies. A Sioux draws his first finger across his throat, meaning that he belongs to the cut-throat tribe, a civility shown to his dead enemies. The Cheyenne draws his hand across his arm, as if cutting it, meaning "to scarify," a common practice with his tribe. The Kiowa makes a peculiar undulating motion of the hand, meaning the prairie tribe, and the Arrapahoe rubs his first finger against the side of his nose, meaning the cut-nose tribe. The Apache, (Lipan), designates himself by a downward motion of the hand, meaning the "poor" band.

A journey is represented by a sort of galloping motion of the hand, and its length by resting the side of the head in the palm of the right hand, repeating that motion for each day, that is so many sleeps, about fifteen miles constituting a sleep or day's journey. A chief indicates the fact of his rank by passing his hand, palm downward, over his head in a curve line towards his back. Each chief has a high opinion of the altitude of his own greatness, and enjoys very much communicating the fact to everyone he presumes not cognizant of the fact. It is amusing to observe the display of egotism. The chief, in signifying his rank, invariably describes a curve so tremendous that he raises on his toes in the effort. By this they mean to convey that they are very big chiefs, and none can compare with them.

Two Indians, approaching from opposite directions, if not certain as to each other, go through this form The first Indian raises his hand, palm front, and moves it backwards and forwards, meaning to halt. If the second Indian be not hostile, the signal will be obeyed. The right hand is again raised as before, and moved towards the right and left, signifying "who are you." If a friend, the other Indian will raise both hands and grasp them as in shaking. If hostile, the second Indian disregards the overtures of the first.

CHAPTER 31

Traditions

Though without any written language, I found among a the plains tribes a rude system of hieroglyphics, by which the leading events in their history were recorded. In the village of Black Kettle quite a voluminous account of the warlike performances of that chieftain and his warriors was taken. It was drawn in an old day-book, which evidently had been captured. A number of leaves were missing, which previously contained, quite likely, the business transactions of some luckless trader of the plains The drawings were designed to represent a war-party. The soldiers of the white man were in wagons, drawn by mules. The coloured troops were indeed quite artistically coloured, evidently with a burnt stick. The chiefs were represented in most desperate encounters. One had as many as two soldiers impaled on the end of his spear, and had hewn down several others with his battle-axe.

The chiefs were portrayed with immense rows of feathers trailing over their heads and down their backs. They were also highly illuminated in person and attire, vermilion and blue predominating. This book is a valuable Indian curiosity. The writer is in possession of a fine buffalo robe ornamented with picture painting by Satanta and Lone Wolf, chiefs of the Kiowas. The figures represent the encounters of those two worthies with the Utes and Navajoe tribes. Under the circumstances they probably considered the subject of their biographical sketches had better turn to a less direct subject than to killing soldiers. This painting cost the writer a pound of vermilion alone. The elegantly burnished physiognomies of Satanta and Lone Wolf, and their friends, during the production of this work of genius, suggested that the eminent artists did not forget the favourable opportunity of a lavish application of art to their own hides.

All the tribes have their own traditions, relating to their origin, the land of their forefathers, and accounts of heroism displayed at different times in war. They also have a number of fables, in which there is a marked resemblance to our own Æsop. It is also strange that the word "*æsop*," in Comanche, means "to lie." Our own fable of the greedy dog with the meat crossing: the stream is also known to them, with the exception that the dog in their case is a wildcat. Whether these fables are of their own origin, or have been communicated by other tribes, is a mystery.

The plains Indians, with the earliest progenitors of their race, recognize the existence of a Great Spirit. They also show great reverence for the sun, the moon, and the stars. Every time he fills his pipe the savage blows the first smoke towards the sun as an offering to the Great Spirit, and as an invocation that he may protect him. The earth also comes in for a share of devotion. Any remarkable occurrence in nature is a subject of superstitious awe. An eclipse of the moon is an occasion of universal uproar, shouting, and jumping, and demonstration in the direction of the obscured luminary, to drive away the evil spirit taking away its light. When the shadow begins to recede fear changes into joy, and a general jollification, in a savage way, terminates the suspense.

Religious superstition also teaches him that the earth is a great plain, and that there is a jumping-off place. When he dies he goes west. A horse is strangled over the grave of the deceased that he may mount the spirit of the animal and the quicker make his journey to the land of the happy hunting-ground. His weapons, and some food, are buried with him, to serve him on the journey, which is long or short, in proportion to the good favour incurred of the Good Spirit when alive.

When a Comanche dies he is generally buried in a sitting posture on the top of a high hill. The usual practice, however, with the plains tribes is to place the bodies in the branches of trees, when convenient, to prevent them from filling a prey to the wolf. Where there are no trees a high scaffolding is built, and the body is placed upon that. It is customary with some of the tribes to burn the bodies of "medicine men."

An Indian burial case, found by Surgeon Sternburg during the campaign, consisted of a cradle of interlaced branches of white willow, with a bottom of buffalo thongs, woven in an open manner. The cradle was wrapped in two buffalo robes of large size. Within these was an aperture eighteen inches square, about the middle of the cradle. Within this there were other robes, held together by coloured bands.

Five robes and five blankets were used in this species of embalming. The immediate covering of the corpse consisted of three robes, with hoods very richly ornamented with bead-work, and spherical brass bells. The remains lay upon a mat, the head resting upon a pillow of rags, in which were a bag of red paint and antelope-skin straps. A beaver cap, ornamented, was on the head, and about the neck were *wampum* necklaces. The body was elaborately dressed in fall Indian attire.

Among their lower classes less pomp of burial is practised. A buffalo robe, or a blanket, wrapped around the body suffices for the poor and humble.

There are frequent occasions of public or private ceremony scrupulously observed by every tribe. The process of mourning is one of the greatest formality and noisy grief. At the grave of a warrior his own and a committee of sympathizing squaws will gather at nightfall and chant their hymns for the dead. The mournful sound, which they only acquire by practice, borne upon the solitude of the night air, is most doleful. The bereaved squaw cuts off her hair for her warrior, and until it grows she is obliged to keep her widowhood. She also makes the same recognition of the demise of a grown relative. If she loses a child, the mother squaw cuts off a joint of a finger. Were her offspring as numerous as among some other nations, digits would soon be in demand. The men in mourning cut off their hair, and discard all paint and ornaments for a certain period.

Each tribe has many dances exclusively its own. Dances of a propitiatory nature, and dances of thanksgiving, are common to all the plains tribes. The great "medicine dance" precedes all great undertakings, particularly of war. The drumming and antics of the "medicine men" disturb the last hours of the sick in a vain and ignorant effort to exorcise the evil spirit of disease. There is also the sick deer dance, the beaver dance, the buffalo dance, and the virgin dance. In the latter the men seat themselves in a circle. Any virgin is allowed to enter the circle, but it is death to those who venture within and are charged as unclean.

The musical talent displayed on these occasions consists of a sort of lugubrious cadence, shouted in unison. There are a few songs which are generally known. One that the writer heard translated reads, "*The moon lives a little while and then dies. The sun never dies.*"

The following is sung by a little girl, the tribe seated around.

There are the bones of our fathers, in another season they are white with the winds, hurry up and do all you can because your bones will soon be lying there too.

Those listening sing in return:

This talk is so, we follow the road of our fathers.

Although the Indian is considered always in a brown study, hatching mischief, he gives thought also to amusement. This is particularly the case with the young men. Racing is naturally a popular sport. Tribes wager against tribes, and the greatest excitement prevails. Buffalo robes, arrows or other articles of a similar nature, are freely put up. The fleetest animal in either tribe is selected, and a suitable course on the plain near the village is marked out. The horses are brought upon the ground. On each is an Indian boy of about twelve years of age, perfectly naked. The horses are without saddle or bridle. At the given signal, the horses start. It is a wild sight.

The horses and riders bounding along with the wind, the eager warriors of the rival tribes seated upon their war-ponies, and in full costume, lining the course on either side. When once started, the race becomes a promiscuous affair. Warriors will try the mettle of each other's ponies. Small groups thus dashing in all directions, perform some extraordinary feats of horsemanship. The race usually terminates in a kind of rude steeple chase, in which the whole number of warriors present by tribes array themselves in opposition. Such a spectacle is exceedingly fine. A hundred or more gaily caparisoned and inimitable horsemen generally compose this general race. Each party whoops and yells terrifically, some firing their pistols in the air.

The other amusements of the Indian, are such exercises as jumping, running, and wrestling, all calculated to give strength to the body. Gambling is a great vice, and all games of chances are eagerly taken up. Arrows generally constitute the prize played for, but sometimes robes and even ponies are put up and lost or won.

It is a singular fact that, notwithstanding their frequent contact with the trader, the Indian of the plains, and it is the same with the majority of the race elsewhere, have no conception whatever of the value or uses of money. If an Indian sees an article which he covets, his first question is "you swap?" You can then make up your mind that he will pay an exorbitant price in robes, ponies, or anything else he may have. Having once determined to have a thing, he is not backward about exchanging handsomely for it. On the other hand, he is equally as fixed in holding on to a thing he desires for his own use. The most extravagant bid will not move him at such times. Indian wealth consists in ponies. In the accumulation of this species of riches, he will assume every risk and encounter every danger and toil.

In all transactions, the medium of exchange is ponies. A fine lodge, or wigwam, is valued at eight to twelve ponies; a less number for one of inferior workmanship and finish. From eight to fifty arrows are worth a good pony, and so for other necessary or useful articles. Arrows are also used, in many cases, in smaller transactions. *Wampum* is often met with as ornaments in necklaces, but is never used in exchange as a regular medium.

In dealings with the trader, the Indian—the squaw, particularly—is susceptible of the soothing influence of sweet things. Sugar and molasses arc held in great esteem. A squaw having a fine robe, worth at least ten dollars, will part with it for ten or fifteen cups of coarse brown sugar, worth, probably, from two to three dollars. I once offered to the daughter of an Arrapahoe chief, as much on account of her beauty, perhaps, as of the beautiful specimen of her handiwork, two, and then three, dollars for a paint-pouch which she had made. She refused, but subsequently accepted five cups of brown sugar, worth about seventy cents.

In dealing with an Indian, it is certain he will never be satisfied with the bargain agreed upon, so that it is always a measure of prudence and foresight to strike the bargain low, and then raise on a fair margin. I remember, at one time, a very fine and powerful bow was offered me by a squaw for a red blanket I possessed. A warrior, who was riding with her, probably her husband, sang out, with great emphasis, "*how!*"

I replied, "how."

"You swap?" said the warrior, taking hold of the corner of the blanket, and pointing to the squaw.

I looked inquiringly. He pulled his bow out of the case, and, handing it over, again began pulling at the blanket. As I was anxious to secure a good bow, I made the exchange. The next day the warrior and his squaw appeared in front of my tent. After loitering about for some hours, occasionally poking their heads into the tent, and performing certain pantomimic gestures, all of which I could not comprehend, the interpreter explained to me that the squaw said she had given me a bow for a blanket, and now wanted something to make the bargain good. I at once sweetened her temper with a few cups of sugar. She left delighted with my liberality.

Besides eating it in enormous quantities, or sprinkling it in a mild decoction distilled from a few stray grains of coffee gathered at the garrison, sugar is also used as a preservative. By a peculiar process of applying it, they manage to keep buffalo-meat for a long time.

In every band there are those who are skilful workmen in the manufacture of implements and war-weapons. These are generally old men, whose days of war are over. In many cases, also, the squaws are very expert, and vie with the men in the character of their work.

The shield is made of a piece of rawhide, very thick, taken from the shoulder of the buffalo. By way of ornament, after being cut in a circular form, the surface to be presented to the arrows of the enemy is covered with buckskin, which has generally, in the centre, a rude drawing of an animal, A loop on the inside serves for carrying the shield, and handling it as a means of defence. Bows are made of various materials, but principally of *bois d'arc* or Osage orange; hickory, cedar, and several other woods are used, but only in the absence of the Osage orange. The more powerful bows are reinforced with sinews, which not only add strength, but the elasticity and spring are greatly increased. Bows made of elk-horn are curious and often met with. They are greatly appreciated. The bowstring is made from the gut of the wild cat, if it can be procured.

In the making of arrows, the greatest taste is displayed. By certain marks—either a groove along the shaft or the arrangement of the feathers—arrows can be distinguished from each other by tribes. The arrows are principally made of wild-cherry. The blade is made of flint, or a piece of strap-iron, cut in the proper shape, polished, and sharpened on a whetstone, and fastened to the shaft by one end being inserted in a notch, and secured by a sinew. Crow and turkey feathers are chiefly employed for ornament and to direct the flight. The eagle feather is held in too high esteem for this purpose—that bird being the emblem of dignity. Eagle feathers are always used in the war-bonnet. The war-club has now almost been abandoned. The pipes are made of red stone, with stems of ash, or some hard wood, with a hole burned through.

The traveller on the plains often meets with cairns upon the summit of hills—large stones arranged in peculiar forms—and pits of singular fashion. Aside from these and the great medicine-lodge, the progenitors of the wild tribes of the plains have lived, killed the buffalo, scalped their fallen foe, and set out upon the spirit of a horse for the happy hunting-ground, without leaving a trace of their existence. No curious remains, as encountered in the early seats of the Creeks, in the south, or the Delawares and the Shawnees, in the valleys of the Scioto and Muskingum, are to be found. Like the Beduin of the desert, upon his fleet steed the American savage has galloped over the plains, from the Missouri to the Rocky Mountains, without fixed haunts, or a solitary spot which he might claim as particularly his own. The antiquarian will search in vain for the monuments of this vanishing race. That this people ever existed, will, in a few brief years, be known only from the page of history!

Chapter 32

An Exploring Expedition to the Witchita Mountains

Although Fort Cobb occupied a central position in the favourite winter resort of the wild tribes, Sheridan had determined to abandon the post as soon as a more convenient one could be found. With this view he sent out a small expedition in the direction of the Witchita Mountains to make an exploration of that wild section. On the evening of December 27, I was informed of the proposed expedition and received an invitation to join the party to leave on the following morning. Although the temperature was not of a character to inspire much ardour in the line of exploration and adventure, I accepted the invitation quite cheerfully. The packing of our establishment in front of headquarters created unusual mirth the next morning as a preliminary of our departure. Our mule, following the example of his progenitors, particularly in the male line, had a will of his own, and on this occasion he took care to use it.

Three stalwart troopers, accordingly undertook to manage the animal, regardless of his views to the contrary. The exercises of the long-eared and agile quadruped were remarkable and ludicrous. Human ingenuity, however, triumphed. A blind was put over the animal's eyes. Unable to direct his efforts, his muleship suddenly became quite tractable. After the tent-fly and blankets were carefully adjusted, the load was finished off by a superstructure in the shape of a champagne basket stocked with ham and hard-tack. By means of straps and ropes the cargo was securely fastened. The mule being laden, the covering over his eyes was removed. The moment the animal observed the transformation which had taken place during the temporary obstruction of vision, he promptly renewed his physical demonstrations amid the orchestral rattle of pots and kettles dangling about his form, with more regard to convenience than beauty. After this prefatory flourish, the animal made several violent dashes in advance, at the same time indulging in that resolute manoeuvre known as "bucking." But the cargo was immovable.

It was nearly nine o'clock in the morning when we parted with the Commanding General and his staff, and a few friends of the seventh, who had come to see us off. Our transportation was put in charge of an orderly, who firmly held one end of a cable while the mule had possession of the other. Our departure was not characterized by any solemn ceremonies, but had decidedly the cast of a farce. When released from his mooring, his muleship again seized the opportunity to renew his performances, which was ably done amid the laughter and shouts of every one. The mule planted himself suddenly, as if deter- mined not to proceed an inch farther. A sentinel, nearby, probed him with the point of his sabre. This unexpected demonstration had a wonderful effect. After a few more sudden pauses for contemplation of himself and reflections upon the situation, the mule finally yielded and went of expeditiously down the bank of the river, the trooper after him at a full gallop with orders to keep in motion.

Having the mule off our hands we joined the rest of the expedition at the headquarters of General Grierson. Here an escort of forty cavalry of the Tenth, commanded by Lieutenant Doyle, were drawn up in line waiting orders to move. Our party, consisting of Generals Grierson, Hazen, and Forsyth, Major Woodward, Captain Clous, and the writer, set out with the escort, moving down the north bank of the Washita. On the way we were joined by McCusker, the interpreter, and Essetoyeh, our Indian guide, and his squaw. After passing the entire length of the Peneteghtka and Kiowa camps, which lay in the valley, we crossed the Washita, pursuing the course of a narrow *cañon* which led to the "divide." The day was delightful. The sky was clear and the air bracing. In advance. a distance of several hundred yards, rode Essetoyeh upon a sorrel Indian war-steed of remarkable beauty, and celebrated for his speed.

Our guide scanned the horizon with all the vigilance and suspicion of his race, and frequently dashed to some neighbouring eminence to catch a more extended view of the surrounding plain. The old savage sported a puritanical felt, such as the infantry wear in the army, with the amendment of a broad tin band around the crown and several streamers of red flannel. The rest of his dress was composed of an assortment of articles of apparel, buckskin leggins, moccasins, breech-clout, an infantry blouse, with a red shirt on the outside, a cavalry overcoat, and a buffalo robe. The squaw followed her master to all his evolutions, always a few paces at his heels. She was perched high up in the air, astride a pyramid of rations in a gunny sack. Essetoyeh evidently anticipated some fine hunting, and he brought his squaw with him to dress the meat, to prepare his food, and build for him a shelter of branches to sleep under at night. The rest of our little party followed the guide keeping along in compact order to be ready to repel any attack.

The country over which we passed during the day was high and rolling, with a greater frequency of running streams, and more timber. In every ravine herds of antelope and deer started in our path, and a few good shots did not fail to secure for the whole party a fine repast. Several small herds of buffalo were seen in the distance, but set off at a gallop as soon as they noticed our approach. At three o'clock in the afternoon we reached a small running stream, with a pebbly bottom. Here it was resolved to pass the night. For protection, as well as convenience of wood and water, we selected a deep *cañon*, backed by the creek, and by high rocky bluffs.

Here the pack-animals were unloaded, and the horses unsaddled, and *lariated* in the broad valley, which swept away for a distance of several hundred yards from the abrupt sides of the narrow gorge. The valley was covered with a thick young growth, protected from the wintry frosts by the dead grass which covered the plain. My Indian pony evidently had indulged in this kind of feast before, and went rooting about with his lips, exposing the fresh green vegetation. Here was a paradise for our animals. After the inadequate supply of food it was assuredly the most gratifying experience of the day to see them enjoying themselves.

The surroundings of our camp had the appearance of a fine place for game, and everywhere we discovered indications that our opinion was correct. As we went into camp a beautiful herd of deer started from the open space near the stream, and darted into the bushes. A small drove of buffalo had just passed over the hill.

As soon as we had designated the site for the camp Essetoyeh, leaving his squaw to look after his comfort for the night, accompanied by several troopers, set out on a hunt.

In the course of an hour our little camp was established, tent-flies spread, fires built and blazing cheerfully, water boiling, provision baskets were overhauled, and preparations were made generally to perform the important and interesting duty of laying in a supply of provender. On this occasion everybody was his own cook. We sat around the fire, each fortified with a skewer, made of a green stick, sharpened at the opposite extremity, on which was impaled inviting strips of buffalo meat, deer, and salt pork. The reader may smile, and say a delightful combination. Hazen, who was somewhat of a connoisseur in camp cooking, had provided himself with a patent broiling-machine, the merits of which were so marked that the general soon found himself quite busy in preparing and distributing specimens of his skill.

Having laid in an enormous quantity of "broiled," pickles, and hard-tack, tin cups were unstrapped and filled with a dense black fluid, in which were huge particles of coffee floating about. The beverage had, at least, the recommendation of strength. With the accession of a camp biscuit, by way of dessert, several gallons of the mollifying stimulant passed out of sight almost imperceptibly, and with little effort.

This exercise wound up the labours of the day. Pipes were smoked, filled, and smoked again. As the potent influence of sleep began to draw about exhausted nature, one by one, we rolled into our blankets, and amid a chorus of snores the night quickly sped away. The lonely sentinel paced his beat. Everything was quiet and undisturbed until the following dawn, when the unwelcome reveille awoke us from our slumbers.

The next morning we early broke camp, and were again on the march. The day was cloudy, and rain momentarily threatened. The air was chilly and dense with dampness. We were now approaching the Witchita range, so as to obtain a closer view of its general outlines. The summits of the higher peaks were veiled in a drapery of mist. The rugged sides, the immense boulders towering aloft, or bending over in giddy precipices, could be well defined with the aid of our glasses. The country was more bold and rocky. The timber was heavier, and grew in extensive belts at the base of the mountains, while their sides were perfectly bare.

At eleven o'clock in the morning, we reached Medicine Bluff. Our Indian guide contemplated this wonderful exhibition of nature with awe and reverence. To the interpreter he said, pointing to the conical summit of the central elevation, "there the great spirit sometimes dwells—there the Comanche goes to drive out the bad spirit." As for ourselves we were wonder struck with the sublimity and magnificence of the scene. The bluff was a mile in length, forming a perfect crescent. At the base of the perpendicular scarp, which constituted the concavity of the crescent, coursed a beautiful stream about twenty yards in width, called Medicine Bluff Creek. In some places the creek seemed bottomless, so that looking into its crystal waters, it had the appearance of a basin of ink, and again pursuing its way in more shallow spots became pure and sparkling.

From the very brink of the creek rose the vertical sides of the bluff three hundred and ten feet in height by actual measurement. The sides had the appearance of a trap-rock, and the *strata* stood almost perpendicularly. At the central and highest point, the *strata* met, separating in the descent. The surface of this face of the bluff was regular and perfectly smooth. A minute species of moss covered the sides with a garb of pale green, which might easily have been mistaken for the rock. By far the larger portions of the face was perfectly bare, though at some places a few stunted cedars had found a lodgement in the crevices. On the opposite side of the creek, in several places, the banks were forty and fifty feet high, rocky, and overhung the stream; but they were, however, mostly low, stretching off into an alluvial plain.

From this side, we amused ourselves by firing several shots at the rocky wall. The detonations were echoed up and down the valley with surprising effect, and alarmed a herd of deer which had come down to drink. The timid animals were now bounding over the plain terrified at such strange sounds.

Medicine Bluff was, unquestionably, the result of upheaval, though an earthquake alone could have detached it from the adjacent rocks. It was remarkable also that the pressure should have applied itself to so small an area. The face of the bluff rose at once from an immense fissure, now the bed of Medicine Bluff Creek.

Leaving our escort in the *cañon* in the rear of the bluff, and taking with us a few orderlies, we rode as far up as the steep ascent permitted, and then also dismounted making the rest of the laborious journey on foot. The Indian guide Essetoyeh when asked to ascend with us to point out and explain the country, merely observed "me no sick" and obstinately refused to go to the top, but galloped off in pursuit of game.

From the rear the bluff presented three knolls, the centre one being the highest. The steep sides were composed of small fragments of rock, indicating that at one time they were made up of boulders. The disintegration, however, was of a character to admit of the growth of large quantities of bunch grass, and a peculiar variety of flowering cactus.

This plant consisted of one, two, and sometimes eight or ten buds, an inch or two in diameter, and flattened on the top. The buds clustered upon a single root, were covered with a heavy mail of spines, and were not to be touched with impunity. The flower was of a purple tint, and formed a tuft in the centre of the ball. Some very fine specimens were collected by our party.

Having reached the central knoll, the view was extremely grand. The course of the Medicine Bluff Creek could be traced, wending its way from the mountains, across the intervening valley, and away down the broad expanse in our rear. Mount Scott, about eight miles distant, stood before us with its pyramidal outline. Clouds swept by its rocky summit. It stood like a sentinel guarding the eastern gate to the mountain range. The country on either side changed suddenly into a rolling plain. Between us and the mountain swept a great valley, A small herd of buffaloes were grazing in a perfect sense of security upon the sides of a small spur of the range. Everything else was without life, and a profound solemn stillness reigned. From our commanding position we looked around upon the face of nature untouched by the hand of art, the very air was pervaded by that profound reverential solitude which, on such occasions, touches the soul with a deep sense of the divinity of creation.

Turning from the view towards the mountains, the eye rested upon a broad valley. Indeed, so extensive, that were it not completely surrounded by a range of low bills, it might have been taken for an endless plain. On the right a belt of timber defined the course of Cache Creek, which about two miles from us united with the Medicine Bluff Creek, the latter then losing its name.

CHAPTER 33

Legends of Medicine Bluff

Medicine Bluff, I afterwards learned, figured prominently in Indian history, superstitions, and tradition. The bluff, from time immemorial, had been held in high reverence by all the tribes who had dwelt or hunted in the vicinity, and by none more so than by the Comanches and the Witchitas. The hill was considered to possess miraculous and mysterious influences. There the Great Spirit often descended, and from the bluff looked over and cared for his people, saw that game was abundant, and that his children were prosperous and happy. Upon the summit of the principal knoll, the Comanche medicine men had erected a cairn of stones about six feet in height. Here the sick repaired, or were brought by their relatives or friends, and were left to the invisible presence and subtle power of the Great Father.

It was told me by an aged medicine man, and with a manner of unflinching confidence in the veracity of what he had to say, that the sick, who were beyond the control of their own powers of healing, were deposited on the cairn and left to be disposed of by the Great Spirit. If the sick had not offended the Spirit they were suddenly healed and returned to their kindred. Sometimes they were transported bodily to the happy hunting-ground. But if they had been notoriously bad, they were allowed to die, and the ravens descended from the air, and the wolf came up from the valley and devoured the body, and the bones were gathered up by the bad spirit and deposited in the land of terrors.

He went on with great vehemence, and in proportion as I appeared to manifest greater belief, he embellished his story with details. In a tone of seriousness and reverence, he said in substance, that in the darkness the Great Spirit descended upon the hill. Upon such occasions the immediate vicinity became suddenly lit up as if by a great fire. The dews of night, the rain and the wind circled about the spot, but within the small space on the very summit, none of these agencies of nature trespassed, and the patient was thus protected better than if sheltered by his *wigwam*.

The old doctor narrated some remarkable cases which he said he knew. One, for instance, of an old warrior, who had long lived among the women of the village. He had long ceased to hunt the buffalo, and had turned out to await his time to join his fathers. The old warrior had struggled to the top of the bluff to die, and be borne away by the Great Spirit. He had been absent three nights. Every night when darkness covered the face of nature, the awe-stricken people of the village below observed a great blaze, as if a signal-fire had been built to alarm them. On the morning after the third night, a young man, equipped as a warrior, was seen descending the bluff, and followed the trail to the village. He looked about him with surprise. He approached the chief's lodge and sat by the fire. The warriors; with their arms, gathered around, gazed at him. No one recognized him.

All remained silent, expecting him to speak. Lighting his pipe, decorated with beads and the feathers of strange birds, he handed it to those present, and each having partaken of the pipe, he told them his story. When he had reached the top of the hill he looked off upon the vast expanse which surrounded him, he saw the village of his people. He could hear the children laugh, the dogs bark, he could hear his kindred mourning, as if someone had been taken from them. He saw the buffalo and the deer covering the plain. He saw the sly wolf lying in wait to pounce upon his prey.

When he looked around and beheld the young warriors in all their pride and strength, he asked himself, "Why do I live any longer? My fires have gone out. I must follow my fathers. The world is beautiful to the young, but to the old it has no pleasure. Far away to the setting sun are the hunting-grounds of my people, I will go there." With this he gathered up all that remained of his failing strength, and leaped into the air from the giddy height before him. He knew no more of the woes of life. He was caught up in midair. He was transported into a smiling country where game was without numbers, where there was no rain, no wind, where the great chiefs of all the Comanches were assembled. They were all young and chased the buffalo and feasted. There was no darkness, but the Great Spirit was everywhere, and his people were continually happy. Beautiful birds warbled upon the trees, the war-whoop never penetrated those sacred realms.

The superstition and credulity of the savage was captivated, and the young warrior at once became an oracle and a "big medicine man" in the tribe. His counsel was all-powerful, and his abilities to cure were considered invincible. The merits of the aged warrior were recounted for the imitation of the young and his rejuvenated successor was feared and obeyed.

The ancient customs of late years, it appears, have been in a great measure abandoned. The tribes have become scattered since the rapid depletion of the buffalo. But the reverence for the bluff is still fresh. The Comanche will not ascend the hill, and during frequent visits while in the vicinity, I must admit, I never saw an Indian make the ascent.

According to accounts, the bluff has also long been a famous place for suicides. The disappointed and the disconsolate have resorted thither to terminate their miserable existences. I was also told that, until very late years, it was a Comanche custom that when a young warrior was about to take the war-path for the first time, he provided himself with a shield and proceeded to the highest point of the bluff for three successive mornings, and in the attitude of warding off an arrow or a spear, presented the face of the shield to the rising sun. The sacred surroundings of the place, and the sun, the emblem of the Great Spirit, casting its rays upon the shield, were supposed to possess it with supernatural powers of invulnerability.

An interesting tradition was told me one day, while sitting by the lodge-fire, of a very old Comanche. Indeed, he was so old that he said that he was the brother of one of the loftier peaks of the Witchitas. I certainly admitted his veracity and set him down as emphatically aboriginal. Many years ago, he said, the Comanches were a great people, their warriors were like the buffaloes, so numerous, and like the wolf, so cunning. They had immense herds of ponies and many villages. Everybody feared them. But there were two warriors, braver than all the rest. They vied with each other in courting the dangers of the war-path and winning the scalps of their enemies. They were rivals in the hunt. They tried the strength and agility of each other in the village games. The warriors obeyed them alike. The children held them in equal awe, and the women coveted alike their favour. This equality was keenly felt by the great warriors, and each made, in consequence, extraordinary efforts to accomplish something which would surpass the other.

One day they were returning from an incursion into the enemy's country. As they rested to graze their ponies under the shadow of Medicine Bluff, one of the warriors, the younger, gazed upon the quivering height. For a moment he was wrapped in deep meditation. Suddenly the young warrior drew himself up at full length, and, turning quickly, in all the pride of confidence, gazed boldly at those who were lounging about on the green grass. His defiant manner startled his comrades. Several sprang to their feet. He explained: "I am the great warrior of the Comanches. No one equals me. I am like the mountain. My deeds tower above you as the mountain does above the plain. Where is the Comanche who dares follow me?"

As he said this, he raised his shield in one hand and his spear in the other. His rival, not to be outdone, approached with majestic tread. "You the great warrior of the Comanches," said he, striking his breast with heavy blows, "then you are the buffalo that leads the herd. I am the old bull buffalo, driven away to die and feed the wolf. You ask me to follow you. I will not follow you—I will go with you!"

All the warriors of the party assembled around. They gazed with wonder upon their stalwart comrades, eager to see what fresh act of courage was contemplated. The rivals arrayed themselves gorgeously. They mounted their favourite war-ponies, which they had decorated with scalps and feathers. The two warriors left their comrades, who were surprised at their singular conduct, and rode away without uttering a word. The party watched them until they disappeared over the adjacent hill. They now gathered in a circle, to talk over the strange scene which they had witnessed.

The rivals crossed the rapid flood of the neighbouring stream. The young warrior now directed his steps towards the sacred summit of Medicine Bluff. When they had reached the highest point, the younger, pointing to the fearful brink not more than fifty feet before him, said to his companion: "You have followed me so far—follow me now!" With these words, he shouted the war-whoop, clapped his heels to his animal's flanks, and plunged towards the precipice. His companion, as quick as thought, fairly lifted his spirited steed from his feet, and, with a responsive yell, planted himself in one of those sublime attitudes calling for desperate resolution, and followed his rival. The edge of the whirling height was reached in a moment. The courage of the young warrior quailed. He reigned his steed upon his haunches.

The elder warrior saw the treachery. He gave a yell of triumph, and bounded off far into the trembling air. The warriors on the plain below heard the terrific yell. They saw their great leader leap from the dreadful height. He sat upright; and, in his fearful descent, was calm as if in council. He shouted, "Greater than all Comanches!"

The warriors beneath hastened to the spot where the fearless warrior and his trusty steed lay. Their mangled forms were conveyed together to a neighbouring hill. Here the solemn rites of burial were performed. All night the wind moaned through the trees. The warriors sat in solemn council, and chanted their songs of mourning. They cut their hair, and smeared their faces in black. In sight of the bluff, the spirits of the warrior and his steed were left, to take their flight to the land of the Great Spirit.

When the war-party reached their village, the old men and the women came out to rejoice. They were met with the wailing of the warriors, and saw their blackened faces. The scene was changed to mourning. The deeds of the dead warrior were spoken. The women nightly gathered in a neighbouring vale to grieve for the loss of the great warrior.

The young warrior wandered from village to village. The very dogs snapped at him. The name of his rival he heard in every *wigwam*—his own was an accursed word with the Comanche. He wandered a stranger in the world, unknown, but inwardly punished. A hunting-party in pursuit of the buffalo, as was the custom, passing in the vicinity to visit the grave of the greatest of the Comanches, found the body of a warrior, half devoured by the wolf. The spear and the shield, and bow and arrows, identified the character of the person when living. The young warrior, disappointed and overcome with remorse, here came to die upon the grave of his rival.

This story was told to a picturesque group of warriors, who had assembled around the lodge-fire, and listened intently.

Story-telling is quite an art with the Indian. It forms an interesting entertainment, and not only perpetuates, probably in an embellished form, some real occurrence, but is calculated to inspire a tribal pride, which is a marked trait in Indian character. At one point in the bluff, about fifty yards towards the right, is an enormous fissure, or, more properly, embrasure, about fifteen feet in width, thirty feet in depth, and at least two hundred and fifty feet from the stream below. In the rear part of the bluff, a small, sharp ravine leads directly up to this opening. The embrasure itself is excessively rugged, its sides being composed of boulders and huge fragments of disintegrated rocks, which look as if they were about ready to fall and crush everything beneath them.

It would seem as if, in the awful convulsion of nature which must have thrown the underlying strata into such an extraordinary position, this, being the weaker part, gave way. In the process of time, this fissure had become filled, leaving but the embrasure described. This would farther appear to be correct, for, in standing in the embrasure and looking down, a sort of groove, filled with broken stones, can be traced to the water's edge. The descent is almost perpendicular, in a direct line, but a few communicating ledges, and apparently winding paths, intersecting this apparent crack, makes it seem as if the descent were feasible.

On one occasion, subsequently, while in camp near the bluff, the writer, with a friend, tried the experiment of a descent. He succeeded in getting down about a hundred feet. The traces of wild animals, wolves especially, had tempted him so far. Here they disappeared, and the further descent was quite cut off. A vertical leap of forty feet extended below. Several rock-slides, occasioned by the displacement of a few stones in the descent, came crushing by and in rather alarming proximity. With considerable effort and danger of losing my footing, I managed to reach the top again quite relieved. This path is known among the Indians as the "Medicine Man's Walk," by means of which, according to tradition, in the darkness of the night, a famous savage doctor, of the necromantic art, passes from a cave in the bluff down to the stream below, or out upon the summit above. Judging from my own experience, the old savage must have been armed with claws.

CHAPTER 34

A Race For Life

Descending the bluff to the point where we had left our horses we rode for a short distance along the hillside, meeting with a variety of springs, saline, sulphur, and chalybeate, all in close contiguity with each other. The saline spring flowed rapidly, though with a small current, and spread over a large basin rock. The spring was evidently the resort of many of the wild animals of the vicinity. Deer and buffalo tracks were numerous. This was a great temptation to pass the night in the vicinity, and take a rare opportunity for still hunting.

Leaving the bluff we joined the escort, and climbing the steep sides of the *cañon* come out again upon the open country. A spirited ride brought us to a high plateau, or swell, in the expansive valley. This was the end of our journey. About a year before General Grierson had passed the spot while on an exploring and scouting expedition towards the head waters of the Red River. This point lay about seventy-five miles from Fort Arbuckle west. The tract consisted of a high level sweep of about two hundred acres. Ten miles distant, west north-west, lay the eastern extremity of the Witchita Mountains.

Medicine Bluff Creek passed on the north-eastern and eastern sides, at the foot of a clay and gravel bluff, about fifty feet in height, and a mile lower down joined Cache Creek. The latter stream is a tributary of the Red River. In the vicinity we found red and yellow sandstone, and an excellent quality of limestone. Oak, cotton-wood, walnut, pecan, ash, elm, hackberry, mulberry, and Osage orange grew in greater abundance than had as yet been seen on the surrounding plain. Buffalo, gamma, and mosquite grasses were met with in great luxuriance, and at the time of our visit, notwithstanding the frequent severe northers, and inclement winter weather, under the lee of the hills the young grass gave quite a green cast to the surface. Game was evidently abundant, including black bear and panther.

Essetoyeh, having declined to ascend Medicine Bluff, had left our party with his squaw, and having cleared the *cañon*, discovered a small herd of buffaloes within four hundred yards of him. He gave pursuit, and after putting several arrows into one of the unfortunate brutes succeeded in bringing him down with his carbine.

When we arrived on the spot the choice parts of the animal had been appropriated by Madam Essetoyeh, and were lying around in heaps on the ground. She was now busily engaged in getting the meat in some sort of a transportable condition, and had already festooned her pony with several yards of hump. The madam having taken her share the escort went to work with busy knives, and in a few minutes a wolf would have turned up his nose at what was left. It was now proposed that we would celebrate the occasion, and honour the locality with a repast, gotten up in true primitive style. The horses were *lariated* on the plateau, and while a guard was left to watch them, and at the same time to look out for Indians, we built fires under the gravel bluff. We commenced broiling small "hunks" of meat in a lively manner. Madam Essetoyeh had set apart a choice portion of the buffalo, broiled it, and now handed it over to us with her compliments. Courtesy prevented our declining to receive the proffered kindness, though we all preferred, under the circumstances, to do our own cooking, and to select our meat.

The dampness of the atmosphere in the morning now more than ever threatened rain. It was proposed, therefore, to set the escort in motion back towards the camp of the previous evening. Our meal was thus abruptly terminated. Grierson, Woodward, and myself were, however, determined to visit some coal veins and bitumen springs known to exist about eight miles farther on. The Indian guide designated the spot to us, so leaving the command to get ready to retrace its steps our little party, with three orderlies, set out on a private tour of exploration.

On the way to the Cache Creek crossing we passed the ruins of an old Witchita village. The Witchitas, according to tradition, were the original owners of the country, and gave names to the different localities. These people, however, under the wear and tear of constant attacks, and a feeling of insecurity at the presence of so many of the warlike tribes, some years before had abandoned the country, and established themselves upon the north bank of the Washita, about forty miles distant. The Witchitas, as far back as tradition speaks of them, either among their own people, or the other tribes, were celebrated as being great deer hunters, and cultivating crops. They seldom went to war, except in defence of their homes. They lived in regular houses, similar in form to an ordinary wigwam, but constructed of thatch and mud, and raised corn, pumpkins, and beans. When I visited the spot the only traces left were heaps of earth, a number of large circular holes, as if the lodges were dug out before the superstructure was put on, and several acres of vines, with bushels of frost-bitten mock-oranges. The whole place was overgrown with these vines.

In the days of their prosperity the Witchitas kept up a brisk trade with the wandering tribes. They bartered corn, and their other agricultural products, for buffalo robes and ponies. All the men did was to hunt for meat, as the improvident habits of the wandering tribes made any dependence on them rather a precarious way of living. The women mostly tilled the soil and raised the crops. The tribe, through various causes, the ambitious young men joining war-parties, and difficulties frequently arising with other tribes, led to trouble. The vast herds of the Witchitas were scattered, and finally the bands themselves were compelled to remove, in order to save what little they had left.

The name Cache is evidently of French origin, the word meaning a hiding place. It must have been applied to the stream by the *voyageurs* in allusion to the custom of the Witchitas to *cache*, or secure in large holes for the purpose, the productions of their labour.

After a ride of nearly two hours we reached a deep *cañon*, in which the traces of coal, with a surrounding of blue clay, were very readily found. An examination indicated that it must exist in considerable quantities deeper in the earth, though that which we handled was too slaty to be of use. The bitumen, however, was less easily to be found. We scoured the summit of several hills before we discovered it. The substance was now quite hard from the cold weather, though it was very apparent that it had oozed through crevices in the earth, owing to a great subterranean pressure. The surface was covered with it in large quantities. An experiment with some small pieces the writer carried to camp with him proved that it was highly flammable.

Having satisfied our curiosity in these explorations, we proceeded to retrace our steps so as to make camp by dark. Instead of following the same route, by which we came out, we headed directly for the trail of the escort, in hopes of intercepting it and following it back. By this time a drizzling rain had begun. Our discomfort was increased by the necessity of crossing numerous streams, and forcing our way through almost impenetrable brakes. By way of a diversion, a steep bank along which we were riding gave way, precipitating Grierson and his horse some twenty feet below. Fortunately they escaped without injury.

The country through which we passed was alive with game. The weather had driven every species of animal life into the sheltered valleys. In several instances we came within a few feet of some stray buffaloes before they discovered us. The number of deer was surprising. Everything surrounding us was in its wildest solitude. The foot of the white man had never trod the soil.

A ride of six miles brought us to the outward trail, but no signs of the return of the party. It could not have been possible that the escort was behind us, and it was not a pleasant thing to suppose that they had been driven out of their path by a body of hostile Indians. We had but one course to pursue. There were but six altogether in our party. We had our arms with us, but no supplies. We got on the trail determined to follow it back to the old camp, and if we found no one there, decided to push, during the night, as best we could towards the Washita.

Darkness soon enveloped us. The impenetrable clouds over head, cast a shadow over the lights of the night, and the rain which was falling, multiplied the discomforts of our situation. The very blackness of darkness reigned. It was impossible to penetrate the terrible gloom. We allowed our animals to take their own course, and kept close to each other by frequently exchanging words. An hour of annoying uncertainty thus prevailed. We scanned the black element in front, in hopes of discovering the friendly light of the camp-fire. We struck the creek. Ascending the bank we were soon relieved by the challenge of the sentinel. A few steps farther on we saw the light of the fires. The rain had now set in harder than ever. Everything in camp was wet, and fires would scarcely burn. Our tent-flies were of little use to us. The rain blew in on all sides. Under these circumstances a supper on hardtack was a luxurious repast, and soon we all threw ourselves upon the ground to pass a wet and cheerless night.

Rain! Rain!! Rain!!! The livelong night the liquid element pattered upon our leaky protection over head. The next morning we found ourselves in several inches of water. The *cañon* in which we had established ourselves, was evidently poorly drained. We were in a sorry plight. Wet to the skin. The animals were jaded, and had not rested at all through the night. It was now necessary to return to the Washita as quickly as possible. Our camp arrangements were gathered and packed upon the animals, and by eight o'clock we left the comfortless spot without regret.

Rising out of the *cañon* we encountered a change of temperature. A fearful "norther" was sweeping over the plain, and the entire face of nature exposed to its force, was covered with a crystal surface. The trees, the high grass, and under growth were covered with ice. The wind and cold rain were directly in our faces. Our animals refused to advance. It required a vigorous belabouring to get them warmed up before they would brave the storm.

We had eight hours ride before us. A trying prospect, wet and half frozen as we were. We ventured to make the attempt, though many were the fears that some would be found missing before we could reach the other end of our journey. There was another danger which the omnipotence of Providence alone could control. That was the element around us. The temperature was now at freezing, and the air began to grow colder. Should the "norther" suddenly change to one of that merciless character often experienced, and so often causing the death of parties, both white man and red, our case was hopeless. It frequently occurs that from a severe rain, a "norther" follows in the course of a few hours, changing the temperature from comparative summer into the depths of winter.

These were our fears. It was known no Indian would leave his lodge such a day as this. The rain fell, and the fierce north wind blew The streams were swollen, and the low grounds flooded. Cold, wet, and numb, each one of our party pushed ahead as best he could. There was no order. Every one now looked out for himself. An animal falling by the wayside, would cost a human being. The temperature was watched with solicitude. Every change was noted, for upon this fickle thread rested our safety.

Late in the afternoon the Washita was reached. The water now flowed in a threatening turbid flood. So near our destination, we were not to be delayed. Away we went, splashing and sinking, and rising, some in the middle of the stream, some heading up, stemming the current, some losing their direction and carried down in the rapid waters. We crossed safely. No one lost. We were now soon in camp, but in a sorry plight, presenting the appearance of a combination of ice, wet, and mud. Reaching camp, the hardships we had endured were more sensible. Swollen hands and feet, painful in the extreme, were the lot of every one. Four of the troopers were unable to dismount. They had to be taken from their horses and sent to the hospital. Several men fainted, overcome with exhaustion. Several horses laid down, never to rise. As for myself, I found It necessary to cut my boots from my feet. With a roaring fire in my tent, I sat for a half hour in the interesting attitude of holding my hands and feet in cold water. Both these extremities felt as if a thousand needles were going through them. An inward application of hot punch and a night rolled up in blankets and buffalo-robes, found me in good spirits the next morning, more than could be said for some days of the majority of our party.

CHAPTER 35

An Unpleasant Predicament

The object of the expedition was satisfactorily accomplished. The Commanding General made up his mind at once to abandon the old camp and establish the troops at the new site, where it was proposed also to erect a permanent post. During the delay, in consequence of the incessant rains which had fallen since our memorable ride, information was received from Indian sources that a column of troopers had suddenly appeared at the western extremity of the Witchitas, about forty miles distant. This column, it was reported, had attacked and destroyed a Comanche village of sixty lodges. At first the report was doubted as a story, fabricated by the Indians around camp. To confirm these rumours, several paid Indian runners and scouts were sent out to communicate with the column, if it existed. All the runners and scouts returned, confirming the Indian stories. It was discovered that this was Evans' column, which had moved out from Fort Bascom, in New Mexico.

Lieutenant Hunter, of the expedition, with an escort, had now arrived at headquarters. Orders were sent out for the column to await supplies on the Washita, thirty miles above. The Commanding General, accompanied by several officers and an escort, rode to Evans' camp. The supplies were also hastened forward, so as to lose no time by delay. Evans left Fort Bascom, the previous November, with six companies of the 3rd Cavalry, one company of the 37th Infantry, Captain Gageby, and four mountain howitzers. Lieutenant Sullivan. December 4, he reached Monument Creek, in the state of Texas, a march of one hundred and eighty-five miles. Here he established a depot of supplies, with a garrison of twenty men, under Captain Carpenter. With his command, Evans now set out in search of Indians. He had not gone far when he struck a trail.

The Lakes—Witchita Mountains

On the twenty-fourth he encountered a hunting-party, which he immediately pursued. The next day, Christmas, he was attacked by a band of warriors, but soon routed them and drove them so precipitately through their village that the women and children had barely time to mount their ponies and flee. In some cases four Indians mounted a single pony. The village was situated at the foot of one of the highest peaks of the Witchitas. Sixty lodges were destroyed, together with five tons of buffalo meat, a hundred bushels of corn, and an abundance of articles of value to the savages. The squaws and children having taken to the mountains, the warriors kept up a lively whooping, and were circling around while the troopers were making short work of their former habitations. Evans again took the trail the next day, but was obliged to withdraw on account of lack of provisions.

The brave troopers had been out twenty-four days in snow and rain, and intensely cold weather, without tent of any kind. They had marched four hundred miles and lost about eighty horses. In the Indian village three men were wounded. This bold dash of so small a body of troops had a decided effect upon the savages, who had retired to the western end of the mountains, in the neighbourhood of the Antelope hills and on the confines of the *Llano Estacado*. A few days after, deputations of chiefs and warriors came in from the Cheyennes and Arrapahoes, to see what the big white chief "wanted."

Orders were given to Evans to scour the country towards the headwaters of the Red and to return to Bascom. Probably never were the occupants of that wild and unexplored region thrown into greater consternation. Afterwards it was learned that a delegation of Comanches went to Bascom immediately after Evans' attack, and wished to surrender. They were in the wildest fright, declaring that, to the eastward, the warriors of the Great Father Washington were as numerous as the trees of the forest.

A large amount of annuity goods, due to the tribes, according to the old "treaties" with the government, having been accumulated at Fort Cobb, orders were sent to the villages that a distribution would take place at a certain time. Early in the morning the warriors, with their families, gathered in. It was the day for the issue of annuities to the Peneteghtka Comanches. The squaws, with their *papooses* and dogs, seated themselves in a semi-circle in front of the goods, which had been tossed from under a tarpaulin warehouse. The warriors of the band sat in a body opposite to the semi-circle. The civil and war-chiefs, and one of the head warriors, were within the circle and had the active part of the distribution in charge. A number of officers of the garrison had also assembled. The goods consisted of the following articles for males: a suit of black shoddy clothes, price paid by the government, thirteen dollars. Value nothing, labour excepted. Hats, red flannel shirts, case-knives paint, red flannel in piece, looking-glasses, coarse and fine-tooth combs. For the women, calico, red flannel in piece, stockings, awls, fine combs and coarse needles. Tobacco for both sexes.

The chiefs, who had the business in hand, felt their importance and kept up a distracting ordering about. Each warrior was called by name. As he approached, the old chief simultaneously seized a hat by the rim, a pair of pantaloons by one leg, or a coat or shirt by one sleeve, and shied them at him. The warrior gathered the goods out of the dirt and resumed his seat. The same form was courteously observed towards the women.

After the distribution was fairly under way, the scene was quite amusing. The first thing done by the warriors was to cut the seats out of the pantaloons and put them on over leggins and breech-clout. Next they put on their coats, and over these their red flannel shirts, and on their heads the puritanical hat, with which they were provided.

The boys did not stop to cut the seat out of their breeches, or to abbreviate their dimensions. A boy of six years was often the recipient of pantaloons large enough for a three hundred pounder. The contractor must have had a diabolical idea of the physical development of a red juvenile. Warriors might now be seen strutting about, each arrayed in two pairs of pants, two or three hats, and three or four shirts, all on. The boys, particularly, fancied sporting their red flannel shirts.

The squaws invariably put on their stockings over their *moccasins* and leggius. The writer interested himself in the enlightenment of a pretty maiden on the subject, greatly to the merriment of a bevy of old hags, who closely watched these elementary lessons in civilization.

After all the goods had been distributed, the band broke up and returned to the village. The next day most of the articles found their way to the tent of the Indian trader, who gave sugar in exchange.

The sixth of January was clear and cold. The opportunity of this change was seized to move camp to the vicinity of Medicine Bluff. The streams were much swollen, and the open plain was almost impassable. The movement of the column was, therefore, slow and tedious. The wind blowing during the day had rapidly dried the high grass. Towards the east the grass had been fired by some lurking savages. The flame, carried before the wind, soon enveloped the entire country in a blaze. During the day it frequently became necessary to halt the column to allow the great waves of flame to pass. The scene that -night was truly sublime. A sea of fire surrounded us, and as far as the eye could reach, sheets of blaze and smoke could be seen leaping before the wind, in the wildest fury, driving the terrified buffalo, antelope, deer, and wolf, from his favourite resort.

The next day the flood-gates of heaven were again opened. The column crept along at a toilsome pace through mud and slush. The advance party, consisting of the Commanding General and escort, reached Medicine Bluff early in the afternoon. The rain descended in torrents. Finding it impossible for the train to come up that day, a courier was dispatched to bring up the headquarters' wagons. After several hours' drenching, the wagons arrived and tents were pitched. The rest of the command was at least ten miles in the rear. During the night, another of the frequent tornadoes of the country visited us. This time, however, it was most heartily welcome. The plain was frozen, so as to relieve the column of its difficulties in reaching its destination the next day.

It was not until the tenth of the month that the weather had settled sufficiently to permit the transfer of headquarters in closer proximity to the camps of the troops, located in the immediate vicinity of the site of the post. A sheltered nook, about a mile and a half farther down the stream, had been selected, and here we fixed ourselves for a long stay. The Medicine Bluff Creek ran in our rear, with a dense forest of cotton-wood beyond. A range of low bluffs rose in front. A short distance up the stream, was the camp of the Seventh, and below, that of the Tenth. The volunteers were in camp two miles nearer the mountains.

The Commanding General was anxious and restless. The trains, which should have arrived from the east, had not yet appeared. The rains again set in with all their fury. The country was inundated. At camp, the prospect was anything but cheering. The troops were suffering for clothes. The animals were exhausted and dying in large numbers. Forage was nearly out, and rations were growing alarmingly scarce. Not satisfied with the course matters were taking, orders were given to relieve the animals from all duty. They were driven in herds, with a strong guard, to a valley several miles from camp, to eke out an existence, as best they could, on the dry grass.

The general himself, with his quartermaster, McGonnigle, and California Joe, as escort and *avant courier*, set out for Fort Arbuckle, in spite of rain and mud. The trains from the east, which he had ordered to be fitted out the preceding fall, had failed him. To farther discourage the future movements of the troops, dispatches were received from Carr's column, which was designed to operate from Fort Lyon, along the Cimmaron and the north fork of the Canadian. The movement was fruitless of results. After marching over a large expanse of country, experiencing terrible snowstorms and the loss of a large number of animals, the command retraced its stops.

The troops were likely to remain some time at the camp on Medicine Bluff. An occasion so favourable to exploration was not to be lost. The Wichita Mountains were a sealed book, as far as any knowledge within their immense walls was concerned.

A week after our arrival in the vicinity, in company with Generals Hazen and Kidd, of the Tenth, an interpreter, and an Indian guide, the writer set out for this wild region. A single orderly composed our escort, and a pack mule our transportation for camping accommodations and rations.

About six miles on our way, we confronted a high ridge, composed of a mass of enormous rocks. Our guide conducted us through by an Indian trail, which made its way in tortuous disregard of a direct line. Upon the crest of the ridge we halted for some minutes to enjoy the landscape. It was varied and extensive. The silver stream, suddenly appearing from its mountain spring, leaped into the valley, the frowning granite scarp of Mount Scott, the grove, and the plain, all blended in agreeable harmony. Large herds of Indian ponies were scattered here and there, watched by Indian boys. The white, cone-shaped lodge of the Comanche, seated in retired groves, and the circling smoke winding into the air, could be plainly descried. These villages, which had followed us from the Washita, had selected this luxuriant section for the new seat of their lodge-fires.

We descended into the valley, and a ride of several miles brought us to a suitable spot upon which to spread our tent-fly and build our fire for the night. We had now reached the north-eastern base of the eastern peak of the Witchitas, on a nameless stream, tributary to the Medicine Bluff. Beyond, about a hundred yards distant, we had as neighbours a Yampariko Comanche village.

After feeding the animals, and regaling ourselves upon strips of buffalo-meat, early in the afternoon, Hazen, Kidd, and myself, saddled our horses for an ascent of Scott. The rest of the party were left in camp. After a short gallop, we reached the base of the towering height above us. We began the ascent on horseback, winding among rocks, scaling boulders, moving along dizzy ledges, with no pleasant anticipations should the animals lose their footing.

During the ascent, while deeply engaged in observing the sublimity of surrounding nature, my attention was arrested by repeated spasmodic efforts in the vicinity of the tail of my horse. It required but an instant to recognize the fact that the animal was making extraordinary efforts to elevate his heels, but the angle of ascent was greater than the horse could overcome. It did not require a second invitation for me to dismount, for had I not done so voluntarily I might the next moment have found myself sliding like an avalanche over my horse's crupper, which the saddle now did without me. With great effort, and certainly with no little inconvenience on the part of the animals, we reached a sheltered ledge. Farther ascent, mounted, was found to be an impossibility. While Kidd, not satisfied, and having a wager in view, set out around the crest of the mountain in hopes of finding some means of attaining the top, the general and myself tied our horses to a stunted pine tree, and proceeded on foot.

The ascent of the main summit was extremely hazardous and difficult. An immense slab of two hundred feet square, presenting that area of exposed flat surface, lay against the side of the mountain at an angle of a least thirty degrees. After considerable exertion, continually experiencing imminent danger of sliding back, we struck the great mass of boulders which constituted the cap of the mountain. As we toiled upward, jumping from boulder to boulder, frequently climbing from ledge to ledge by means of cedar trees growing in the fissures of the rock, we encountered several enormous caverns, which were evidently the habitations of the savage beasts, the sole and undisputed possessors of that wild and secluded spot.

An hour of the severest physical exertion brought us to the end of our journey. The summit of the mountain consisted of a sunken bed, surrounded by rugged walls of granite, having much the appearance of the crater of an extinct volcano. This level space was covered with fragments of rock and earth. The latter was thickly overgrown with a wiry grass. The sun was setting. The view was sublime. Fifty miles distant southward could be traced the dark line of the valley of the Red River. Towards the west lay the confused mass of the bold precipitous mountains and towering peaks. At the other end stood Mount Webster, rising upon the heavens like a dense black storm-cloud. In all other directions spread out the boundless plain. Immediately at our feet coursed the sparkling waters of the Medicine bluff, connecting a series of small lakes. Upon their banks were situated the villages of the Comanches, who, satisfied with war, had returned to their favourite haunts to enjoy peace.

While admiring from an overhanging cliff the solitude and sublimity of the prospect, which lay around us, a voice from beneath our feet attracted our attention. It was Kidd, who had succeeded in reaching a point at least three hundred feet below us. After great effort he had managed to get his horse that distance, and had left him while he climbed to the top of an immense boulder, from which he was getting a partial view of the country.

At the suggestion of the major we determined to make the descent by his route, which we imagined would bring us back more expeditiously to our horses. As it was fast growing night we took a last survey, through the darkening atmosphere, and began to find our way down. We soon came to the conclusion that the laws of force, as regarded mountains, acted in reverse. We found it infinitely more difficult to get down from our elevated position than we had experienced in getting up. By the application of divers gymnastic feats we made our way to the foot of the larger boulders only to find ourselves hemmed in by great and almost impenetrable patches of scrub oak and briars.

To increase the perplexities of our situation it was now quite dark. We groped our way through, heading as best we knew how, to get around the mountain to our horses. We were in constant danger of stepping into some of the numerous yawning fissures in the rocks, or perhaps wandering over the frightful scarp of the mountain, which lay on our right. In consequence of these weighty reasons I proposed to the general, who was pretty well blown after the exertion of the afternoon, to find a place under the lee of a boulder, and there to remain until morning. It was clouding up, and a storm was certain.

The general did not favour my proposition, so onward we trudged through brambles, tumbling over rocks, and liable at any moment to receive the affectionate embrace of a bear, or the more tender and emphatic demonstration of some one of the formidable species of felines known to inhabit those mountain resorts. The general was determined to find the horses, and to get back to camp. I had given that up as a fruitless task. At all events, as we went on together, I took occasion to have my weapons handy.

Another dash brought us out of the thicket. It was now lighter. The moon was about making its appearance, and, having cleared the shadow of the mountain, it was possible to see farther than a nose's length.

But about the horses? The gathering clouds portended rain. In hopes of hearing an occasional neigh, we seated ourselves on an isolated rock. We listened in vain for any disturbance of the still air that might point out the direction of the horses. Horses brought up under military discipline, it was apparent were different from other quadrupeds of the same species. A half hour must have passed absorbed in profound deliberations over our situation, broken by repeated shouts and a vigorous whistling. But no response from the horses. They certainly appreciated the virtue of patience. Whatever may have been the promptings of instinct, they took their desertion with calmness.

We had now given up all hopes of finding the horses that night, and as a heavy mist began driving by the mountain, we made up our minds to endeavour to find our way back to camp on foot. We set out by a direct course into the gorge where we struck, as we supposed, a tributary of the stream in the valley. It now commenced raining in earnest, and again grew disagreeably dark. Our overcoats were strapped to our saddles. Following the creek for some distance, frequently getting into the water, and equally as often falling headlong over the confused mass of rocks, or getting fast in the wild vines and briars which grew along its bank, we came out on the plain. This was at least a relief. We quickened our steps until we reached what we took to be the main stream. We had pursued this but a short distance, when we were assailed by an array of Indian dogs, which having discovered us, came out from the Comanche village on the other side. The canine army was fortunately particular to leave the stream between us. The danger was that they might arouse the warriors of the village, who were always ready to improve such a favourable opportunity to steal a scalp.

Returning up the stream to a point we knew by the location of the Indian village, must be within hailing distance of our camp, we set up a few shouts which were promptly responded to. We now soon had the pleasure of being greeted by our companions. The major and his horse had returned but a few minutes before. After demolishing a hearty supper of wild turkey, we turned in to enjoy a sound slumber.

The next morning the guide went up the mountain, and having

trailed the horses to the spot where we had left them the night before, returned with them after an absence of several hours. The poor animals seemed to show some signs of satisfaction at getting back to camp. A double feed, out of the scant supply of grain, we had brought with us soon made them oblivions of the past.

The Witchita Mountains, at the time of our visit, were unexplored, and known only on the maps by location. Within their lonely walls was an unknown region. These mountains had always been known to be a favourite resort for Indians, as a refuge of the weaker tribes against the attacks of the stronger. Here numbers were of no avail. Skill, agility, and endurance, were the main requisites of defence. According to Indian tradition, many terrible encounters had taken place in these dark defiles. The bear, the panther, the wildcat, and the buffalo, made their haunts within its sheltered solitudes. The savage never, except when driven there.

Mount Scott which we ascended was fourteen hundred feet in height It was the eastern abutment of the range, and rising as did the entire chain, immediately out of a vast surrounding plain, the height was greatly magnified. Towards the west two main ranges extended as far as the eye could reach. The landscape was composed of bold ridges, great piles of boulders, with an occasional valley, small in dimensions, but presenting a beautiful prospect.

CHAPTER 36

A Hunt by Moonlight

The following morning we saddled up as soon as the horses were fed. The rain of the previous night had
ceased, and the day was clear and bright. The atmosphere fairly sparkled with purity. We rode deeper into
the mountains, the Indian guide pointing out a gorge through which we could get around, and proceed back to camp by a different route. According to our guide all the mountain peaks were considered sacred by the Indians. He narrated some miraculous cures accomplished as the reward of a toilsome journey to the summit of Mount Scott. While, in early days, all went there to prolong life, the majority found it a place of sepulture. We took our course by what the guide called the Caddo-trail. It had evidently not been recently used, as I could see no footprints of man or beast. This trail, at all events, led us into what was said by the Indian to be the only pass through the mountains for a distance of thirty miles. On our way we passed the chain of beautiful lakes seen from Mount Scott. They were surrounded by the wildest description of scenery. Perpendicular heights, immense trees, with occasional cascades from their mountain sources pouring over dizzy heights in the foaming abyss below. We saw no fish, though, according to the guide, all the lakes and streams abound in beautiful trout.

As we rode along almost every moment deer and antelope started with terrified expedition from their haunts. Wild turkeys seemed to be without number. One drove, which we halted to watch passing, not over a hundred yards distant, must have contained three hundred birds. At the summit of a bald ridge, about five miles west of Mount Scott, we halted for a half hour to take a survey of the surrounding country. On the right were several small valleys, in one of which we saw at a distance a herd of beautiful elk. A strong temptation it was to pursue.

A mountain, twenty-three degrees north of west of Mount Scott, distant three miles, I took the liberty of naming Mount Sheridan, after the Commanding General. It was by all means the finest mountain of the range. Its north face was a clear perpendicular height of eight hundred feet, the total being twelve hundred feet. Its crest was composed of towering shafts of granite, split in the most marvellous manner, resembling the teeth of an enormous comb. Across a narrow gorge, and isolated from the main mountain, was a solitary cone of solid rock, which stood out like the sentinel of the mountains. Our Indian guide, pointing to Mount Sheridan, said that was the father, and pointing to Mount Scott, that the eldest brother. This aboriginal geology is not authenticated by any cotemporary authority, though tradition would make it appear so. The mountain lying in the same line of direction was an immense mass of closely packed boulders, and about a thousand feet high. We now turned back, resuming the Caddo-trail, which led us between Mount Sheridan and the detached masses of Mount Scott. An hour's ride over a dark and lonely path we reached the open spaces on the other side.

The number of tracks of all sorts of savage animals was amazing. A fresh bear track we encountered was characterized by one of those sudden explosive sounds on the part of our Indian, which indicated an animal of prodigious size. We found it impossible to track him, and being without a dog had to go on.

A halt of an hour in an open valley, on the south side of the range, was consumed in resting and feeding the animals, after which we set out for camp, arriving several hours after dark.

The more prominent peaks of the Witchitas I was told were often used by the Indians for signalling. Hazen and myself, during our presence on the top of Mount Scott, set fire to the dry grass and branches of the cedar which we could gather. In a very short time the entire summit was in a blaze, alarming the savages for miles around. They seemed to interpret it as the signal of a fearful state of strife.

The mountains derived their name from the Witchitas, who are admitted by the Comanches to have been the first occupants of the country. During our journey we saw but very few buffaloes, when the traces of the animal, particularly the skulls, were so abundant that there was no questioning the fact that not long before they must have subsisted in these luxuriant valleys by tens of thousands. This, the guide explained, was one of the consequences of the war. Such a thing as scarcity never having been known in the country before.

The accounts which we had brought back of the game in the mountains, induced the Commanding General to get up a party of his own a few days after. In addition to the general, were Crosby, Forsyth, and Asch, of the staff. Weir and Yates, of the Seventh, and myself. This time we had matters arranged more systematically, taking with us an interpreter, Indian guide, cook, three orderlies, six scouts, and four pack-mules. A heavy fog prevailed the morning we started. The party become scattered, especially the pack-mule with the rations of the party. It was noon before we got together again, particularly the rations. The orderlies and attendants were halted on the stream at the base of the mountain, while the general and the rest of the party undertook the ascent.

The effort this time was no less difficult than I had experienced with Hazen. By the time we had reached the top, the whole party was well blown. At least an hour was expended in studying the topography of the surrounding country. Before leaving, the contents of a bottle of brandy was replaced by a list of the names of the party, and an account of the circumstances of our visit. The bottle was for the edification of some future enthusiastic admirers of nature, who might reach that elevated station in the physical world.

After admiring the scenery sufficiently for all, we made the descent on the south side and encountered the same obstacles which Hazen and I had met with in our descent on the north. The brambles and briers turned out to be a dense growth of blackberry and raspberry bushes, strengthened in their impenetrability by a diminutive variety of plum-tree. From the difficulty we experienced in getting through by daylight, I was struck with amazement when I reflected upon my first experience in the darkness of night.

By the time we reached the foot of the mountain, the scouts had selected a charming site for a camp, and had spread the tent-flies. Several fine wild turkeys had been killed and greeted us with a savoury odour. Our journey was attended by one misfortune, the loss of the general's stag-hound. Several of the scouts made a fruitless search for him. With the loss of the hound, half of the sport of the excursion was lost.

After the moon had risen, we divided up into parties and set out from camp in search of turkey roosts. All the game had evidently been frightened away by the scouts hunting in the afternoon. After wandering over the country several hours into the night, getting but a few shots, and meeting with all sorts of mishaps, we returned with an evident relish for a smoking supper, which was about to be distributed in true primitive style.

The fatigues of the day soon drove all to the blankets, from which it was with great reluctance, before daylight the next morning, we were called, by the orders of the night before, to make an early start.

The next morning we rode through the gorge passing under the frowning cliffs of Mount Sheridan. Our particular object in taking this direction was a bee-tree, which had been discovered a few days before by an old frontier's man, who had been "in the mountains a sarchin bar." We had the old man with us to point out the tree.

Mister Carr, the title being punctiliously applied on all occasions, had joined the campaign in its earliest stages. He was over sixty years of age. His presence in the army was an act of paternal devotion often met with on the plains. In the massacre on the Saline, he had a son murdered, consequently "he just joined the army so as to kill a few red skins out of revenge." Mister Carr had spent his whole life on the frontier, moving farther west as civilization advanced. The old man was strong and hearty, and had a certain amount of the finer qualities of human nature, which made him an agreeable companion on such occasions. As far as killing red skins was concerned, in the battle of the scouts, on the Arrickaree Fork, he did his share.

The honey-tree being reached, Mister Carr, as the discoverer, by courtesy, was entitled to the superintendence of cutting it down. We dismounted in the timber, and allowing our animals to graze about, formed an anxious group to observe the chopping. Mister Carr, not satisfied with the awkward hacking of a couple of orderlies put at the work, took the axe, and with a broad, familiar, graceful swing, made huge pieces of timber fly right and left, clearing a space of respectful dimensions around the tree. In a few moments the tree began to career over. A host of curious bees, anxious to learn the nature of the outside demonstrations upon their domicile, were buzzing around the knot-hole aperture, which led into the tree.

A few of the more courageous of the formidable little insects, made a charge upon our party, causing a hasty suspension of operations and a general stampede. At last the noble tree fell. A few well directed strokes of the axe penetrated the deceptive exterior and lay open a huge cavity. A mass of dried comb was at first exposed. The bees had already devoured the inviting sweet. Farther down, however, we reached the commissariat of the hive. Innumerable bees were hard at work demolishing their store, when interrupted by our voracious party.

Every person helped himself freely to a huge cake, and perching himself on an adjacent rock, made short work of the labours of that little community during the previous summer. On examining the tree, the claw marks of bears could be detected on the bark. How often had old bruin visited that tree, and succeeded no farther than to smack his chops at the entrance to the hive, without tasting the delicacies within.

While seated around the hive, all busily eating, our Peneteghtka guide perpetrated the best bit of humour I had heard for many days. At a moment when laughter and shouts had ceased, the Indian looked up from an immense piece of comb he held before him, and with one of the drollest expressions said "*Bueno*, you all Peneteghtkas."

"Good! Good!!" was the unanimous rejoinder. Peneteghtkas the name of his band meant "Honey-eaters." The Indian, not thinking he had said anything very witty, in a most serious manner returned to his honey. If his band got their name from a fondness for eating honey, Essatoyeh certainly did justice to his people.

Having eaten to satiety, the remainder of the honey was put into a large kettle to take into camp. We now remounted and resumed our journey, following the romantic banks of Wild Horse creek. The country over which we passed, presented beautiful landscapes in constant succession. In several of the rivulets tributary to the stream, wild celery and watercress were found in large quantities. We halted for some minutes to gather a supply for our table.

It was dark before our party again reached the encampment. Our excursion had been full of novelty in the discovery of new scenery, but in the products of chase, it was anything but a success. At headquarters our first greeting was from the general's hound, he having returned to camp that morning.

The necessary inactivity of the army, was a burden to the free spirits, which composed at least one half of its number. The volunteers made up of men, who had always been accustomed to leading a sort of roving life upon their native prairies, since the army reach Medicine Bluff, had passed much of their time in hunting or wandering about within a circuit of twelve or fifteen miles. A few of these men tired of the campaign, or its delays, took occasion to wander beyond the limit prescribed, and not being seen again, it was supposed undertook the hazardous and toilsome journey of reaching the settlements, trusting to their rifle for sustenance, to instinct as a guide, across those interminable intervening plains, and to chance for eluding any prowling band of savages who might feel an inclination to "lift their hair."

In the absence of other excitement the volunteers pried into every nook and corner in all the country round, and frequently discovered marvellous things. Among these was a rattlesnake den.

One afternoon early in February, in company with several of the officers at headquarters, I visited this latest wonder. At the base of the cliff, opposite the most lofty portion of Medicine Bluff, reached only by a narrow and dangerous ledge, sometimes but six inches in width, leading down to the water's brink, was an opening underlying the large masses of super-incumbent rock. The crevice ran horizontally, being about twelve feet, and in height or width about twelve inches. At one end was an elongated opening of about two feet. In front was an immense barren rock which extended to the water. Farther down was a small space of soil covered with grass.

The cliff here had a slight concavity, the extremities abutting abruptly upon the water. The space thus cut off from all access, except by water or the ledge already mentioned, did not cover an area of over fifty feet in length, and at its widest part six feet. The cliff rose fully a hundred feet above. What inducement could ever have tempted any one to make this perilous descent, in the first instance, was a mystery to me. It was with extreme difficulty, having first climbed down a scraggy cedar, which obstructed the upper end of the ledge that I could make it. I managed it only by getting down all fours, sometimes lying flat out and by degrees working down. But one of my companions followed.

The space below was covered with a sickening spectacle. A mass of enormous "diamond" rattlesnakes were lying about in all states of mutilation. Some were without heads. All without tails. The largest and in fact the majority were completely skinned. As I learned afterwards the hideous skins were used by the "Kansas boys" for belts. The skins and rattles were also considered as possessing mysterious medicinal agencies. It was rather appalling to be in the midst of such a population of the most dreaded and venomous reptile of the plains, even though lifeless. My imagination would sometimes invest the horrid mass with motion. The effect was startling, I invariably felt a proclivity to get on the high ground overhead.

Several of the largest of these reptiles, poked out and laid at full length, measured not less than eight feet from head to tail—that is, what was left of those extremities—and, at the thickest part, were six inches in diameter. It may be imagined what a sight a knitted mass of raw, purplish flesh, and of such shapes, must have presented. The main pile of defunct reptiles would have made a cart-load, and, besides, the rocks and crags had also been elaborately decorated by the "boys."

The space leading to the den had the appearance of having been the scene of hibernation of the snake family for centuries. The hard rock was worn and slimy. When these indications of some sort of creature making the den its abode were discovered, the adventurous explorers secured a long pole. While one was poling up the unknown occupants within, the others stood around the entrance with pistols and carbines loaded ready to greet the first appearance of the denizens, whatever they might be, of that inaccessible abode. After a few minutes poking, a huge old monster of a rattle-snake, which seemed to be the patriarch of the community, crawled out in a semi-torpid condition.

His snakeship was promptly dispatched, and his enormous length drawn out of the den. Not supposing that this was the rightful possessor of the premises, a little more lively poking brought to light a few more offended monsters, which were likewise dispatched. The business, according to these invaders of the snake dominions, now became quite lively. The snakes on top, exposed to the rather chill atmosphere of the den, dragged themselves along slowly. Those that came after, were a little more active, and kept the besiegers quite busily employed.

Over two hundred snakes were thus drawn from their comfortable quarters and promptly dispatched. I saw, at the time of my visit, the remains of one hundred and fifty-eight. A number had been thrown into the stream, and not a few had been packed off to camp by the discoverers, as trophies of the engagement. Subsequent visitors also carried off a snake or two as a souvenir.

From the old plains men I learned that, in autumn, these reptiles gravitate, instinctively, towards some spot where they hibernate in large masses. This fact simply, however, was not as remarkable as to find them in such a place as the den in the cliff. It seemed beyond comprehension, that the snake should visit a particular spot to winter, and that by water. Yet such appeared to be the fact.

An old Kiowa medicine man, speaking about the den, said that many years before an Arrapahoe chief was old and about to die. He wandered over the bluff, and finding this den, entered it, and was never seen again in human form; but every spring great numbers of terrible snakes came out and scattered over the country. According to his explanation, the Arrapahoe tradition declares that this old warrior turned into a snake, and became the father of all the snakes in the country—a large and interesting progeny indeed. The medicine man, when asked whether there were many snakes, opened his eyes and mouth in a most fearful manner, exclaiming "Heaps, heaps! Big, so!"—holding his long arms out at full length, indicating the different sizes, and then seizing his thighs to show their diameter.

We returned to camp with wonderful stories of the day's adventures. For my part, the same night wriggling fabrics resembling serpents, and monsters generally, formed the disturbing visions of my dreams.

CHAPTER 37

Closing Events

Although by February all the wild tribes had sent in their representatives, promising submission, the tribes themselves were slow to fulfil. The Arrapahoes of Little Raven's band, who had made the boldest professions, had been loitering at a distance for several weeks. When their men visiting our camp were interrogated why their people were so slow, the invariable answer was, the weather, and forlorn condition of their animals. It was quite apparent that this high-spirited band reluctantly yielded to an imperious necessity. The war had driven off the game; they, therefore, had but to starve or surrender. Their dogs had been consumed, and horse-flesh had even been resorted to in their extremity. Their ponies found difficulty in travelling. Surrounding them were interminable plains, now destitute of animal life. The Commanding General naturally supposed the Arrapahoes were playing the shrewd part of diplomacy. This band was evidently desirous of awaiting the opening of spring, and then quietly to disappear, join the Cheyennes, and once more, with sustenance for their ponies, resume the war-path.

The general was not to be thus gulled. Having exhausted his patience in waiting, Colonel Wier was directed to organize a squadron of picked men and horses, to move out suddenly, and compel the Arrapahoes to come in. The weather was suitable for the expedition, as the then recent rains would prevent the flight of the savages. His men and animals, though worn from the effects of the campaign, moved out, as if enjoying the relief from the monotony of camp-life. In the direction pointed out by the Indian runners, the column proceeded, and after a ride of thirty-five miles, struck the Arrapahoe camp. The savages were surprised. The chief, Little Raven, came out to meet the troops. He made excuses and asked time. He was informed that he

Elk Valley

had had time enough. He must get ready to march in the next morning, or the camp would be destroyed, his people taken prisoners and punished. The colonel having taken the precaution to surround the village, there was no chance of escape. The same night a council was held, when the diplomatic savage warriors very discreetly resolved the wisest thing they could do would be to accompany the soldiers to their camp.

Having received information that Wier was near at hand with his charge, I rode out with a party of officers a distance of five or six miles in the direction of the approaching village The village consisted of sixty lodges, and was strung out over a distance of a mile, and scattered over a width of fifty yards. The squaws, and papooses, male and female, old enough, drove the laden animals. The warriors formed the advance and rear guard, and a chain of flankers stood as sentinels on hills along the route. The women were chatting as if pleased at their relief. The warriors were sullen and downcast.

The moving village was halted, and planted in a sheltered spot, selected for its contiguity to our camps, so that this suspected community might be watched. Little Raven, the chief of this branch of the Arrapahoes, I found to be a remarkably intelligent Indian. He was rather stout, about fifty years of age, having the appearance of one who lived well and took the world calmly.

As soon as he had pointed out the place for his lodge, and had given some instructions to his people, he rode to head-quarters, where he made some explanation of his conduct. Rather a bitter task for the independent spirit which struggled within his breast.

While watching the erection of the lodges, and the domestic details of the village, my attention was called to a young lad of about twelve years of age. I was told that he had been captured when but an infant by a column of troops, and had passed some years subsequent to that time at an educational institution in St. Louis. I made several attempts to induce him to converse, but all overtures he persistently refused. He leaned against a fallen tree, and wore a most rigid expression. He comprehended the questions put to him, but, with the exception of an odd word, and an affirmative or negative shake of the head, he might have been a stone, for all that he would say.

It occurred to me that he feared to say anything on account of the warriors who were standing around, and who might have imagined that he was communicating intelligence of the tribes. The child drooped and pined away when taken from his native plains. He longed to be among his wild kindred; a wish afterwards granted. Like the buffalo, take him from the boundless freedom of his native state, and the red man sinks into a premature grave.

Custer set out in the latter part of January with a small escort to visit the Cheyennes and main camps of the Arrapahoes, as it was supposed, on the headwaters of the Red. Arriving in that vicinity, it was believed, more than ever, that the savages were anxious to protract their absence until spring. Although signs of their recent presence were visible, the tribes themselves could not be found. The expedition having been absent two weeks, and being out of supplies, returned.

Notwithstanding the peculiar conduct of the savages that had not yielded submission, it was certain that they were in no condition to assume the offensive were they so disposed, and it would be well into summer before their animals would have sufficiently recruited to respond to the exertions of a fresh outbreak. These considerations admitted of a possibility of the tribes in question carrying out their professions of coming in as soon as their forlorn condition would admit.

From the Arrapahoes it was learned that the tribes still out were in a condition of lively alarm. The success of Evans' column, and the presence of Carr, in addition to our own troops, had satisfied them of the futility of further opposition. At the time Custer set out, his movement was communicated by the Cheyenne and Arrapahoe *videttes*. The two tribes took to their heels, fearing the object of the expedition was of a hostile character. Having fled towards the Red River, they followed for some miles the bed of the stream, so that all traces of the direction of their flight would be effaced upon the first flood. This flight led to a division in the Arrapahoe camp, which resulted, as we have seen, in the surrender of Little Raven's band.

As far as the savages were concerned, every day made it more evident that they had received more than they expected when they undertook the war. Fresh deputations of warriors had arrived to renew their professions of peace.

The Commanding General, willing to test the professions of the savages, towards the middle of February released Satanta and Lone Wolf, of the Kiowas, from their two months' lodging at the government expense. He also agreed to hold a talk with the chiefs of all the tribes.

On a bright afternoon in February, about fifty warriors, with all their trappings, in a semicircle, seated themselves in front of headquarters for the Great White Chief to talk. The head orator occupied the centre. He was dressed in great state, wearing a brigadier general's coat and a sabre. Before the council met, he strutted about in his bare legs with an air of great importance, calling attention every now and then to the fact that he was a big chief; in evidence of which he pointed to his shoulder-straps and brass buttons.

The general came out and made his first speech. He told the warriors, in substance, that he had come from his home, where soldiers were like the trees of the forests, so great in numbers, to punish the red man for murdering white men, women, and children. That he was willing to let the past be buried; but if the red man must have war, he could give it to him as long as there was a warrior left. But it made the Great Spirit sad to see his children fighting among themselves. That the same Great Spirit ruled over all, and he liked to see peace.

The warriors, in turn, got up as they felt the impulse move them. They spoke of their lands and of their vanishing race. They wanted peace, because after war they were weak, like a feeble old man ready to die. They were willing to lay down the hatchet, and do as the great Washington (the president) wished his good children to do.

The manner of some of the orators was very striking. Tall and majestic in figure, with an air of boundless freedom, a grace of gesture, a flexibility of intonation, and harmony of expression, these savage warriors were the embodiment of dignity and elocutionary effect. After the speaking, which was done through an interpreter, the warriors one by one arose, and shook the general vigorously by the hand, exclaiming emphatically, "*How! How!*"

The final scenes of the war were drawing on; but it was still necessary to make a movement towards the laggard tribes, to let them see that the "white soldiers" were still able to fight. Such a contrast with their own forlorn condition could not fail to have a powerful effect. It would explode forever in the savage mind their belief in the impenetrability of their limitless plains during the pitiless and stormy period of winter. The hardships of the campaign, the terrors of the freezing weather, and the infinitely more trying rains which had now set in, had already told severely on the troops and animals. Worse than all, the arrival of supplies was delayed to such a degree that matters were looking serious. A large number of animals had died, and a larger number were barely able to keep their feet.

The troopers, however, were unusually healthy. A few cases of scurvy, only two of which assumed a serious form, and some colds, were the substance of the sanitary condition of the command. Still, the

Commanding General was resolved upon a move. While these matters were being discussed, Colonel Audenried, aid-de-camp to the then lieutenant general, arrived at headquarters on a tour of inspection.

As it was probable in a few days we would break camp, Hazen, Audenried, and myself planned an elk hunt. This would close my own adventures in that wild country. One morning in February, therefore, we set out with an Indian guide, an orderly, and camping arrangements. About the middle of the afternoon we spread our tent fly on a beautiful stream, a tributary of West Cache Creek, near the southern foot of Mount Sheridan. The camp was peculiarly picturesque. Lofty mountains and bold crags towered about us. The valley was covered with giant trees.

It was proposed, as we had several hours before night, to make the ascent of Mount Sheridan. Leaving our orderly to look after the camp, we set out on our journey. The Indian accompanied us for a short distance, and then set out to beat up game. Our route lay first through a dark forest, from which we emerged upon an open space, leading towards an accessible place of ascent. The higher we got the more difficult became our task; until, the last few hundred feet, we were obliged to crawl from crevice to crag up a perpendicular wall. The feat was accomplished, but, looking back, it was sufficient to astonish our courage in undertaking so dangerous an exploit.

Crossing the summit from the comb of the mountain, and looking over the trembling height, the view was the finest I had yet seen. The streams and groves were portrayed in delicate miniature. The position of the mountain also afforded a view up the long line of passes and valleys between the ranges as far as they extended. Through a glass. Mount Webster, at the western end, could be distinctly seen,

I never was better repaid for a journey than upon the occasion of this visit, and I felt better satisfied than ever that the mountain was worthy of the name and great deeds of Sheridan, and particularly to commemorate the success of *the winter Campaign on the Plains.*

Out of the dry grass and dead branches of scraggy cedars growing among the rocks we made an immense fire A few minutes after our return to camp the Indian came in with the hides of two splendid cow elks, the carcasses he having put in a tree out of the reach of the wolves. A good supper, prepared for us by the orderly, was readily disposed of. After a social smoke, and planning a hunt for the next morning, we "turned in," much fatigued from the day's excursions.

At daylight, the colonel, accompanied by the Indian, set out in advance. An hour later, the general and myself followed. A walk of a short distance brought us to a beautiful valley, completely surrounded by hills. Everywhere traces of elk and deer were visible. Owing to this fact, we gave the place the name Elk Valley. The sun had just risen. The dews of the morning sparkled on the plain; a thin veil of mist swept by the loftier mountains. A beautiful stream ran in winding course across the valley. The Indian trail wound through rocks and wood towards the mountain passes.

While standing upon the summit of a low hill commanding a fine prospect across the valley, my attention was attracted by the general shouting. Considerably surprised at his enthusiasm, I brought down my rifle, not knowing but that we had fallen among savages.

It was but a moment, however, when I saw less than sixty yards before me a majestic elk staring directly at me. While struggling through the thick under-brush, having withdrawn the cartridge from the chamber of my rifle, I drew the piece up and pulled the trigger. No detonations responding, I tried again. Again the rifle refused to fire. This time cocking the piece, I brought up a third time; once more it missed. All this time the elk stood with his large, beautiful eyes fixed upon me. My motions must have excited his curiosity the more.

Having sufficiently recovered, I rammed a cartridge into the chamber. But having witnessed all this preliminary stupidity, the elk was satisfied, and bounded off. Before the animal was a hundred yards distant, I sent a bullet after him. It was a good shot. The animal flourished his white tail, suddenly changed his course, at the same time quickening his graceful gallop. The old adage, "*make haste slowly,*" never was more perfectly illustrated. It struck me that it was a mild type of "Buck fever."

We now set out, under cover of the hill, to intercept the animal, on the way getting a shot at a deer at close range. By the time we came in sight the elk was still bounding away in the dim distance. The deer was wounded, but not fatally, and hobbled off.

While the general and I were wandering about without any very definite ideas of what we were hunting, but acting under the general principle of taking a shot at everything that came within range, the colonel and the Indian, who were mounted, were galloping rapidly across the valley after a herd of fourteen elks which they had started. The herd had headed towards a gorge in the mountain. The hunters were close after. Reaching a wood, the Indian jumped from his horse and started into the timber on foot. A few minutes after, a shot was heard echoing among the mountain walls. A fine buck responded to the messenger of death. The Indian having succeeded in turning the herd, as it again emerged from the wood, the colonel, who was lying in wait, made a fine running shot and bagged his game.

Towards midday we returned to our camp. Preparations had already been made for a hasty departure homeward. On the way, several herds of elk and a few deer were started. A few long-range shots from horseback were made, but had no other effect than to expedite the movements of the timid fugitives. We reached headquarters before sundown, with goodly quantities of elk meat and the hides of the animals killed as trophies of our success.

A few days after the release of Satanta, the village of the Kiowas was thrown into confusion by a domestic scene. The hero was the son of the wily chief, a youth of more than ordinary manliness of face and figure, and the pride of the nation, in the daring he had already displayed in the chase or the war-path. The young warrior was enamoured of the squaw of one of the chief warriors. His attentions were not liked by the warrior, and, out of fear of receiving a severe flogging, were shunned by the squaw. The young chief, knowing his passion was reciprocated, continued his advances, often fearlessly confronting the husband, to the imminent danger of a conflict. At last the affair culminated in a most singular way. The young warrior, approaching the lodge, entered into a verbal controversy with the husband. The squaw, alarmed, fled towards the lodge of the young warrior's father.

Young Satanta seeing this, set out in pursuit, while the husband brought up the rear. As they were crossing the village, the mother of the youth intercepted him. She called him a "fool." The young warrior, stirred to the quick, drew his pistol, but, strange to say, discharged the contents into his own body. He reeled and fell, but was not mortally wounded. Hearing the report of the weapon, the warriors rallied in a flash. The whole village, in a few moments, was a scene of uproar and lamentation. The young warrior was removed to a lodge set apart for him. The medicine men were called. Satanta performed those usual acts of medicinal liberality, such as making presents of lodges and ponies promiscuously, to invite the kind interposition of the Great Spirit as a response to his generosity. Three medicine men were employed to exorcise the spirits of evil. Drumming and shouting and *pow-wowing* were kept up without intermission for hours, to drive out the bullet and keep away the spirit of death.

Satanta, the father, the morning after the occurrence, visited headquarters and told what had befallen his son. The General offered the services of his surgeon. The old chief replied: "No; the red man's medicine man must try first; then the white man's. If white man first, then medicine man say, if die, bad medicine. Our medicine man no good. White man much good." Satanta evidently did not have much faith in the boisterous and pretentious doctors of his own race, but diplomatically preferred letting his own people try as a recognition of their native prejudices. The boy afterwards recovered, with the assistance of the white man's medicine.

The savage bands, having become settled under control of the troops, the Commanding General found himself besieged on all sides by a new enemy—a number of Texans, who had performed journeys of several hundred miles in hopes of recovering horses which had been stolen from them during the raids of the savages within their borders. This was a knotty question for adjudication, and was likely to excite afresh, or at least to kindle, a feeling of dissatisfaction. There was another question which had to be considered. These invaders, not, by any means, the best part of the population of Texas, were claimant and witness at the same time. The Indians soon discovered the object of the presence of these strangers.

After considerable talk and bad humour, the Indians gave up a few of the horses, and were informed, should they ever go on any more raids, they would be compelled by force to give them all up. Those Texans who had arrived having received their horses, orders were issued prohibiting any one, without permission, from coming into the Territory west of Fort Arbuckle. No more equine questions were brought up.

CHAPTER 38

The Administration of Indian Affairs

Before bringing this narrative to a close, I desire to incorporate a few facts and reflections concerning the past and the future of the American Indian. It was natural that the presence, and particularly the aggressive spirit of the early settlers, should inspire in the breasts of the primitive dwellers upon the American continent a feeling of suspicion, uneasiness, and hostility. Occurrences so visibly opposed to their interests and safety, were calculated to effect the results which followed, involving upon the one hand a conflict for the perpetuation of race, and the preservation of tribal hunting-grounds, upon the other territorial acquisitions, to make way for the building up of a new and modern civilization, in the wilds of a new world.

Over three centuries have elapsed. This has been a period of bloody, and desperate wars, and horrible atrocities. Whether the savage is to blame for his natural aversion to civilized habits, and the sanguinary part he has acted, or whether the superior white race is open to censure for the means too often resorted to for the acquisition of the vast territory today under its control, is a question now too late for consideration. What remains of this aboriginal people within the limits of the United States, is left to the alternative of civilization or rapid extinction. The spread of population, art and science, will not wait for the slow process which characterized the efforts of a century or less ago. The two conditions of the savage, and the enlightened of the species cannot live peaceably, and with equal prosperity, together. While this is a deplorable element of human intercourse, the weaker must give way to the stronger.

A retrospect of the history of this continent as regards the two races, demonstrates very satisfactorily, the causes of the depletion of the Indian population, and the same processes are still at work. In the contests between the rival nations of the old world, for territorial aggrandizement, taking advantage of the simplicity and passions of the aborigines by means of promises and presents, this unsuspecting people were induced to participate in the endless wars which ensued. These hostilities led to feuds and rivalries among the savages themselves, and where the thirst for blood was so fully gratified, the radical change of nature required by civilization, occupied the least portion of their attention or desires. The natural result was a melancholy and rapid decline of numbers, and the few still in existence perpetuating the tribal names, and very few of the nobler qualities of their progenitors, point to an inevitable fate.

The civilization of today is selfish and aggressive. The multiplicity of new avenues of development realized in the application of steam and electricity, are not to be trammelled by such abstract considerations as philanthropy. Humanity may arouse feelings of magnanimity on the part of the strong, but philanthropy is an ideal sought after, and too often results in a misinterpretation of the condition, and capacity of the weak. It is easier to imagine philanthropy without understanding it, than to elevate and ameliorate an abject, or a savage race, by the mere process of bestowing charity for the accommodation or convenience of physical necessities

An inherent spirit of progress must certainly exist before any advance in the scale of improvement can be anticipated. If a savage prefers his native wilds, to the anxieties, perplexities, and higher condition of intellect incident to civilization, no flowery sentimentality nor sympathetic expressions of the heart will avail a particle of good. A natural energy of mind and body, stimulated by an ambition to rise in the scale of human life, will more speedily accomplish results, than all the external influence that could be brought into existence. The spread of civilization must either be retarded to allow those whom we wish to benefit, to catch up or go forward, and engulf those who are unable to ride upon its rolling wave.

The Black Hawk war of 1831-'32, the Seminole war lasting seven years, the Creek war, the Sioux war of 1852, the Cheyenne and Sioux outbreak of 1864, and the Cheyenne war of 1867, together with repeated less-important troubles, have resulted with large expenditures of money and a considerable loss of life, on both sides, in opening to settlement and profitable use a vast extent of domain, reaching nearly two thousand miles west of the Atlantic coast. For the past twenty years the same scenes have transpired to dispossess the savages of their profitless occupation of the valuable territory on the Pacific slope, and to clear the way for that career of affluence and empire which first found its way upon those remote shores through the golden gate.

The total Indian population, now living within the limits of the United States, is less than three hundred thousand. Of these about seventy-six thousand are found within the limits of civilization, while very nearly three times that number, or over two hundred and nineteen thousand, inhabit the plains and Rocky mountains. Both these regions, less inviting to the husbandman, or undeveloped, respecting their mineral wealth, have become the last point of refuge for the race.

The Indians, in their new resorts, have found facilities for pursuing their wild habits, and trusting to the natural defences thrown around them, experience, at least, that temporary respite from harassing and depleting wars, inspired in defence of their hunting-grounds, and retaliated by the whites from necessity and protection against the horrible outrages which belong to savage warfare.

The Indian question now comes up in its latest phase, and is brought to a final issue. For more than twenty years an exclusively civil administration has been tried, and in no instance, when the whole subject has been investigated, do we find a single act which has advanced the savage materially above his primitive condition. A gigantic system of pauperism has been inaugurated, in which the savage has reaped the least share of the benefits.

Let us take a casual glance at this machinery of civil government. By act of Congress, about twenty years since, the management of the Indian tribes, within the United States, was placed exclusively within the control of the Department of the Interior. The Secretary, representing the head of this branch of the Executive of the Government, turned the active management over to a bureau officer, known as Commissioner of Indian affairs. A mere subordinate, this officer undertook the government of the large population of human beings entrusted to him. In his official character, he had not even the appearance of executive functions. The Secretary trusted to the Commissioner, while the latter attempted to fulfil his duties within the limited powers he possessed. The office, not tempting in its honours and legitimate rewards, did not invite as high an order of ability as its requirements demanded.

An effort was made to bring about an organization by classifying the Indian tribes within certain prescribed limits, under the immediate supervision of superintendents and agents. An army of representatives was sent among the tribes. Annually large appropriations have since been voted by Congress, as an annuity fund, to pay the travelling expenses of Indian delegations visiting "the Great Father," at Washington, to foot the bills of Peace Commissioners, sent out at intervals to bribe the refractory tribes to a nominal recognition of authority, in compensating contractors having charge of the periodical removals of the tribes from an old reservation to a new one, in purchasing or leasing ceded lands from one nation for the use of another, and for other purposes, which seems to have constituted a no less important item. In the expenditure of these large sums of public money, as well as in the general management of the Indians, there has never been any visible responsibility. An agent secured a large amount of funds, which he felt it his duty to disburse, and upon this principle, apparently, thousands of dollars have found their way, out of the Indian appropriations, without even keeping the Indians at peace.

Another fact which has come under our personal observation, is the wholly unaccountable dealings with the different tribes. It is known very well by the Indians themselves, that to be hostile to the government is more profitable than to adhere faithfully to the obligations of their treaties. In December, 1868, we witnessed the distribution of the annuity goods to the Peneteghtka band of Comanches. This band, through every contingency of threats from their own race and neglect at the hands of the government, for ten years had been friendly, and had committed no acts of violence, as a tribe, against the whites. Yet, at the time alluded to, I was told by the chief, that that was but the second distribution of annuity goods during the long period of their friendship, although, in the treaty, the government had pledged itself to an annual recurrence of these favours.

This has been precisely the policy. Those who deserved to be rewarded, were the very ones who suffered. If anyone thinks an Indian, because he is a savage, is, in consequence, ignorant of the arts of diplomacy, that person is very much mistaken. Not bound by any moral obligations, his promises are good as long as he is benefited by their fulfilment; but it is a slight transition from peace to war, when he conceives fresh claims upon the liberality and indecision of his agents. The Cheyennes, Arrapahoes, Kiowas, leading bands of the Comanches and Apaches, wise in policy as they are restless in spirit, as representative tribes of the southern plains, have long discovered their power, having received more than their share of goods as a reward for their abundant promises of good behaviour and periodical marauding expeditions upon the frontiers of Texas and along the line of the Arkansas, The tribes mentioned are known and recognized as the richest upon the southern plains, and have received, in addition, as a reward for their arrogance and threats, the lion's share of the gifts of the government.

But, unquestionably, the greatest anomaly in the Indian management has been the farcical *pow-wows* called treaties. These "treaties" have been consummated in the following manner: A few bands take the war-path from inclination, or neglect, as they claim, on the part of the government. The bureau, or Congress, if the war be of dimensions, sends out its representatives to open negotiations, and to secure a restoration of peace. The Commissioners, having arrived on the ground selected for the council, and with them having a variety of goods and trinkets for presents, send out runners to communicate with the hostile bands. A small party of Indian scouts are met. The runner is captured, and undergoes great risk of losing his hair before credulity is brought in harmony with the cupidity of the savage.

The assurance of "heaps of presents" is followed by sending off one of the party to communicate with the main camp. The expression of the tribe is obtained by a council, at which the chief presides and the head men give their views. Meanwhile the runner is held by his captors, who amuse themselves in insulting him, and talk about how they will kill him if he "speaks lies." If the talk of the council is "good," word is sent back by the runner, that the tribe will "bury the hatchet." A delegation of head men of the tribe follows. If everything is satisfactory, the warriors come in with shouts and the discharge of firearms, dressed in war attire, and painted in all sorts of fantastic devices, generally producing a particularly terrifying effect upon the Commissioners.

The savage feels his importance, for it is satisfactory to his mind that he comes in, not because he is compelled to, but as a victor, because he is willing. In this condition, he is not backward in demanding and securing any terms he pleases, and he struts about as if he felt it were only his magnanimity that forbade him seizing the goods lying in wait for his acceptance, and, as special trophies, taking with him the choice locks from the heads of the Commissioners.

The formality of the council or "talk," is gone through with, the savage smokes in silence and puts on one of those looks of profound reflection and overflowing sincerity, for which he is celebrated. The "treaty" is consummated. The presents are distributed, and the savage negotiators, without the ceremony of an acknowledgement, decamp, while the Commissioners scamper off, as if doubtful of their personal safety, until they are far within the confines of civilization. A few months later, and many of these same savages will be found again on the war-path and ready for another "treaty."

Again, we find a deplorable lack of knowledge or true interpretation of Indian character. As a race, the condition in which we find the American Indian of today, is not one step above his condition three centuries ago. If any change have taken place, it has been for the worse. Influenced by the most absurd and exacting superstitions, with a spirit incapable of the restraints of a regular mode of living, with no ambition above the acquisition of scalps, as an evidence of valour and the accumulation of ponies, or other objects of Indian value, as constituting wealth, with no conception of the uses of money, with no law, save that of custom, bowing to no authority but that vested in the voice of the tribe, treacherous in his intercourse with others, depending upon the chase for food, and in most instances, for a rude covering for his body, we have the American Indian as we really find him. A savage, by nature, he persists in leading the live of a savage. He delights in scenes of blood, and spoils wrung from his neighbours, serve him as the road to fortune.

It cannot be said that the Indian so well preserves his character as a savage, because he has not been subject to the influences calculated to improve his condition. The missionary, landing upon the shores of the continent with the first adventurers, gave his earliest thoughts "to the conversion of the heathen." The devout monarchs of those days, made the " teaching of the gospel to the savage inhabitants of the country," a paramount obligation in the granting of new territories.

This same interest has been manifested ever since, but all the energy, piety, contributions of money, and sacrifice of personal safety and comfort, expended on behalf of the savage, during these long years, stand in bewildering contrast with the miserable handful of impoverished individual instances, rated under the head of Christian Indians.

It is to be said of these men, who hazarded the enmity and caprice of a savage foe, though their efforts were barren of results, worthy of their pious labours, as the explorer, traversing new countries and opening to the world fresh and valuable accessions to the store of geographical information, as well as opening an acquaintance with the people among whom they journeyed and lodged, they advanced the interests of knowledge if they did not enlarge the boundaries of religion.

An effort to improve the condition of the savage has not formed the least feature in the official administration of their affairs. The means adopted to accomplish this result, through the tangible evidences of food and clothing, are generally part of the specifications in the treaties with the tribes. None of these "treaties" take note of the intermediate stages from the savage to even a semi-civilized condition, there is no executive provision to enforce compliance on the part of the refractory. It is attempted, by tribute, to win the savages over to the new condition of things. They are furnished with clothing in too small quantities to clothe them all the year round, so that one-fifth of their time they dress in a civilized attire, and the remaining four-fifths appear in a savage costume. The pittance held forth as an inducement to tempt them to go upon the reservations, is probably the best commentary that can be made upon this policy, yet, until recently, it has been a fair sample of the most enlarged official efforts to better the condition of the red man.

The terms might be accepted and complied with, readily, by some wretched, poverty-stricken, and subjugated bands, reduced to a servile condition by the misfortunes attendant upon perpetual wars with their enemies. To the same extent that such instances of submission are natural, and the only cases of sincere friendship, it is absurd to imagine that the wily Kiowa, the powerful Comanche, the warlike Cheyenne and Arrapahoe, for instance, with their herds of ponies, numbering by thousands, their magnificent lodges, and all the comforts which wealth and savage luxury and ingenuity can secure, are to be won over, permanently, from a condition of Independence and a congenial mode of living, for one suit of clothes, one hat, a red shirt, and a pair of stockings.

CHAPTER 39

The Administration of Indian Affairs Continued

A source of constant complaint among the Indians I found to be the inferior quality of the few goods issued to them, though the prices paid by the government would secure a far superior article. I examined, with a number of army officers, the goods for over two thousand Indians, these having been regularly purchased sometime before the recent changes. The suit of substantial clothes consisted of a coat and pantaloons of coarse cotton stuff, and looked as if dyed in writing fluid. Several of the coats could not even hold together long enough to give several Indians of obese figure a chance to select a fitting size. This was the leading feature of the civilizing process which, until recently, had been going on at a vast expense of millions of the people's money, and, as we have seen, with no practical benefit to the savage. A few missionaries to teach the use of coats and pantaloons were also needed.

A comparison of the progress attained by the Indian population in the various sections of the country shows the following figures before the present policy was adopted:

The Plains—Population, 112,366; acres cultivated, 23,949; frame houses, 549; log houses, 5,070; schools, 21; scholars, 1,681; teachers, 56; missionaries, 48.

The Rocky Mountains—Population, 107,442; acres cultivated, 13,605; frame houses, 13; log houses, 14; schools, 1; scholars, 16; teachers, 1; missionaries, none.

East of the Mississippi—Population, 26,848; acres cultivated, 30,573; frame houses, 657; log houses, 1,475; schools, 52; scholars, 2,090; teachers, 52; missionaries, 33.

The Pacific Coast—Population, 49,338; acres cultivated, 7,888; frame houses, 672; log houses, 692; schools, 10; scholars, 237 teachers, 12.

In the mere matter of cultivating the soil, which is the first most important step the savage makes towards a change of life, it is certainly a matter of encouragement to discover that the remnants of the tribes east of the Mississippi, numbering less than one-tenth the whole Indian population, cultivate nearly one-half of the entire number of acres tilled by Indian labour. Half of the remainder of acres are cultivated by the bands living within the limits of Kansas, and the seated tribes of the Indian Territory

In this connection it should, however, be remembered that the tribes east of the Mississippi, who cultivate such an overwhelming proportion of the entire number of acres, are but perpetuating a means of sustenance, even more universal at the time of the first appearance of the white race than now. The seated tribes of Kansas, in a majority of cases, formerly resided east of the Mississippi, and were an agricultural people. Those seated in the Indian Territory, like the Cherokees, also eastern nations, were far in advance of their cotemporary tribes, and are an exception to the rest of their people today.

In the examination of Indian statistics, with a view of eliciting some guide by which to determine the leading causes which induce the Indian to leave his primitive way of living, it is found that in every instance those tribes that have yielded have done so from necessity. That the step has not been an act of their own desire to rise in the scale of development, but forced upon them by the depletion and ruin brought upon themselves by constant wars.

Although not done with the sanction of the tribes, individual warriors, upon their own account, frequently unite with other tribes in predatory expeditions, and it frequently occurs that Indian bands, tired of the hard lot of so-called semi-civilization, take the first chance to incorporate into a more powerful tribe, following its habits, and controlled by its preponderating influence. The remnants of the only nations which have resorted to fixed rules of government and modes of life are the Cherokees, Creeks, Choctaws, Chickasaws, and Seminoles. These nations have adopted a rude model of government, with executive, legislative, and judicial departments; have a capital, a few primitive towns, cultivate the soil, and raise stock. In manners, living, and dress, they imitate the whites.

In all their pride, power, and affluence, when occupying the fertile lands of Florida, Georgia, Alabama, and Mississippi, according to contemporary writers, these people lived in towns, had a regular government, and raised extraordinary crops of maize. They do nothing more today, except to exchange their primitive customs and forms for a rude imitation of something modern. The length of time that has elapsed, with a proper application of its opportunities, since their first contact with the whites, would certainly lead us to expect more. There are individual instances of very superior men, by education and talent in all these nations. There are a few establishments, on a more extensive scale, indicating refinement and education; but, so far from being an example for imitation, they have, in a great measure, proved a cause of the degradation and impoverishment of the helpless and ignorant.

A review of our Indian difficulties shows, also, that the Indian has been treated frequently with the greatest injustice and falsehood. It is natural, as he sees his race declining in numbers, his former hunting-grounds annually growing less to make way for the settler, that he should feel sad in spirit. Acknowledging the stern necessities which surround him, either by force or compensation, he yields up his lands. In exchange he was to receive certain annuities. The government failed to perform its obligations. The money was appropriated, yet the poor savage complained that "their agents lie; they get nothing, and are forced to resort to war to save themselves from ruin." They invade the settlements. These settlements, they say, are upon their own lands, and they want to drive the white man away. This is natural, because the government promised, but failed, to pay them for their lands; therefore they are going to fight to get their lands back.

This is the Indian's argument The secret of the majority of wars, though the blame is attributed to the whites in general, is, in reality, the fault of mismanagement Where the settler goes beyond the legitimate limits of the government title, he exposes himself to consequences which should receive no sympathy, and be recognized as the punishment which he deserves for a violation of the faith which the government agreed to keep. But to say that the whites are to blame for acts which have been indisputably, the logical results of faulty administration, b a charge which grossly misrepresents that hardy, adventurous, and industrious class of our population, who sacrifice the comforts and security of established society to open the way to the peaceful industries.

Those who are capable of comprehending the great issue now before the government in regard to the western frontiers, will admit the utility of steam and telegraphic communication between the Atlantic and Pacific. Where there are railroads, there must be stations at intervals, for the accommodation of the workmen, and a surplus population to provide for their subsistence and living. This constitutes settlements. For the safety of trade and human life, something must be done to provide the Indian with a sufficient and a responsible government, to compass his physical wants, and to compel the insubordinate to quiet.

It must be accepted that the savage cannot be controlled by moral influences, and to buy peace is to gratify his vanity as a victor. The only law he recognizes in his local administration is force, and the only authority he will respect in his relations with the national government, is the same which, by inheritance, nature, and discipline, he has been taught to fear.

The system of reservations, for the benefit of the Indian, is a good one if properly enforced. It is sure in the present state of affairs, the Indian must be reduced, and confined within certain limits, or the white man must abandon his railroads and telegraphs. Public enterprise and public convenience demand that these should exist. For the sake of future security a belt of country, extending from the Arkansas, to a line fifty or a hundred miles north of the Platte River must be removed from all contingencies of Indian attack. An extensive system of reservations north of the north line, for the northern tribes, and another south of the Arkansas, for the southern tribes already exists. The Indian should be informed of the country he is to occupy, and if he refuse to go there, should be whipped into submission.

More than two years ago, the Indians agreed by "treaty" to occupy these reservations, but the imbecility or timidity of the civil administration, at that time, put over him, failed to move him one step towards the fulfilment of the wishes of the government. The representatives of the government, in order to keep peace, yielded everything until the demands of the savage exceeded their ability to satisfy, and their red charge went to war to earn fresh claims to their benevolence.

The civil policy has been one of continued submission. The true motto in keeping with the ideas of the savage, is to demand nothing but what is just, and never give up that which has once been claimed and acquired. A savage never asks, but demands. To acquiesce from any motives, whatever, is to him a surrender by compulsion or through fear. The reservations set apart for the wild tribes of the southern plains, compose some of the finest lands to be found west of the Mississippi River. The Indian territory has long been the seat of a large Indian population. The Indian territory extends from the Kansas southern boundary to the Red River, and about eight degrees of longitude at its greatest breadth. The reservation of the Cheyennes and Arrapahoes, carved out of that portion of the territory known as the Cherokee country, abounds in a variety of natural grasses, and is a favourite range of the buffalo. The Comanche and Kiowa reservation lies west of the Chickasaw nation, and in the southern part of the territory bordering on the Red River.

This country is if possible superior to the other, and is acknowledged to embrace the finest lands in the Indian territory. Notwithstanding the expensive presents expended at the treaty of Medicine Lodge Creek. the tribes which pledged themselves to occupy their reservations, did not make the first move towards putting into effect their promises until they were compelled. The war inaugurated by the Cheyennes and Arrapahoes, and supported morally and physically by the Kiowas, Comanches, and Apaches, is probably an incontrovertible argument that the Indian parties to the treaty, had no intention to comply until disturbed in their contemplated aggressions, on a large scale, by the unexpected presence of the army in their midst.

We have seen that the Indian can only be controlled by force. This being the case it is certain that no administration, to be effective, can be enforced without the co-operation of the army. And in many respects the army recommends itself as more competent than the civil power. The army combines executive functions with the capacity to exact compliance. No one would believe, for a moment, that the army would wantonly exercise unnecessary severity.

It is an historical fact that, for year after year, expeditions have been sent against the Indians, to be defeated by the intrigues of the agents of the government.

Refractory bands have been punished, and the government, at the instance of its agents, has reimbursed them for their losses at a vast outlay of the public money. An act of obedience on the part of one branch of the public service has invariably been denounced as a fiendish and atrocious massacre of innocent people by the other. The savage, it is undeniable, must be kept in certain localities. Contact with the whites is a sore precursor of extermination by disease, chronic inebriation, or drunken brawls. His days of unrestrained freedom upon his native plains is a thing of the past. When the wild Indian understands that on the reservation means peace, and outside of it war, the government may look for quiet, and the settler on the frontiers for perfect security. Then the large hearts and affluence of the humanitarians of the nation would be able, with an assurance of safety, to put into practice the benevolent intentions, which might, at least lessen, if they could not conquer, the savage instincts of the Indian.

Upon the reservation the Indian would be accessible and a safe one to meet. Upon the plain to find him would be the toil of months, and when found his hospitality would be uncertain. Restrained in his longing for war, by the fear of punishment, the red man might find some object in bettering his condition. The issue to be solved is the preservation of what remains of the Indian race by an administration which he fears, or a continued warring against him, brought on by his own acts, and the encroachments of the settlers, both the natural result of an authority without a head to reason or arms to strike.

Chapter 40

Off for Camp Supply

The valleys around were already beginning to assume the garb of spring. The feathered harbingers had already made their appearance. The groves, bordering the streams, were already joyous with such music as we had not listened to for months. This opening scene of the year enlivened all. The trooper lolled about in the genial atmosphere. The animals showed signs of life and spirit The change which was now passing over the face of nature was the more agreeable, as the termination of the hardships and rigors, to which the command had been exposed. In the far southern latitude we had reached, we now found all that salubrity of climate and advance of vegetation.

The campaign for the winter having ended, Sheridan determined to leave for the northern posts and observe what had taken place during his absence in the field. A few wagons, sufficient to transport the smallest allowance of baggage, blankets, and supplies, together with the led horses, were sent a day in advance to Fort Cobb. The Commanding General, three staff officers, myself, an interpreter, five orderlies, a cook, one servant, and thirty-eight of the scouts, constituted our party. Our transportation, two ambulances and three army wagons. The headquarters' train was left in charge of Colonel Moore, with instructions to move with Custer's column.

At seven o'clock on the morning of February 23rd, we set out, having before us a journey of over four hundred miles in the saddle, through a wild and desolate country. As we passed through the camps, the officers and troops had turned out to witness our departure. Farewells and cheers to the general, rose, as he rode through the lines of men. We soon crossed the Medicine Bluff Creek. It was almost with regret that I left the familiar tent and the free life I had so long enjoyed, for a return to the turmoil and bustle of civilization. A life of

THE TABLE LANDS

such boundless freedom inspires a feeling of aversion to the personal restraint, necessary in organized communities. I felt that I could now appreciate the fascinations which lure men from the comforts and security of established society, to brave the dangers and exposures of the frontiers.

We turned from the subject of our farewell thoughts. The smoke of the camp-fire, as it wreathed its way heavenward, was the last we saw of the camp on the Medicine Bluff.

We now galloped away down the hill and across the plain. The mountains rapidly became a blue and indefinable mass. At four o'clock in the afternoon we overtook the advance, sent out the day before, in camp, near Fort Cobb. At Fort Cobb, Captain Rife, of the 6th Infantry, was still in possession. His position, certainly, was not one to inspire envy. Himself, a lieutenant, and forty infantry, had wintered there. The nearest post was the camp on the Medicine Bluff, miles away. At the invitation of the captain, we cheered his hermit board, as his guests, to dinner. His isolated life was not ill spent. A profusion of game, taken from the woods, and fish from the stream, appeased our sharpened appetites. I should add, that the turkey, placed before us, weighed twenty-six pounds, and the cat-fish thirty-eight pounds.

The next morning, at daylight, we resumed our journey, leaving the captain and his lieutenant to their solitude. Our animals, when we left camp, were packed with a view to the extended journey. The route, the general proposed taking, was one that had not yet been traversed. The trail of the column lay far to the west.

Our route on the second day was on a due north line. The country was broken and sandy. At noon we found great difficulty in crossing several lagoons covered with thick cane-brake. During the day we passed several crystal lakes, surrounded by trees. Twenty miles from the Washita River, our route crossed a broad, ascending plain. The surrounding country presented a remarkable conglomeration of hummocks of red rock, from fifty to one hundred feet in height One of these rocks resembled an immense turret. It stood in the centre of an expansive, open plain, and was surrounded by six immense table-lands, perfect in form, and several hundred feet in height. At another point I counted no less than sixteen of these table-lands within a single sweep of the vision. At one point, farther on, we passed by the foot of a natural fort with bastions and curtains.

Early in the afternoon we reached the "divide," between the Washita and the Canadian Rivers. At the summit stood conspicuously, a rock, sixty feet in height, familiar to the early banters and traders as Rock Mary. The general, desiring to make the ascent, I accompanied him, eager to take advantage of so rare an opportunity for a view. The scramble up the bold face of the rock was no pastime. The view, as I anticipated, was sublime beyond comparison. Standing above the highest level of all the surrounding country, a blue line in the dim distance, defined the Witchitas sixty miles distant. The surrounding plain could be traced until heaven and earth joined in hazy unison.

The same afternoon we crossed the old Fort Smith and Santa Fé trail, famous years ago as the great route for trains from the "states" to New Mexico. The same night we pitched our tents on Deer Creek, forty miles' journey from the camp of the night before.

Having made an early start, by eight o'clock, on the morning of the twenty-sixth, we struck the high, perpendicular red clay bluffs overlooking the Main Canadian. We descended to the stream by a tortuous pass, narrow and deep, and furrowed by deep water courses and buffalo trails. We were here more than a hundred miles east of the crossing we made in moving south. The ford, we found, was better, in every respect. The bed of the stream was about three-fifths of a mile in width, but the running water not over two hundred yards. On the opposite side we encountered a number of sandhills, from which we rose gradually to the main "divide."

Early in the afternoon we entered a prairie-dog town. The diminutive mound-like domiciles lay upon the side of an extensive rise in the plain, and could be seen in all directions as far as they could be distinguished at all from the flat surface. The busy little occupants, alarmed at our invasion of their dominions, at first sight raised on their haunches, made two or three indignant, but feeble barks, and then scampered off for positions of convenient proximity to their subterranean homes. The dogs, upon reaching their mounds, in the centre of which were the means of egress and ingress, would once more throw themselves upon their haunches and look around them with an exceedingly comical air of patriotic rage. Here they would wait, throwing their heads up in the air. and barking until we came within a few yards, and then, with a flourish of the tail, would dive into their holes.

For a distance of eight miles we were constantly riding through this immense "town," and did not reach the end until the next day. The area covered by this remarkable community was not less than twelve miles in length and two broad. The "town" covered at least twenty-four square miles. Allowing but twenty animals to the acre, and we have three hundred and six thousand two hundred inhabitants of this city of pigmy dogs.

At one o'clock in the day we reached the north fork of the Canadian, a distance of thirty miles. Having made this journey without a rest it was proposed to halt here, to give the horses, which were already showing the effect of the heavy tax on their feeble energies, a long respite. They were herded in a valley nearby, and enjoyed the luxury of freedom until nearly sundown.

The next morning, the twenty-seventh, we crossed the North Fork of the Canadian, and pitched our tents at three o'clock in the afternoon on the north bank, making thirty-two miles.

The general, towards the end of the march, being in advance with a few scouts, and having selected a beautiful site for the night's rest, sent a courier out on the open ground to signal the rest of the party where to turn. Being thus notified several of us rising in the rear struck into the thick timber, by way of making a cut-off. We had proceeded but a short distance when a brisk fire was encountered in our front. We dismounted quite expeditiously. We could see nothing, but naturally the first thought was that we had fallen into an ambuscade laid by some straggling war-party. We could not discern anything, but our sense of hearing was kept in lively recognition of an enemy in front The bullets flew thick and fast, the latest, up to that time, buzzing with oracular effect close to my head. I changed position in the rear of a large cotton-wood. The rest had already adopted this wise precaution. We also took care to hold on to our horses, notwithstanding their efforts to change front also.

The firing came closer, and the enemy seemed to be developing more strength. All this time, which in the aggregate was but a few minutes, we were waiting for some tangible foe. Suddenly a crashing of underbrush was heard not more than twenty feet off. Our rifles were loaded ready for use. We were watching anxiously, when a huge buffalo made his appearance, frothing at the mouth, and with streams of blood rushing from his nostrils. We now let go our horses. Evidently glad to avail themselves of an opportunity to get out of the way, at least, judging from a lively flourish of their heels, they set off with astonishing alacrity.

The buffalo charged our line, and penetrated it. He evidently was not aware of our presence. As he crossed in our rear we opened a peppering fire, which seemed to astonish the monarch of the plain.

He stopped for a moment It was fatal to him. Asch, from behind his well-adjusted spectacles, gave his majesty a dose of physic, which went through him with excellent effect. The old buffalo no sooner got his dose from the doctor than nature succumbed to science. He fell on his fore knees, and made several efforts to gain his feet. A quiver shot through his frame. In a moment more the monster animal rolled over upon his side. He gave one convulsive start—a tremor passed over him. With a deep sigh of relief life and body were severed.

An instant after a half dozen scouts came out of the brush in hasty pursuit. The animal was too old even for our sharpened appetites, so the immense carcass was left for the benefit of the wolves.

Towards dusk, considerably to our enjoyment, we discovered we had encamped near a turkey-roost The Commanding General, an old turkey-hunter, had already announced this piece of intelligence, and gave orders that no one should leave the immediate limits of the camp without permission. This was to prevent the "birds," as they gathered from the surrounding valleys, from being alarmed and driven off.

At sunset, leaving a strong guard in camp, a party consisting of the general, and eight or ten others, started into the thick wood adjoining camp. At first the orders were to lie in watch. The wood occupied the low grounds of a valley. A large drove of fine birds came tramping down the hill side. In front was a fine cock, which seemed to be the chief bird of this feathered concourse. The chief carefully surveyed everything, looked about him, and then at the trees. Feeling assured that all was right, he gave a quick shrill whistle. In an instant the whole flock raised with a great flutter, ascending to the tops of the larger trees. Firing now commenced. It was a general engagement. Each hunter set out for himself. The crack of the rifle was heard in every direction. The turkeys seemed to be bewildered, and flew from tree to tree, but always kept in the same vicinity. As it grew dark, the number increased. Soon it became night, but every dark object defined upon the blue back ground of the firmament was taken for a turkey, and was peppered accordingly.

It was fully nine o'clock before the last of our party got in. Stray shots from the scouts prowling about were kept up all night

An inventory of "birds" taken before "turning in that night" showed that we had sixty-three. The general killed eleven of the number.

For the next few days we were quite busy stuffing ourselves with turkey, in order to reduce the number, as we could not well carry so much additional weight in the wagons. Wild turkey as a regular diet we found to be a gastronomic question admitting of controversy.

We were now not less than seventy-two miles from Camp Supply, two good day's journey. We had entered an exceedingly rough country, covered with sand-hills and sage brush. The animals suffered severely from these impediments in the way of convenient travelling.

At two o'clock on the afternoon of the first of March, the stars and stripes were seen, dimly in the distance, waving over the stockade fort at Camp Supply. Our arrival was entirely unexpected. At first we were taken for Indians. The sentinels discharged their arms to give the alarm. The herders hastily drove in the animals, which we could see dashing from all directions towards the corrals. When the mistake was discovered, the affair was much enjoyed. Three long months had elapsed since we left the comforts of "Supply," for the wild country on the Washita.

CHAPTER 41

Homeward Bound

The second of March, 1869, was a busy day at Camp Supply. Wagons were loaded to join the column under Custer in the south, and a train was fitted out to move to Fort Dodge for more supplies for the Camp of Supply. The Commanding General had here received a dispatch from the President elect to visit Washington at the earliest moment This changed the original programme of joining Custer's column, and returning north with him. There was, however, no longer necessity for his detention in the field but his own desire personally to see the troops return to their summer camps.

The next day, at seven o'clock in the morning, the Commanding General, Crosby, McGonnigle, and Asch, of the staff, myself, and two servants, in three ambulances, and with three mounted orderlies as escort, set out for Fort Dodge, over one hundred miles distant. The escort was left behind, not having fresh horses. Our personal baggage was strapped on five pack-mules, in charge of an experienced packer, named Wilson, who had passed some years in the service of the Hudson Bay Company.

The day was wet and cold. Before noon a drizzling rain set in. At dark, the same night, we halted on Bear Creek, after a journey of fifty-two miles. During the day, we were constantly driving immense herds of buffaloes before us, and at night we were surrounded by them. Attracted by the light of our fires, they approached so near that the low bellow of the bulls could be distinctly heard. A cordon of wolves also posted themselves around our camp, and kept up a dismal howling.

For fuel we had a solitary log, and that was wet After considerable chopping, we got a few dry chips with which we started a fire. A very frugal meal was our night's portion. At eight o'clock in the evening the rain turned into a heavy storm of sleet The wind howled fearfully. As our sleeping accommodations were limited, we divided, part sleeping in the ambulances, and part outside under a tent-fly near the fire. I preferred the latter, and wisely, as the atmosphere changed to an intense dry cold during the night, which made the fire quite acceptable.

The next day we continued our journey against fearful weather. The air was filled with a fine snow, driven in our faces before a fierce wind.

At Bluff Creek it was necessary to halt. The animals were terribly blown, and, as for ourselves, a few more degrees of cold would have been insufferably notwithstanding we were hardened by four months of constant exposure. With great difficulty, we managed to build a fire, grateful indeed to all of us. While enjoying a good baking, two mail-couriers came galloping down the valley. They were halted, and after assorting out the headquarters' mail, we separated—the couriers, hardy fellows, striking out once more into the cold and cheerless waste.

It was dark when we reached the Arkansas River. The stream was frozen over, and impassable. Here was a dilemma. Nearly a mile distant, on the opposite side, was Fort Dodge. It was necessary to arouse the garrison before we could cross. We fired volleys from our rifles and shouted. It was a cheer- less predicament. The glimmering lights of the rude but comfortable quarters of the fort in sight, and yet compelled to tramp about in darkness, wind, and cold, unable to move an inch farther. A half hour now passed disagreeably enough; but, having succeeded in raking together a quantity of dry grass, we contrived to start a fire, by the light of which we were able to gather sufficient brush to keep up the illumination.

At this juncture the sentinels at the fort appeared to discover us, and gave the alarm. Borne upon the night air we could hear the long-roll beating the men to arms. A squad of troops was sent across on the ice. From them we received the complimentary and gratifying intelligence that the disturbance we had made was heard from the beginning, and, judging from our unearthly yells, we were taken for savages.

An effort was made to open a passage through the ice, but this having failed the Commanding General, with his quarter master, walked to the fort, while the rest of our party passed the night with the ambulances.

The next morning a fatigue party of soldiers managed to get the ambulances over by means of ropes, and running the wheels on planks.

The animals were left on the south side.

By noon, on the fifth of March, with a complete "outfit" of "shave-tails," we darted out of the fort. Every jump or two a set of heels might be seen exposed in the air. The drivers kept the lively long-eared quadrupeds in the trail. A run of a few miles disposed of their ardour very effectually.

The next day, while approaching the Smoky Hill, a courier was seen coming towards us at a rapid gait. Our outrider challenged him as he came. up. "Special courier for the Commanding General," shouted the horseman, at the same time dashing by the outrider at a gallop.

The outrider, wheeling, pursued. The courier halted. When told the general was approaching the courier met the general, saluted, and, with unexpected wit, remarked, "I have the honour to deliver a dispatch to the Lieutenant General." The general, for the first time during my acquaintance, was much affected as he read aloud the telegram announcing his promotion.

Upon the banks of the Smoky Hill we drank from the last cherished drops in our canteens *to the health of the Lieutenant General and the close of the campaign.*

But twelve miles still separated us from Fort Hays. With pleasant reflections upon the success of the campaign, with a sense of pleasure inspired by the agreeable and appropriate moment of the general's promotion, with feelings of joy at the refreshing anticipations of a speedy return to civilization, the closing scene of the campaign, and the last stage of our journey, were equally gratifying.

At half-past three o'clock in the afternoon, on the sixth of March, unannounced, we drew up on the drive, in front of the quarters, of the commandant at Fort Hays.

The next day, Sunday, on the iron highway of Kansas, we sped from the land of the Indian and the buffalo—from the scene of savage war—to the security, peace, and comforts of civilisation.

★★★★★★

Evans and his gallant men had returned from their trying march on the Main Canadian, and the Red, to the comparative comforts of Bascom. Carr and his troopers, from their fearful gallop on the North Canadian, once more enjoyed the hospitable shelter of Lyon. Custer, with the battle-scarred veterans of the Seventh, and Crawford, with his rugged and daring Volunteers, had given the savages on the headwaters of the Red the final blow of the campaign. The Seventh was in quarters near Fort Hays. The Volunteers, after their rough experience had gone to their homes. Such was the end of the campaign before the close of the spring of 1869. The purposes of war were fully realized. The savages were severely punished. The belief in their security in the winter season was shattered beyond a question, even in their stubborn minds. All the tribes south of the Platte were forced upon their reservations. Thus, by the powerful and efficient aid of Sheridan's Troopers, the wild tribes were made accessible to the generous heart of humanity, and the tempering influences of industry, education, and Christianity.

ALSO FROM LEONAUR
AVAILABLE IN SOFTCOVER OR HARDCOVER WITH DUST JACKET

THE 9TH—THE KING'S (LIVERPOOL REGIMENT) IN THE GREAT WAR 1914 - 1918 by Enos H. G. Roberts—Mersey to mud—war and Liverpool men.

THE GAMBARDIER by Mark Severn—The experiences of a battery of Heavy artillery on the Western Front during the First World War.

FROM MESSINES TO THIRD YPRES by Thomas Floyd—A personal account of the First World War on the Western front by a 2/5th Lancashire Fusilier.

THE IRISH GUARDS IN THE GREAT WAR - VOLUME 1 by Rudyard Kipling—Edited and Compiled from Their Diaries and Papers—The First Battalion.

THE IRISH GUARDS IN THE GREAT WAR - VOLUME 1 by Rudyard Kipling—Edited and Compiled from Their Diaries and Papers—The Second Battalion.

ARMOURED CARS IN EDEN by K. Roosevelt—An American President's son serving in Rolls Royce armoured cars with the British in Mesopatamia & with the American Artillery in France during the First World War.

CHASSEUR OF 1914 by Marcel Dupont—Experiences of the twilight of the French Light Cavalry by a young officer during the early battles of the great war in Europe.

TROOP HORSE & TRENCH by R.A. Lloyd—The experiences of a British Lifeguardsman of the household cavalry fighting on the western front during the First World War 1914-18.

THE EAST AFRICAN MOUNTED RIFLES by C.J. Wilson—Experiences of the campaign in the East African bush during the First World War.

THE LONG PATROL by George Berrie—A Novel of Light Horsemen from Gallipoli to the Palestine campaign of the First World War.

THE FIGHTING CAMELIERS by Frank Reid—The exploits of the Imperial Camel Corps in the desert and Palestine campaigns of the First World War.

STEEL CHARIOTS IN THE DESERT by S. C. Rolls—The first world war experiences of a Rolls Royce armoured car driver with the Duke of Westminster in Libya and in Arabia with T.E. Lawrence.

WITH THE IMPERIAL CAMEL CORPS IN THE GREAT WAR by Geoffrey Inchbald—The story of a serving officer with the British 2nd battalion against the Senussi and during the Palestine campaign.

AVAILABLE ONLINE AT **www.leonaur.com**
AND FROM ALL GOOD BOOK STORES

www.ingramcontent.com/pod-product-compliance
Lightning Source LLC
Chambersburg PA
CBHW031623160426
43196CB00006B/253